BON

The L. Ron Hubbard Series
───────────────────────

BRIDGE PUBLICATIONS, INC.
5600 E. Olympic Blvd.
Commerce, California 90022 USA

ISBN 978-1-4031-9880-8

© 1997, 2012 L. Ron Hubbard Library. All Rights Reserved.

Any unauthorized copying, translation, duplication, importation or distribution, in whole or in part, by any means, including electronic copying, storage or transmission, is a violation of applicable laws.

Special acknowledgment is made to the L. Ron Hubbard Library for permission to reproduce photographs from his personal collection. Additional credits: pp. 1, 15, 59, 83, 105, 217, 229, back cover Tribalium/Shutterstock.com; pp. 12/13 trekandshoot/Shutterstock.com; p. 14 Sport and General Press Agency; p. 17 National Archives; pp. 18, 24, 28, 32, 36, 40, 48 Slobodan Djajic/Shutterstock.com; pp. 56/57 europhotos/Shutterstock.com; p. 58 *East Grinstead Courier;* pp. 80/81, 84 Dimitri Vervitsiotis/Getty Images; pp. 102/103 Alex Gul/Shutterstock.com; p. 225 Keystone Press Agency/Hulton Archives.

Dianetics, Scientology, E-Meter, HCO, Saint Hill, Freedom, Hubbard, L. Ron Hubbard, LRH, Scientology Cross (pointed) and *Ron Signature* are trademarks and service marks owned by Religious Technology Center and are used with its permission.

Scientologist is a collective membership mark designating members of the affiliated churches and missions of Scientology.

The Way to Happiness is a trademark owned by L. Ron Hubbard Library and is used with permission.

Narconon is a trademark and service mark owned by Association for Better Living and Education International and is used with its permission.

Citizens Commission on Human Rights, CCHR and *CCHR Logo* are trademarks and service marks owned by Citizens Commission on Human Rights.

Bridge Publications, Inc. is a registered trademark and service mark in California and it is owned by Bridge Publications, Inc.

NEW ERA is a trademark and service mark owned by New Era Publications International ApS and is registered in Denmark, among other countries.

Printed in the United States of America

The L. Ron Hubbard Series: Freedom Fighter—English

The L. Ron Hubbard Series

FREEDOM FIGHTER
ARTICLES
& ESSAYS

Bridge
PUBLICATIONS, INC.®

CONTENTS

Freedom Fighter: Articles & Essays

An Introduction to L. Ron Hubbard | 1

Strong Voices in the Land | 9

On Government | 15

Patriotism | 19

On Writing to Governments | 25

Government and Revolt | 29

Constitutional Destruction | 33

Unite and Win | 37

Unconstitutional Government | 41

Constitutions | 45

The Evolution of Totalitarianism | 49

On Justice & Jurisprudence | 59

Fast Justice | 63

Justice | 67

Riots | 71

The Justice Department versus Americans | 75

On Economics | 83

Economics | 85

Economics—War and Tax | 95

On Psychiatric Subversion | 105

    A Reason Psychiatric Front Groups Attack Scientology | 109

    Druidism and Psychiatry | 113

    Today's Terrorism | 117

    Pain-Drug-Hypnosis | 121

    Failures | 127

    Diplomas | 129

    Psychology and Psychiatry, the Sciences of Saliva | 131

    The Planned Revolution | 135

    Sciences of Saliva | 139

    Control "Sciences" | 143

    The Bland Personality | 147

    Quackery and Fakery | 151

    How to Win an Argument | 155

    Crime and Psychiatry | 159

    Our Intentions | 163

    The Unholy Stick Together | 167

    Cultural Deficiencies | 171

    The Fight for Freedom | 177

    Drug Problems | 183

Tangled Terms | 185

Being Good | 189

Drug Addiction | 191

Cultural Destruction | 195

Old-Fashioned Holdovers | 201

Criminals and Psychiatry | 205

The Criminal Mind and the Psychs | 209

The Cause of Crime | 211

On Researching the Humanities | 217

A Summary on Scientology for Scientists | 219

Citizens Commission on Human Rights | 229

A Closing Note | 241

Appendix

Alphabetical Listing of L. Ron Hubbard Articles | 245

Chronological Listing of L. Ron Hubbard Articles | 247

Glossary | 249

Index | 317

An Introduction to
L. Ron Hubbard

BETWEEN THE MID-1960S AND EARLY 1980S, AND FOLLOWING from a greater geopolitical study of what most plagues this world, L. Ron Hubbard authored an extraordinary series of essays on "cultural inadequacies" of the late twentieth century. Primarily intended for *Freedom* magazine—where the bulk of these works, in fact, appeared—virtually every aspect of our social, political and economic existence was addressed: forms of government, questions of individual liberty, the structure of monetary systems and the preservation of human rights. That the Founder of Scientology would provide us these essays—and quite in addition to all else he provided for the advancement of Scientology through these years—is fully consistent with his view of the church as a traditional force of freedom and decency. Thus, as he tells us, "If there is this fruitful source of suppression, then it is a legitimate field for comment." That these essays further provide us an utterly incisive grasp of just what went awry in the twentieth century is likewise consistent with the larger LRH vision. For in the final analysis, as he also tells us, "Understanding is a sort of a total solvent. It's the universal solvent. It washes away everything."

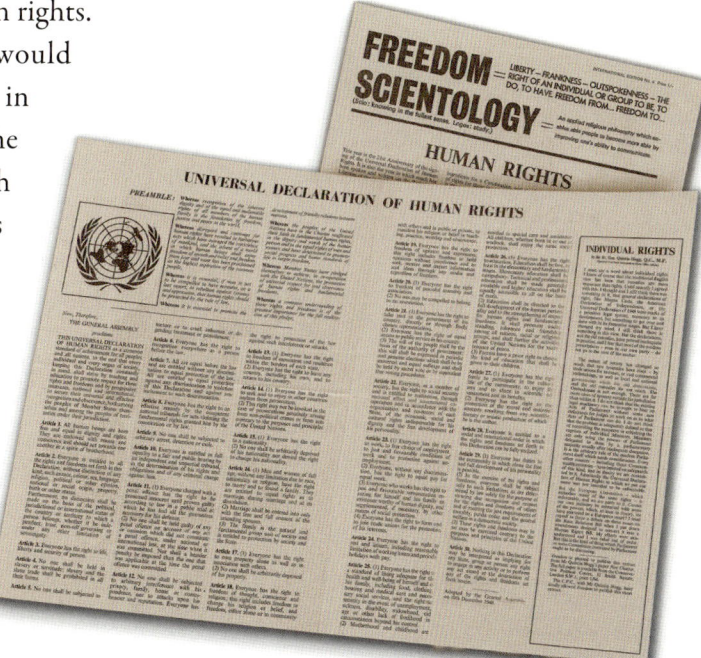

Below The original *Freedom* magazine of 1969, reintroducing the original Universal Declaration of Human Rights from 1948. Until the advent of *Freedom* magazine, the Universal Declaration was largely forgotten and all but ignored.

But what has not been publicly known, or at least until now, is the fact these essays were only part of a larger project. Specifically, LRH was at work, from the late 1960s right through the 1980s, on a book he entitled "The Cause and Prevention of Revolution." Thus what these articles actually represent are but a *byproduct* of a greater body of research to a much larger work-in-progress. In that regard, these essays represent not a comment on society's ills, but LRH discoveries on what actually lies at the root of those ills.

In what then constitutes a very special issue of the *L. Ron Hubbard Series,* we present a selection of LRH essays on all he deemed culturally inadequate: tyranny of government, inadequate justice, oppressive economics and the pervasive terror of psychiatry. Those familiar with other issues of this series will recognize the form. For here is yet another view of the man not generally seen—or more accurately, herein lies an LRH perspective so vast no other publication can reasonably convey it. Those particularly familiar with the issues of the *L. Ron Hubbard Series* focusing upon his humanitarian contributions will especially appreciate the point of this publication. For here is the worldview from which he provided his means for the rehabilitation of a drugged society, his answer to moral decay and criminality and his tools for literacy and learning. In that regard, here is not merely another condemnation of repression and inequity. Rather, here is the perspective from which our most relevant humanitarian examined a deeply troubled world and here is what he had to offer in the way of genuine answers.

How he arrived at the perspective from which these essays were written is, of course, an immense story. Included in the vista are his now legendary Asian adventures between 1927 and 1929. Although chiefly remembered for his trek through Tibetan lamaseries where few Westerners had trod since Marco Polo, Asia

Below
The United States Capitol Building as an ever-hopeful symbol of political freedom; photograph by L. Ron Hubbard, 1958

was also where he would write of an overarching misery in overpopulated and undereducated lands. Hence that perennially quoted passage from L. Ron Hubbard's "My Philosophy":

> *"I have seen people uncaring and stepping over dying men in the streets. I have seen children less than rags and bones. And amongst this poverty and degradation I found holy places where wisdom was great but where it was carefully hidden and given out only as superstition."*

Also foreshadowing essays herein were his papers from Princeton University, where he attended the United States School of Military Government in an anticipation of service with US occupational forces in 1945. It was a transitional time for both the United States and United States Naval Lieutenant L. Ron Hubbard. He had previously seen combat in three theaters, for which he was highly decorated and grievously wounded. While separately and very personally, he had come to hate war very deeply. These papers, then, reflect that passion and compassion. Accordingly, the view is perfectly parallel to what will follow through these pages—the same outspoken cry for humanity, the same uncompromising plea for justice and the same Strong Voice in the Land. And it is all the more pronounced inasmuch as he wrote amidst wartime hysteria and rampant bloodlust that ultimately cost the lives of some twenty million human beings.

Thus the poignancy of this:

> *"A child starves in a few days; a man can't last sixty hours without water; an epidemic can start while one thinks about it. Only those who have been carved down to the basic elements of existence can appreciate the hollow stupidity of politics at such a time."*

Left
The repatriated L. Ron Hubbard after more than a year amongst the extremes of exquisite splendor and grinding poverty that was colonial Asia before the Second World War

Right
Lieutenant L. Ron Hubbard, 1944: he who employed his considerable literary power on behalf of the "undignified dead" and the "weeping wounded"

There was more and it is equally pointed: Those who have been bombed, shelled, machine-gunned and otherwise brutalized do not think abstractly, he writes. They think in terms of full bellies; they think in terms of base survival; they think in terms of foodstuffs, sanitation and protection from looters. They do not think in terms of an untidy *political* meal war has made.

Thereafter and unceasingly so, Ron continued to employ his considerable literary power on behalf of the powerless—the "undignified dead" and "weeping wounded," as he so plaintively phrased it, "the dislocated, demoralized and homeless."

Nor would he ever cease employing his considerable acumen to reveal root causes of conflict and oppression. Why civilizations vanish, why economies collapse and why populations are subjected to unforeseen catastrophes—all these matters and more were subject to LRH examination through the latter 1960s and early 1970s.

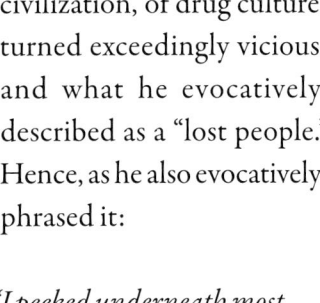

The case in point was his incisive sociological study of American society circa 1973. Conducted in and around Manhattan, it proved revealing in the extreme, for here was the beginning of a stupefied civilization, of drug culture turned exceedingly vicious and what he evocatively described as a "lost people." Hence, as he also evocatively phrased it:

"I peeked underneath most everything...to look for the smile and the warmth that was there once."

And hence the inception of the Scientology Volunteer Minister Program under that phrase now heard everywhere: *Something Can Be Done About It!*

So, yes, here is a most expansive view of the world in which we live and the secret history of how it came to be. That is, and very bluntly: Here are the roots of popular unrest. Here is a carefully woven net of financial entanglement, oppressive taxation and economic policies to *create want*. Here is also judicial inequity, political chaos and social decay. Moreover, the roots are not only still intact, but much of what he foresaw as of 1969 has indeed come to pass... or continues unfolding to this day.

As a further historical word on the era of these essays, let us briefly consider what historians have described as "a world which lost its bearings." For example, we shall read of a "long mass of riots and civil commotion" and the phrase is entirely appropriate what with two hundred American cities erupting in riots between 1968 and 1969. (Although the figure is somewhat debatable since a United States Justice Department attempted to reclassify all incidents of looting, arson and mayhem lasting less than twelve hours as a mere "serious disturbance.") All the same, the department could not reclassify the thirty-five thousand assaults on federal offices and agents, nor the four thousand politically motivated bombings. Similarly, we shall read of an unprecedented university revolt and again the phrase is apt, with seventy-three American campuses suffering mass and premeditated student violence through the first week of May 1970, and commensurate figures across Western and Eastern Europe. Then again, we shall read of a business community listlessly gazing upon "economic ruins," a United States executive branch spitting on the Bill of Rights and an equally corrupt Federal Bureau of Investigation—all further underscored by such catchwords from the era as "Rust Belts," "Watergate" and the little "black book" of J. Edgar Hoover.

Yet the real cancer through these "crisis decades"—as historians have also dubbed

Below
New York City, 1973: site of Ron's incisive sociological research from whence came so many LRH programs for social reform; photograph by L. Ron Hubbard

An Introduction to L. Ron Hubbard   5

this era—is what the mainstream historian has generally missed and what LRH reveals with a depth found nowhere else, i.e., the deeper cultural subversion from a psychiatric and psychological establishment as variously represented by an American Psychiatric Association, an American Psychological Association and a World Federation for Mental Health. As we shall see, LRH additionally has much to say on the psychiatric presence within a United States intelligence community—originally enlisted under a banner of behavioral control or mind control, but eventually serving as an even darker psychopolitical cog within the Cold War machine. Finally, we shall also read of a psychiatric intrusion into the educational realm with a "science of saliva" and the commensurately "sinister implications" of psychiatry's invasion of judicial systems.

But the larger point is simply this: If the name L. Ron Hubbard was to finally prove a psychiatric obsession—with at least two million psychiatric dollars directed to the destruction of his work as of 1955 and untold millions since—that obsession is only peripheral to the story he reveals. In fact, psychiatry looms large in these essays because it embodies a worldwide terror directed against whole landscapes and whole populations. Moreover, and even more to that larger point: "It is *not* a 'symptom of the times' that things are going wrong in the West. They are carefully planned that way."

So unquestionably we are about to tread upon some fascinating ground, for among other topics of those carefully laid plans discussed here: the targeting of minorities, the deterioration of

Below
The Washington Monument, Washington, DC—perennial symbol of United States democracy; photograph by L. Ron Hubbard

individual liberty, the manipulation of media to mold popular opinion, tinkering with economics toward the fraying of a social fabric and the chemical re-engineering of a human personality into a submissive and "good dog" mentality.

As a final introductory word, let us reiterate the bulk of essays here followed from a much larger project aimed at writing "The Cause and Prevention of Revolution." And although that work was never completed, we do possess what LRH intended as the opening chapter, "Strong Voices in the Land."

In a word, that chapter would seem to summarize not only all works in this publication, but the greater crusade of Scientologists everywhere—or for that matter, anyone who stands as a Scientologist at heart for his dedication to the dignity and freedom of Mankind. But in any case, the opening statement to follow most certainly reflects an enduring LRH view that all those who work for individual liberty represent a voice no government can ignore. It also reflects the fact that, as LRH continued his research and the authoring of essays here, the bulk of Scientologists were likewise soon encouraged to raise a strong voice and so also earned the title Freedom Fighters. ■

Left
At his famed southern English estate, forever remembered as Saint Hill Manor

CIRCA AUGUST 1972

The following was intended as the opening for "The Cause and Prevention of Revolution" and originally appeared in this publication.

STRONG VOICES IN THE LAND

by L. Ron Hubbard

WHEN THINGS ARE NOT running right, when the public, unable to perceive why, drift down to an apathy below perception, when a culture, already misguided, drifts further and further toward ruin, the nation is fortunate indeed that it has men with the genius to recognize approaching doom and the courage to speak out.

Fought, discredited, reviled by a blind system in the hands of a power elite careless of all destinies but their own short span, contemporary philosophers are called "Revolutionaries," "Communists," "Agitators," "Malcontents," "Rabble-Rousers" and any other harsh word which the captive press and the arrogant, pompous and blind Establishment can find in their dictionaries.

Heedless, deaf to all reason, psychotic in their righteousness, the "pillars of society," the "safe men," like the treacherous rams of the stockyard who lead the sheep to the slaughter pens, refuse to hear any faintest criticism of their senselessness and fight back with an underhanded ferocity that seeks by any discrediting means to still any and all new thought.

Yet a nation should be warned. When times decay and the death march for the system can be heard still faintly but growing stronger, there are strong voices in the land.

The System, the Establishment, the Government, call it what you will, is a thing which has collected to itself all the self-seeking righteousness of decades. It is an accumulation of yesterdays and the heir to all the errors and opportunistic solutions and mistakes of another age.

Men have been born into it to carry forward unthinkingly the "tradition" (and privileges) of its leadership. Men die out of it, hallowed names on tombstones and city street signs, whose fame was not remarkable for anything but stupid, obstinate devotion to government of the many, by the few and for the profit of the clique.

The possessions and resources of the state, in a party-regulated "democracy," become a prize won by an election victor at stated intervals. Political victory is an opportunity to enjoy the spoils for a stated time. The system is a whore whose favors are won by "popular election" by some new incumbent. But somehow each winner is just a member of the same machine.

So long as it is profitable to the power elite, who cares what consequences are accumulated? The "next regime" can handle those. It suffices only that the system is perpetuated and that the holders of offices of the moment can ensure favors to themselves and to their friends.

Whether one has a monarchy or an aristocracy, an oligarchy, a republic or a military dictatorship, the pattern becomes the same.

A system is established by chicanery or false promises or force, usually in the face of danger to the state from real or imaginary external threat. It develops into a form. It hardens. It ceases to serve. It temporizes. It ceases to listen to any voice but its own and believes only that which serves the short-term profit of its leaders and their friends. It tyrannizes. It begins to die under the weight of opportunistic decisions and senseless crimes.

And at some time during its course, strong voices begin to be heard in protest and in exposure.

But the power elite listens only to the dead words of approved writers safely and anciently dead, from whom excuses and "reasons" can be culled to make the system's actions seem right.

"George Washington said—" "Our Founding Fathers—" "According to Hegel—" "Pavlov stated—" "Disraeli—" "Alexander Hamilton declared" "—the old safe ways—"

"These modern agitators—" "Half-wits—" "Enemy agents—" "—was jailed, you know...." "Can't have it—" "Thinking citizens know that this is all inspired by paid—" "Jail is the only—" "Call out the riot squad—" "—the Army will—" "Get them some other way." "Surely there is some law—" "The recent findings of the Secret Police—" "—hereafter Army deserters will be hanged—" "Perhaps a new war abroad would—" "This is Dr. Kutzbrain, gentlemen. I want him to tell you of his new method of dealing with overactive mentalities—"

And having refused to listen to the voices of today, labeling every suggestion or question or challenge or idea for change as "subversive," "misguided," "harebrained," "enemy-inspired," we eventually hear the requiem of the old boys.

"At least we can die like gentlemen—"

And the wheel has turned its long, long revolution and new faces are seen on the political signboards and new words are heard in the official bulletins of the day.

If a system could hear, if there were somebody to talk to, if it cared, if the men in charge did not become so devoted to their own interests to the callous exclusion of the sufferings of all others, one might achieve political evolution to saner plateaus rather than revolution.

Today we are well progressed on the cycle. The Establishment pays little heed to the times, is blind to the consequences of error, is heedless in its blindness and the men in charge, at least to the great masses of the public, look more like the madmen in charge than leaders of the public destiny.

But there is still time. If those with influence and authority would listen, something could be done before it is too late.

For there are voices in the land, voices of wisdom, voices indicating a way to go that leads elsewhere than to the long, long common grave where old regimes are buried, usually without the dignity of any tombstone other than a blot in the next generation's history book.

CHAPTER ONE

ON GOVERNMENT

On Government | 15
Patriotism | 19
On Writing to Governments | 25
Government and Revolt | 29
Constitutional Destruction | 33
Unite and Win | 37
Unconstitutional Government | 41
Constitutions | 45
The Evolution of
   Totalitarianism | 49

On Government

WHILE ADVOCATING NO PARTICULAR POLITICAL system beyond a system for and by the people, L. Ron Hubbard nonetheless had much to say on the governing of nations. His concern with the matter is simple enough to explain in light of what we find within the very Creed of the Church of Scientology:

"We of the Church believe that all men of whatever race, color or creed were created with equal rights" and *"that all men have inalienable rights to think freely, to talk freely, to write freely their own opinions and to counter or utter or write upon the opinions of others."*

Then again, as we have said, any "fruitful source of suppression" becomes a "legitimate field for comment." But in considering the LRH essays as regards governmental form, governmental redress and governmental tyranny, we are considering a far more extensive LRH commitment to individual liberty. As the classic case in point, he references his warning to former South African Prime Minister Dr. Hendrik Verwoerd and his subsequent banishment from the nation. In fact, psychiatric interests in both South Africa and Rhodesia had declared L. Ron Hubbard *persona non grata* for proposing constitutions calling for the end of apartheid and the adoption of universal suffrage.

As regards the state of governments in the era in which he wrote, let us add a few more words of explanation. In discussing the psychiatric front within United States federal corridors, he is touching upon that secret Cold War partnership between an American military and psychiatrists of ad hoc psychological warfare departments—principally a Psychological Strategy Board charged with input on nuclear counter-strike policies and what was described as the psychological components of a thermonuclear bluff. Also on the agenda were psychiatric recommendations for the policing of frightened populations and the actual instilling of fear—as in the calculated propagandizing of

Saint Hill Manor, England, 1963

Soviet missile-strike capabilities to engender support for annual military expenditures consuming up to 50 percent of the national budget.

In discussing an American Government at odds with both the United States Constitution and Bill of Rights, LRH is touching upon the exceedingly dark term of then President Richard M. Nixon. Among other fully unconstitutional schemes hatched in the Nixon White House—and one that is particularly relevant here—was the compilation of an infamous "Nixon Enemies List," including, incidentally, LRH and the Church of Scientology. Those appearing on the 1969 list, and thus those opposed to the Nixon brand of totalitarian government, were subjected to intense federal harassment from the Department of Justice, Federal Bureau of Investigation and co-conspiratorial Internal Revenue Service agents. In the main, that harassment took the form of unrelenting investigation and continual tax audits. For an idea of just how effective were these methods, one should consider this: Of the one hundred names on that original "Nixon Enemies List," a full ninety-five were left bankrupt, collapsed, disbanded and otherwise dead. Indeed, of the names of individuals and organizations on that infamous enemies list, two survived and still exist today: L. Ron Hubbard and the Church of Scientology.

That LRH wrote of those matters as early as 1969, or a full four years before the world would learn of the real "Tricky Dick," is also highly significant. For if nothing else, Nixon stands as among the most vindictive figures in American history and one did not criticize the man without real conviction and courage.

Finally, in discussing popular revolt through these years, LRH is touching upon such matters as the 1968 Democratic National Convention where some twelve thousand dissidents—primarily students in protest of American involvement in Vietnam—descended upon Chicago for a bloody confrontation with local police, while another eighty million Americans viewed it all on television. ∎

We the People of the United

insure domestic Tranquility, provide for the common defence, promote the
and our Posterity, do ordain and establish this Constitution for the United

Article. I.

Section. 1. All legislative Powers herein granted shall be vested in a Co
of Representatives.

Section. 2. The House of Representatives shall be composed of Members
in each State shall have the Qualifications requisite for Electors of the most numerous

No Person shall be a Representative who shall not have attained to the
and who shall not, when elected, be an Inhabitant of that State in which he shall

Representatives and direct Taxes shall be apportioned among the several S
Numbers, which shall be determined by adding to the whole Number of free Persons
not taxed, three fifths of all other Persons. The actual Enumeration shall be ma
and within every subsequent Term of ten Years, in such Manner as they shall by
thirty Thousand, but each State shall have at Least one Representative; and un
entitled to chuse three, Massachusetts eight, Rhode-Island and Providence Pla
eight, Delaware one, Maryland six, Virginia ten, North Carolina five, South

When vacancies happen in the Representation from any State, the Exe
The House of Representatives shall chuse their Speaker and other Offic

Section. 3. The Senate of the United States shall be composed of two Senators
Senator shall have one Vote.

Immediately after they shall be assembled in Consequence of the first E
of the Senators of the first Class shall be vacated at the Expiration of the second Y
Class at the Expiration of the sixth Year, so that one third may be chosen every seco
Recess of the Legislature of any State, the Executive thereof may make temporary Ap
such Vacancies.

No Person shall be a Senator who shall not have attained to the Age of thi
not, when elected, be an Inhabitant of that State for which he shall be chosen.

The Vice President of the United States shall be President of the Senate, but
The Senate shall chuse their other Officers, and also a President pro tempore
President of the United States.

The Senate shall have the sole Power to try all Impeachments. When su
of the United States, is tried, the Chief Justice shall preside: And no Person shall be convic

Judgment in Cases of Impeachment shall not extend further than to rem

Pursuant to all LRH delineates as intrinsic to a patriotic spirit is all the Church of Scientology has come to represent as a force for honesty and human rights in government. That is, and accepting no citizen can support a secretive government, the Church of Scientology has pioneered what is, in effect, a worldwide movement for governmental accountability—most notably through efforts to broaden the scope of the US Freedom of Information Act, commensurate laws at state level and popularization of their use. Moreover, for nearly half a century, Scientologists have played a decisive role in realizing Freedom of Information legislation in other nations, including: France, Canada, Australia, New Zealand, Italy and Belgium. Just as worthy of note are Scientologists' efforts in spearheading a Taxpayers' Bill of Rights and an annual Religious Freedom Week, both now matters of US law, and countless other similar efforts in numerous countries—all in the name of making human rights reality rather than rhetoric. Or, as a former US Justice Department official stated, "Secrecy is the mortal enemy of democracy. The more secrecy, the less democracy. Through their championing of the rights of all citizens in respect to government files, the Church of Scientology has significantly contributed to the preservation of democracy for everyone."

Finally and likewise following from what LRH advocates, here is all the Church of Scientology has come to represent as the premier champion for the Universal Declaration of Human Rights. Originally adopted by the United Nations in 1948, the document was generally forgotten until the 1998 inauguration of Scientology's worldwide human rights campaign. Entitled United for Human Rights, it is a multimedia and multitiered program designed to broadly raise awareness of human rights in general and the thirty articles of the Universal Declaration in particular. All told, it has brought word of human rights to nearly a billion people and so earned unqualified praise from the human rights community. Indeed, even most vocal advocates within the United Nations readily admit the Church of Scientology has accomplished more in the name of human rights awareness than the UN itself.

1 March 1969

PATRIOTISM

by L. Ron Hubbard

For an officer who worked hard and dangerously with all the rest of the Allies and even gave his health to rid the world of Nazi violations of human rights, it is a little hard to understand when his own government and their allies after the war not only turned a blind eye on a new outcrop of Nazi violations in their own countries, but actively financed to the extent of billions and began to take the orders of those whose practices differ from Nazi only in the absence of a Swastika.

To see a health minister like Robinson write in his own book that unlawful and easy seizures of anyone must become the order of the day, to know he is really the vice-president of a private psychiatric group, to know his financial irregularities on behalf of his group, and yet to see a government obey him implicitly, is a matter sufficient to make one a bit cynical, to say the least.

For more than twenty years I have watched governments in the West make it easier and easier to seize people without warrant or process of law. I've seen "insanity" redefined as someone who disagrees with the social autonomy. I've seen with my own eyes men and women being tortured and killed in "institutions." I've listened to psychiatrists detail their inhuman experiments and brag about their sex orgies with patients and sterilization of those with whom they wanted "sport."

In all this time I've not seen ONE person helped or cured by them.

But I've seen plenty of their patients who were ruined.

I don't think the average citizen could watch one of their shock "treatments" without throwing up.

In one area, four out of nine people we see have been brutally injured by psychiatrists.

My mail every day has several letters in it from their patients pleading for help and relief from their agony.

So with all this evidence around, how can one still believe any Western government is ignorant of the true state of things?

So a lot of us went out and fought and bled and died to make the world safe from Nazi extermination camps. And we turn around and find our own governments not only run them and finance them, but also that any honest effort to help, to find better answers, is mauled and shot at and refused.

All during World War II I found apathy and shrugs on every side of me, not only in our own but also allied forces. These officers and men were not fighting for anything. Most fought under protest. In the firing line 50 percent of them never discharged their weapons.

I didn't understand it then. I do now.

These men had no real cause to fight for. They were willing to destroy the inhuman Nazi. But somehow they knew with certain cynicism that their own masters had more than enough shortcomings to cancel out any advantage to be won for the world.

They were not patriotic. They were occasionally outraged by the enemy. But if a recording had been made of almost any casual chatter by any WW II military group in any wardroom or mess and sent back home, the generals probably would have court-martialed the lot.

And what has happened since? The expatriate loyal governments of our allies were forgotten. Their countries were turned over to Communists or revolutionary hands. Name them off, they are many. Seven hundred and fifty million human beings, at a modest estimate, were tamely passed under the Communist yoke. And through inept "peace-making" and incompetent foreign relations, since 1945 there have been wars and more wars.

The United Nations came up with the answer. An absence of human rights stained the hands of governments and threatened their rules. Very few governments have implemented any part of the Universal Declaration of Human Rights. These governments have not grasped that their very survival depends utterly upon adopting such reforms and thus giving their peoples a cause, a civilization worth supporting, worth their patriotism.

It is vital that all thinking men urge upon their governments (for the government's own sake if no other) sweeping reforms in the field of human rights.

Human rights do *not* mean corn and games. That was the Roman idea and Rome was torn to rubble in the civil wars that had as their fundamental causes the abuses of rights under law.

False accusations. Unlawful seizure of persons and property. The torture and oppression of the individual and social groups. These were what destroyed the Roman Empire.

Such things mocked any pride in "being a Roman."

Eventually her troops did not win battles anymore. They did not care. And so the curtain fell on the "grandeur that was Rome."

The infamous "lettres de cachet," granting as they did the right to seize any person at the whim of any noble and imprison him for life, brought the foremost empire of its day, France, to the tumbril and guillotine at last.

Most governments live on in the myth of their own tradition. They see it in the law book. They teach it in the school. They brag about it in the press and patriotic speeches. And personal experience calls it a lie. A man is accused. Some mountebank has said that he is insane. Bang, he is in prison. Crash, his property is seized. A shower of sparks or the flash of a knife, he is castrated, depersonalized. And very soon dead.

A whispered malicious word. A man is implicated in a murder, he knows not how. He is imprisoned "awaiting trial." His name, repute are wrecked, his life ruined whatever the outcome.

Even in the little matter of a parking ticket he is at risk. It is put under the windshield wiper, not properly served. It blows away. He never sees it. He is brought to court, fined for something he knew nothing about.

So, in the long run, injustices big or small add up to insecurity, to a feeling one is being attacked or could be. The citizen is expected to protect the government. He looks at his tax-shredded paycheck, sees no way out. He decides it isn't a two-way proposition. So he ceases to protect and begins to attack the government. His attack may be as small as simply not acting.

When a government puts up a gross public example of attacking decent people for no crime, as in the case of the Church of Scientology, and when it is obvious that such an attack is under the influence of a blood-soaked terror symbol like the psychiatrist, the feeling of security of thinking men receives a distinct jolt.

Time passes. Some insurgent force whispers "that government is no good." The average citizen may not join up. He only nods quietly to himself, a silent "We know that."

Time passes. Revolutionaries with a new cause rise up.

Machine guns start up in the streets. The conscript army quietly drifts away.

The government cries, "Citizens! Rise up! Repel the invader!"

And in turn they get a cynical if hidden smile.

So the nation falls. The government officials are torn to pieces by the mob.

Why? Because they let patriotism be slain by the thousands, the millions of false accusations, by deafness to any plea for human rights, by shrugging off injustices out of arrogance or contempt.

It is not for nothing that the phrase "a just cause" was coined. No cause is worth fighting for unless it contains justice for all.

"Very few governments have implemented any part of the Universal Declaration of Human Rights. These governments have not grasped that their very survival depends utterly upon adopting such reforms and thus giving their peoples a cause, a civilization worth supporting, worth their patriotism."

We in the Church of Scientology are seeking to help prevent the collapse of Western civilization.

We ourselves have been mauled and oppressed for two decades of false accusation at the hands of an enemy so blood-spattered he looks more like a vampire than a man.

Our studies have brought to light crimes and injustices against the populations of Western nations sufficient to condemn many "best people" if they were ever tried in a Court under the Nuremberg Code.

"Even in the little matter of a parking ticket he is at risk. It is put under the windshield wiper, not properly served. It blows away. He never sees it. He is brought to court, fined for something he knew nothing about."

We are not weak. We are not powerless. We number millions. But our main strength is that we are decent people with the highest respect for law and order.

When we are lied about and banned and we see the governments who attack us letting our accusers, who are condoned in the most heinous crimes, go free, then we know how late it is.

We have straightened up our own house with regard to fair justice.

We are not thinking about ourselves. We are oppressed but vital.

To us these are only symptoms of a society that, unless reformed, will die.

We are putting our shoulder to the wheel to make it see the light, to make it reform its processes of justice on a fair and equitable basis so that once more the men of the West can say they fight in a just cause.

Notwithstanding the consequences of "Writing to Governments," readers should bear in mind the following: In referencing the "drawn gun raid," LRH is alluding to a 1963 United States Food and Drug Administration seizure of E-Meters and literature from the Founding Church of Scientology in Washington, DC. What ensued stands as among the most contentious legal confrontations between the United States Government and any religious organization. Ultimately, however, the Church not only emerged with sweeping recognition of religious bona fides, but the court ordered the return of all seized materials. Parenthetically, however, one might note the last of those seized materials were not actually returned for another four years, or until the mid-1970s. Moreover, and although no explanation was ever provided for that four-year delay, there is much to suggest those E-Meters were not simply stored in a government warehouse, but were actually instruments of intense and fascinating federal study.

In referencing a 1969 British Parliamentary Inquiry of Scientology, LRH is alluding to an eventual ban of all persons seeking to enter the United Kingdom for the study of Scientology. Again, however, and following from extended Church efforts over a decade, that ban was eventually declared wholly discriminatory in 1980 and lifted by the Secretary of State for the Home Office. Finally, regarding Ron's dismissal from Southern Africa as a threat to apartheid, let us not forget apartheid is no more and South Africa now enjoys precisely what Ron had worked for as regards one man, one vote.

Yet if there is a greater lesson to be learned from the outcome of events, it is this: that ill-fated raid on the Church, the ill-fated banning of Scientology students in Great Britain and attempts to suppress LRH efforts toward freedom in Southern Africa—all of it finally and simply proves what LRH declared from the start:

"The old must give way to the new, falsehood must become exposed by truth, and truth, though fought, always in the end prevails."

2 March 1969

ON WRITING TO GOVERNMENTS

by L. Ron Hubbard

GOVERNMENTS THESE DAYS ACT very strangely when one writes to them.

In late 1962 I wrote the US president, after a year had been spent working with flight surgeons in an aircraft squadron which, due to Scientology, went the whole period without a single accident, to state that we could help pilots.

The letter was polite and offering help to the government.

Shortly thereafter longshoremen, posing as marshals, armed with a false warrant, made a drawn gun raid on our Washington Church and seized prayer books and instruments.

In 1966 I wrote Dr. Verwoerd, the South African Prime Minister, a letter that I had information that a dangerous situation might exist in his vicinity. He wrote back thanking me.

I was suddenly made *persona non grata* in Southern Africa.

Shortly afterwards Dr. Verwoerd was assassinated by a psychiatric patient.

In 1967, about July, I wrote Home Office Immigration offering to help them with any student immigration problem, as I had found that some of the people they said were Scientologists weren't. And that perhaps I could get the UK Church directors to cooperate. A very polite letter.

The Home Office promptly told the papers my UK visa was cancelled—and even informed me, some three weeks later. They barred out all students, even Commonwealth citizens, and barred my daughter, who is a British subject.

In December 1968 UK Parliament said there would be no Scientology Inquiry.

As I had been barred out only on the word of now-fired Kenneth Robinson, the psychiatric frontman, in January 1969 I courteously wrote the Home Office that as the government had not produced any evidence against me, could I please have my unlimited landing card back.

The new Health Minister promptly appointed an "Inquiry into Scientology" and the Home Office rejected my request.

Those are the only four letters I've written governments.

They were all pleasant, courteous, routine.

Each one seems to have caused a violent, even terrified, explosion out of all proportion.

It's as if someone on government lines in each case was frightened that Scientology would be accepted or used.

The psychiatric front groups control immigration services through "health" connections. They flood health and immigration files with false accusations against any possible rival. I've seen the files and they contain false documents and pretended literature.

All I can make out of it is that the psychiatric front groups are going all out to protect their billion-per-year handouts and no effective activity need apply.

If the US had accepted our pilot help, they might not be losing their plane a day over Vietnam.

If Dr. Verwoerd had accepted my warning, he would not be dead.

If the UK Immigration had accepted my offer of help with students, Robinson might still be Health Minister.

I don't know what will happen on this Star Chamber "Inquiry." But if it has any similarity to the rest, it won't be successful to the opposition.

That's all I can make of this. Our psychiatric brethren, alert on the lines for anyone that would upset their stranglehold, is not about to let anyone who knows his business get into communication with a government. It might upset their free gift appropriations and the best-laid plans of rats and men.

But they can't keep it up forever. Murder will out.

It's rather an amusing picture one gets though. Of governments in a sort of cage with a psychiatrist as guard.

"It's rather an amusing picture one gets though. Of governments in a sort of cage with a psychiatrist as guard."

12 MARCH 1969

GOVERNMENT AND REVOLT

by L. Ron Hubbard

THE HISTORY OF REVOLTS has had one thing in common: a policy of government by the few, for the few and oppression of the many.

Special-privilege groups dominated and were listened to by every government in history which has fallen to a peoples' revolt.

The keynotes of such special groups is help for nobody but themselves and hate for everyone including themselves.

The Equestrian order of Rome, the Aristocracy of France and Russia, the superselect Nazis of Germany, the international financiers and the psychiatric front groups now dominating Western governments had much in common.

They operated for themselves alone and used the people as though they were animals.

It is no coincidence that psychiatric front groups teach that men are only animals to be herded, used and butchered at a whim.

The Roman Equestrian order, the upper classes of France and Russia, the Nazis and the psychiatrists all fixated on this mode of idea. Man was an animal.

By this, of course, they meant Man was their personal animal. Anyone else who sought to communicate to Man was looked on as an animal thief, an interloper.

But aristos and Nazis and psychiatrists have another thing in common: they are fixated, snobbish people—they cannot change, they do not believe others change and they overlook utterly that times change.

Such people easily go out-of-date. They get stuck in yesterday. The "old times were best" attitude stops all progress. For instance, the psychiatrist is stuck utterly in the nineteenth century. His practices and attitudes have not changed in all that time.

"It is no coincidence that psychiatric front groups teach that men are only animals to be herded, used and butchered at a whim. The Roman Equestrian order, the upper classes of France and Russia, the Nazis and the psychiatrists all fixated on this mode of idea. Man was an animal."

He considers himself a "best people." He associates only with the rich. And he considers Man his personal animal to use or slaughter as he wishes. And he thinks of himself (towers of madness) as part of the government—which of course he is not, any more than the local butcher is.

Governments composed of "the best people" (or snobs if you will) are in actual fact very unstable.

Instead of going forward with the times and keeping abreast of progress, they play at Stop the Clock.

Anyone with a new idea is looked on with ferocity, as an animal thief.

Therefore each new person who steps forward with improvements or suggestions is made at once into an enemy by the violence with which he is greeted.

Thus, in a special-privilege governmental scene, all the new developments are outside the closed circle. The anointed few by this rejection came more and more to stand alone.

One day the people and those with new ideas are all on one side of the fence. The snobs are on the other side.

All progressive people are thus forced into close association with Man.

The special-privilege group sees the danger, hires guns, hoodlums, hoods, bodyguards and tries to control "their animals" with force.

Man, not agreeing he is just a domestic animal, resents it. He turns around to the clever progressive ones on his side of the fence and says, "What do we do now?"

Well, history is too full of gory examples to make further description of what happens profitable.

It surely happens!

A government can always estimate how close it is to being revolted against by counting up how many bright willing men it is excluding from participation. It does not matter how the exclusion is done—aristos used pedigree, Nazis used Aryanism, psychiatrists use "degrees"—the result is the same. The bright ones are with the people, the special ones have only guns.

And that is the real genus of revolt.

Governments by, for and of special privilege are doomed the moment they set up the first barrier to the many. It becomes a barricade.

9 June 1969

CONSTITUTIONAL DESTRUCTION

by L. Ron Hubbard

For any group to engage fully and knowingly upon the destruction of the Constitution and any liberty or freedom it may guarantee is less startling than that they should also be accepted as the dominant force behind many politicians.

"National" Mental Health groups in any country are all members of the World Federation of Mental Health. The former president of the WFMH, the Communist Brock Chisholm, and any and all officers of this group and its "National" Mental Health members freely confess that they have as a primary target the eradication of their country's Constitution.

In the US this is a criminal offense, to advocate the overthrow of the Constitution. But many unprincipled State and Federal politicians not only turn a blind eye upon this, but also condone illegal seizure, torture and murder of citizens by these groups.

Hitler once said that his primary weapon was the "incredible." No one would believe what was actually being done by the Saboteur forces of the Third Reich because their plans were incredible.

These psychiatric front groups have a very thorough program of Western destruction:

1. Destruction of the Constitution.
2. Eradication of boundaries.
3. Easy seizure of anyone.
4. The "right" to torture or kill.
5. Eradication of all churches.
6. Destruction of sexual morality.
7. Deprivation of future leaders by the creation of dope addiction in schools.

All these things and more are to be found throughout their campaign literature, their advices to members and their puppet political supporters.

The "Health" ministries of almost every Western nation are occupied by their appointees.

The "technology" they use is entirely *control* technology. They do not pretend in any way to heal anyone. "Treatment" to them means injure or kill.

They have redefined *insanity* to mean "anyone who is incompetent." They define *competent* to mean "people who do not oppose them."

In California any citizen can now be seized and held seventy-two hours and tortured or killed. The "practitioners" and the secret officers who execute the action are made immune by law from any suit.*

All this sounds very familiar. About two-thirds of Hitler's espionage agents were "doctors."

Electric shock and brain operations to depersonalize dissident elements were developed by Hitler. They never were curative.

The turmoil of schools and universities trace back to the agents of these groups and their advices to corrupt puppet politicians.

This is the Utopia now in action.

The destruction of all liberty and civil rights. The hypocrisy that these are the best people who know best are all the ingredients of revolution.

But all of these groups, whose control is uniform over the world and whose lines go straight to Russia, may be in for a terrible surprise.

Since Scientology became aware of them, they have lost seven of their top dozen leaders.

Since their documents and plans were uncovered, they have been facing bankruptcy.

Every single lie, false charge and attack on Scientology has been traced directly to this group's members. They have sought at great expense for nineteen years to crush and eradicate any new development in the field of the mind. They are actively preventing any effectiveness in this field.

But seven of their top men are wholly out of action.

And their group is going bankrupt because we have shut off their appropriations.

It was an unlucky day when they began to attack Scientology. It was not even in their line of country. It had no interest in them.

The primary threat to freedom in the West has been fought by just one group, the Scientologists.

If you want freedom and peace in the West, join Scientology.

The Scientologists are the only vital new effective force in the world today.

And Scientology is the only game on Earth where everybody wins.

Specifically, LRH is referencing the Lanterman-Petris-Short Act, allowing for a 72-hour psychiatric confinement of citizens suspected of unbalanced behavior. The act further allowed for the drugging and electroconvulsive treatment of detainees. In the mid-seventies, however, and largely owing to efforts of Scientologists, the guts of that act were removed under California State Assembly Bill 1032. —Editor

"About two-thirds of Hitler's espionage agents were 'doctors.' Electric shock and brain operations to depersonalize dissident elements were developed by Hitler. They never were curative. The turmoil of schools and universities trace back to the agents of these groups and their advices to corrupt puppet politicians. This is the Utopia now in action."

Although, as he previously remarks, Scientologists represent the "only vital new effective force in the world today," LRH long acknowledged the efforts of others to at least decry oppression and tyranny. In particular, he would seem to have been referencing the many student organizations then working to end a Central Intelligence Agency presence on campus, the many civil rights organizations working on behalf of minorities and the various citizen organizations opposing oppressive taxation. In any case, the political landscape of 1969 had indeed been teeming with hundreds of protesting bodies, frequently in competition with one another and vying to be heard.

13 June 1969

UNITE AND WIN

by L. Ron Hubbard

THERE ARE INNUMERABLE INDEPENDENT groups and societies in the West who are fighting to halt the encroaching tyrannies and oppressions which menace the West.

These single voices are relatively ineffective only because each seeks to act alone.

The enemy is the Utopia-minded social and economic planner* whose arrogance is destroying the cultural standards of the people and supplanting them with the untried and insane concepts of total social control.

The West was made by free men. It is being unmade by tyranny.

At the hand of most government leaders today are social or economic agencies which seek to impose unsound and unproven controls upon a formerly free society.

As and when he takes office, the politician is promised a roseate and marvelous result by men who could not manage a petty cash account or control a puppy if their lives depended on it.

These wild-eyed Utopians have all but destroyed Western Universities, Western economies and Western civilization.

Each protesting public body is crying out at its own particular oppressor. Yet all these oppressors together are the real collective target.

Public groups should unite in a forum and choose their particular target and then apply all efforts at righting that type of wrongness by united effort. Then they should choose another target and handle that.

---

*As a word on the "Utopia-minded social and economic planner[s]" to whom Mr. Hubbard refers, he explained in January of the same year that "Today we have government by special interest. It ignores to a huge degree what the average citizen really wants. This winds up usually in some weird, special-interest-Utopia mess like the book George Orwell's *1984*. The number of Utopia planners around would amaze you. The average individual shuns Utopias like the plague. One has to go to the individual member and go to many individuals in many strata of society to find out what's really wanted. It's usually pretty simple." (Note: This is from Hubbard Communications Office Policy Letter 31 January 1969, HUMANITARIAN OBJECTIVE AND GUNG-HO GROUPS.) —Editor

It will be found that the enemy is well united and that he uses the full force of credulous and incompetent governments to crush the whole people.

It is *not* a "symptom of the times" that things are going wrong in the West. They are carefully planned that way.

Each public group that is protesting is today divided from the rest so that no united public voice calls erring agencies to account.

In the West our affairs are in the hands of experimenters in social control. The result is disorder and disaster.

There *is* such a thing as Western government devoid, as it used to be, of social and economic Utopians.

In one way or another, every protesting group has as its purpose the halting of further faulty experimentation and the restoration of the sound and wise policies in government.

While we still have something left for which to fight, all public societies and groups should unite to halt the tyranny and oppression which threatens to engulf us and destroy forever the society on which we depend.

The West came to greatness under the banner of liberty. But all liberties are gradually withered away where a public is not alert.

Revolt is *not* the answer. Firm and united counseling of the government by groups which defend our culture and our liberty alone can serve us all.

"The West came to greatness under the banner of liberty. But all liberties are gradually withered away where a public is not alert."

To have described President Richard Nixon in this June 1969 essay as "spitting on the Bill of Rights," LRH truly represented a fearless voice. As history shows, he was also absolutely correct. For in addition to previously cited excesses over and above the United States Constitution and Bill of Rights, Nixon was eventually named as party to at least the following: the illegal wiretapping of political opponents, the burglary of private offices, the misappropriation of campaign funds, the misuse of government agencies for personal ends and what amounted to the blackmail of enemies. Although succeeding president (and former Nixon vice-president) Gerald Ford was to finally pardon the man for crimes committed in office, many among the Nixon staff eventually served time in a federal penitentiary.

27 June 1969

UNCONSTITUTIONAL GOVERNMENT

by L. Ron Hubbard

THE EXISTENCE OF A Constitution does not guarantee a people a Constitutional Government. Written or unwritten, Constitutions usually set up the form of the government and guarantee the people certain rights.

Governments usually formulate them and point to them as evidence of their liberality. Often, to gain popular support, they add to them very worthwhile Bills of Rights guaranteeing individual freedom, trial by jury, confrontation of one's accusers, freedom of religion and speech and other desirable features.

But the end product is a "con game" of wonderful scope.

The elected and appointed members of the government and their employees are all found to be "above the law." *They* are not compelled in any real way to act within the Constitution or a Bill of Rights.

The government's departments and bureaus routinely act completely without regard to the Constitution.

In the US, the Supreme Court exists to reverse government unconstitutionality. But one seldom reaches it with a case unless one has tens of thousands of dollars for legal fees and even when one wins a Supreme Court decision, the government employee or bureau whose unconstitutional actions caused the trouble in the first place goes unpunished and unscathed.

Almost all the trouble in a country is the government, through its employees, acting in a thoroughly unconstitutional fashion.

This reacts on the public as a disbelief in the actual government and a disavowal of it.

As the government employees, elected or appointed, do not act within the framework of the Constitution, the public thinks of them as frauds or conquerors and alien.

Revolutionary groups spring up. Any foreign enemy finds adherents. Criminals are protected by the public. No one goes near the police. And the final product is at best a revolt and at worse the death of a civilization.

The government "public servant" is supposed to act of, for and by the people in a democracy. But the public sees in him someone peculiarly exempt from law and a servant of only special-interest groups.

The aspect of a government mouthing the Constitution and yet acting as a Superman caste undermines patriotism by defying belief. The public reacts to this untruth with defiance. More and more force is needed to control the population and at last there is a revolt or the nation degenerates and dies.

As the public cannot strike at the government individual who is acting in an unconstitutional manner, it strikes at the whole government. No government can afford even one tyrannous petty clerk much less unconstitutional behavior in all its departments.

In America the people are fond of the Constitutional freedoms promised by the Founding Fathers.

Yet the existing government in all its executive departments spits on the Bill of Rights a thousand times a day. And executive orders defy them in an avalanche. These departments are actively at war with religion, freedom of speech and ordinary legal procedures to a degree that observing the Bill of Rights is a remarkable exception to their normal conduct.

The courts will accept no complaints or summonses for these "public servants." They cannot be sued. There is no crime which they cannot commit with complete personal safety. And they control the bayonets and full force of the state and use it to serve themselves and their friends.

In gathering case histories of the unconstitutional conduct of these agencies, one is overwhelmed with the volume of instances and feels the futility of even beginning to list them.

At state and county level, abuses of power and violations of rights are so flagrant that few voices indeed dare raise themselves in protest.

National and state, county, and city laws, reviewed against the Constitution, present a spectacle of studied defiance. Illegal seizures of persons and property, detention without trial, are the common routine of officials.

Yet they wonder that the public does not support them actively, but tends to withdraw in fear.

When a public is faced with unconstitutional officials, it becomes insecure. When the insecurity becomes high enough, they join any revolutionary force. When further oppression is leveled at them, they revolt.

The common answer of one of these governments is money handouts in an effort to buy support. It does not work.

Trying to remove all leaders or active people from the population by some unholy alliance with psychiatry, not only does not work, it accelerates the downfall of the state, involving as it does even more flagrant rights violations.

So many empires and nations have gone this route—Rome, France, Czarist Russia, Germany, Poland, Hungary, Czechoslovakia, etc., etc., etc., etc., and so many are furiously floundering down the same path that it is a wonder that men in government have not spotted their trouble.

"When a public is faced with unconstitutional officials, it becomes insecure. When the insecurity becomes high enough, they join any revolutionary force. When further oppression is leveled at them, they revolt. The common answer of one of these governments is money handouts in an effort to buy support. It does not work."

THE VAST MAJORITY OF GOVERNMENT EMPLOYEES ARE HONEST, DECENT PEOPLE. BUT THEY ARE COMPELLED, OFTEN AGAINST THEIR WILL, TO ACT UNCONSTITUTIONALLY BY SOME OF THEIR LEADERS OR FELLOW EMPLOYEES WHO FLOUT THE RULES OF DECENCY IN THE NAME OF THE STATE.

Perhaps the taste of tyranny is so delicious and the sadism of despotism is such an addiction that even if they knew their lives depended utterly on becoming bound by and acting according to their Constitutions and Bills of Rights, they still could not forego it.

The dope addict may know his vice is killing him. Yet he cannot end it. Possibly this is the case in unconstitutional bureaucracy.

Men go quite mad with power. And madmen commit suicide easily. In fact, they never do anything else.

One wonders rather sadly why these fellows insist on committing suicide so expensively.

But Democracy, republics, even monarchies, will go on decaying and dying—and killing the rest of us—until the government official is forced to act in all his acts within the framework of the Constitution and all guarantees of individual rights.

One cannot perpetuate the monstrous untruth of a Constitution and Bill of Rights guaranteeing security and liberty while the most powerful class in the land is Superlaw and is in no way bound by it.

28 June 1969

CONSTITUTIONS

by L. Ron Hubbard

A Constitution is an instrument founding or modifying a government.
Most national Constitutions are written, but some are partially written and partially understood. Some early Greek Constitutions were unwritten.

Nearly all modern Constitutions are incomplete and only the Constitution of Eire is binding upon its government leaders and employees as well as the people. In all other states the politicians and employees are "above the law," which of course results in a total nullification of the Constitution in that the people who run the state are not bound by the founding instrument of the state, making their Constitutions a sort of "con game." The discrepancy between the Constitution and the actual conduct of the government is a primary cause of revolt.

A Constitution ideally would be composed of four subjects or parts:

A. The Purpose of the State
B. The Composition of the Government
C. The Rights of Citizens
D. The Penal Codes

In instrumenting a Constitution, the concentration is on appeal. The instigators have first and foremost the problem of persuading a population to accept an instrument of government.

Like many political promises, the effort to persuade is not entirely sincere. Therefore, one or more of the essential parts of a Constitution are omitted and are added later as "laws" by "men who know best."

For instance, it was not the intention of the Founding Fathers of the United States to have anything but a republic, while intimating, then and ever since, that they founded a "democracy."

A Republic is a government wherein the "best people" represent the people and act for the "good of the people." Once elected, a "Representative of the People" goes his own way, most often following the orders of the special-interest groups who financed his career. A Democracy is government directly by the people, a thing seen in France in recent times where no serious action was undertaken without referendum to the people.

Politicians seem to have a recurring problem of how to pretend to guarantee liberty while actually reserving the right of despotism. We see this in any Constitution which omits or later disregards one of the essential parts of a Constitution while offering one to the people.

The original US Constitution omitted both the Bill of Rights of the citizen and the Penal Code. A few years after its adoption, Shays' Rebellion and other public commotion forced the United States to quickly add a Bill of Rights, known now as the first ten amendments.

However, the politician later dropped part A, saying "the Preamble has no force in law" and thus robbing the state of a purpose, condemning it thereafter to idle wanderings in policy and setting up a new channel for tyranny.

The Australian state Constitutions are unblushingly ignored in totality, thus omitting all parts of a Constitution at once by flagrant neglect. These Constitutions were pure examples of a mere public relations stunt without other meaning.

The recent Greek Constitution not only lacks its essential parts, but the referendum adopting it was still fluttering on billboards when the government violated it on all counts despite its acceptance by the people. It is one of the purest examples of a public relations trick on record.

Once a populace has accepted a Constitution, it has surrendered the rights to act otherwise. Therefore, intentional despotism can be attributed to a Constitution which leaves essential parts unsaid or which delegate their settlement to a privileged few.

Changes in Constitutions are usually activated in the direction of further limitation of liberty and are usually attended by disaster.

The 1905 change in the US Constitution which nullified the clause prohibiting "Poll Tax" opened the door to the hideous nightmare of an Income Tax system operating its own courts and condemning any citizen without regard to the Bill of Rights.

The infamous Prohibition Act forbidding liquor began the trend of financed crime and accelerated the decay of a country already dying because of the Poll Tax change. Prohibition was eventually removed in the Constitution, but not until crime was well financed.

A Constitution which omits any one of its essential four parts is an invitation to tyranny, as these missing parts will be supplied by legislators and continually changed.

A Constitution which contains no clause to make violations of it actionable by the individual public on individual government members elected, appointed or employed is not worth the effort to print it, as it will become focus of revolt since it fosters the public belief that its government is not its government, but something else.

A Constitution is a good thing only if it gives due and sensible attention to all the above. Otherwise it is a bad thing and an invitation to a trap in which the whole population can become oppressed.

"The infamous Prohibition Act forbidding liquor began the trend of financed crime and accelerated the decay of a country already dying because of the Poll Tax change. Prohibition was eventually removed in the Constitution, but not until crime was well financed."

25 November 1969

THE EVOLUTION OF TOTALITARIANISM

by L. Ron Hubbard

TOTALITARIANISM IS DEFINED AS "of or relating to a political regime based on subordination of the individual to the state and strict control of all aspects of the life and productive capacity of the nation, especially by coercive measures (as censorship and terrorism)."

The world has seen it in the raw ruthlessness of many despots of the past and Hitler's Germany and Stalin's Russia in modern times.

As Totalitarianism is easily the most detested form of government and the most difficult to cast off, some thought should be given to how a Totalitarianism evolves.

Basically the political life of a nation is divided into two types of groups.

First there is the GENERAL-INTEREST GROUP. This is a broad, open group such as a political party or an association of teachers or a church. What distinguishes them as a general-interest group is the fact that they stand for what they say they stand for and do what they say they do. They have beliefs, they scuffle about, but they are in the open and their influence is direct and visible.

Then there is another type of group. It can be called a SPECIAL-INTEREST GROUP. It could also be called a "hidden" interest group. It is characterized by having some fixed idea, but advertising something else. They are composed of zealots who work to the exclusion of all other interest as well as the exclusion of the well-being of others who are not "aligned" with the fixed idea of that group.

These special-interest groups are commonly distrusted since they fail to announce their actual intention and sell their fixed idea behind a facade of often-clever steps and propaganda.

The citizen who suddenly learns that Senator Belch was really a "front" for the oil interests or that Minister Bray was really trying to increase armament company profits is, as a good and unsuspicious citizen, usually dismayed when "all is revealed."

Fixed ideas are usually buried in the mind and a person, as often as not, is unaware of what underlies his revulsions and prejudices. Similarly in the broad masses of the society, a special-interest group is obscured from view—one only sees its ploys and falsified "information" and is left to believe them, reject them or neglect them.

A suspicion that government is more and more guided by special-interest groups and less and less determined by general-interest groups, such as political parties or advertised social intent, has become a practical part of citizenship in modern times. When nations do not seem to be guided by good sense, the citizen begins to suspect "special interests" must underlie government policy. He is often so right that cynicism has displaced patriotism in most Western nations and we read that the day of idealism is dead.

As a matter of fact, only about 8 percent of the population is estimated to be "aligned" with special-interest groups of one sort or another even in moments of national stress. Ninety-two percent of the population, even in a country undergoing insurgency or revolt, are not "aligned" at all. Other social and political estimates show even less "alignment."

Thus, whether one is talking about a hidden or covert interest in specialized publics or oil or railroads, special-interest groups form a very small minority of the population in peace or war. The vast majority of the people are caught up in the clever statements, maneuvers and "unavoidable decisions" of a very tiny number of people.

"Public opinion" as stated by a special-interest group is seldom actual. The special-interest group alleges "public opinion" and by various means uses this statement to maneuver their will upon their opponents or the treasury or the law books.

Democracy tends to lend itself to the special-interest group in several ways, the most notable of which is a candidate's necessity to have campaign money with which to be elected. Some of these candidates for democratic office could not run at all without the funds furnished by or the influence of special-interest groups.

Thus the special-interest group can buy a voice to press its special interest, for the politician, no matter how honest, finds he is now supposed to utter certain opinions and espouse certain measures and defy the opponents of the special-interest group which supplied the influence and cash to win him his election or appointment.

Thus a democracy, as it deteriorates into special-interest hands, tends to be not of, by and for the people (who are more than 92 percent), but becomes of, by and for special-interest groups (which are less than 8 percent of the total population).

Even the honest politician, unaware that one of his colleagues is putting out false information and pressure from a hidden source, can be swayed by the special-interest group.

Such groups often covertly control certain press. They also infiltrate into general-interest groups and push some version of their fixed idea out disguised as a part of a hitherto-honest general-interest group.

For instance, the newspaper magnate Hearst used his papers to develop the "Yellow Peril" (which led to the 1941 war). But it is now known he was solely concerned not with the "evil Japanese," but with the threat open immigration of these skilled agriculturists posed to his own irrigation, produce and land interest. He was part of a group of moneyed landowners whose hidden special interest was their own holdings, but who spoke of patriotism, self-sacrifice, racial purity, nationalism and glory just to fatten their private purses. The Hearsts of the world rather spoiled an era of civilization. It was nothing to them how many men died believing the surface shouting. Another generation saw through it and patriotism, idealism and other values died because they had been corrupted to serve the hidden selfish ends of this special-interest group.

From time to time in history, small groups with fixed ideas have allied themselves together sufficiently to penetrate the political, economic and social life of the nation and taking advantage of some general disaster have emerged suddenly as the force triumphant.

Their real aims remained disguised until the very last moment and the population abruptly finds itself oppressed by special-interest men holding all key posts and all forces.

Freedom vanishes. Political life suddenly hardens into the fixed idea. Coercion and terrorism crush all opposition.

> *"When nations do not seem to be guided by good sense, the citizen begins to suspect 'special interests' must underlie government policy."*

Even those who assisted in the overwhelm, but whose own special interests are not needed any longer, are smashed down with the rest of the population.

A Totalitarianism has been born.

History is strewn with the wreckage which follows the operations of special-interest groups. Even Athens lost her glory and freedom due to the hidden inner workings of the "Macedonian Party" which, in her own Senate, covertly undermined Athenian democracy to serve their own private ends. Bribed by Philip of Macedon, these men sold out all Greece and brought on a Totalitarianism from which Greece never fully recovered.

In our own century Hitler, working under cover, recruiting at first the very Jews whose industries and newspapers he needed, promising anything but what he really was about to deliver, emerged abruptly in 1933 with all important posts and organizations covered.

We know the rest of this grim Totalitarianism.

Whenever a nation is struck by some disaster, some special-interest group may see its chance. And no nation is without such groups.

Being mad, the majority of special-interest groups are seldom successful in erecting a Totalitarianism. They fail to infiltrate enough high levels, enough general-interest groups. Or they fail internally. When the disaster for which they hunger strikes, they try. That they do not always succeed does not make them less dangerous.

The whole test of what is a special-interest group is "Do they do and try to do what they and their spokesmen say they are trying to do?" If so, they are just a general-interest group.

If a group has one advertised set of purposes but is generated by secret and hidden ambitions, it is a special-interest group.

Rightly the public abhors and fears a special-interest group. Unfortunately many a special-interest propagandist seeks to assign hidden interests to some innocent general group which has none—it is a common propaganda trick.

The proof of the pudding is the actual documentation of the hidden special interest.

Sometimes the proof never appears but the actual intentions of the group do—denoting a singular failure on the part of security forces.

"From time to time in history, small groups with fixed ideas have allied themselves together sufficiently to penetrate the political, economic and social life of the nation and taking advantage of some general disaster have emerged suddenly as the force triumphant. Their real aims remained disguised until the very last moment and the population abruptly finds itself oppressed by special-interest men holding all key posts and all forces."

Such a sudden emergence into the light is not always political: The US 1932 bank takeover wherein the huge chain banks used political frontmen to smash all private banks and grab the assets of a nation. Countries have been in economic slavery ever since. It was such a sudden emergence and so well "explained" that it took economists a quarter of a century to begin to realize there was a total revolution in economics and finance and that a new banking "Totalitarianism" existed where not one independent banking voice could be raised successfully. All Western nations are now totally dominated by just one group. And they run things sufficiently badly (what with inflation and political dictation) that a large majority are privately convinced these fellows have something else in mind. People are worried. Perhaps rightly, perhaps wrongly. But this group now reaches into the pockets of every man in Western nations directly, positively and mercilessly.

Stalin's Totalitarianism is an example of a special-interest group within a special-interest group. That emergence is still reverberating.

The psychiatric front groups are special-interest groups by documentation. To the public they talk on and on about mental health. But in every conference, in their private inner-circle publications, they speak about and listen to eradication of all boundaries, the destruction of all constitutions and other political matters which spell only ambition for world domination. Their political and organizational infiltration is extensively queer for a lot of headshrinkers. Their interest in easy seizure of people and their conduct in institutions are all at variance with their public facade of "mental health."

They have clearly shown that they can get any bill passed in a majority of legislatures. They are at the elbow of major political figures. They dominate the think of armed forces.

These are interesting boys. Mentally they act as mad as any totalitarianist ever spawned.

Even in the US civil defense manual, in event of a national disaster, the role assigned to these fellows is "to seize anyone who tries to do anything about it."*

People in the field of the mind who are really in that field usually talk about *cases*. You get around Scientology auditors and you hear about *cases*. You don't hear about getting publishers and politicians and the military under control. That's because they belong to a general-interest group that does what it says it does, processes and trains people about the mind.

But the psychiatric front people *don't* do what they say they do. They heal no one. And under hysterical duress in the press they repeatedly screamed that their aims were completely incompatible with those of Scientology. So if they didn't say what their aims were, although Scientology aims are just making people well, one is a bit surprised.

Why can't these psychiatric front groups announce their aims in public? You'd know if you read them. And I don't think the public would appreciate those psychiatric aims. "Us psychiatrists are interested in destroying boundaries and tearing up all constitutions." Sound kind of funny if they said that in public, wouldn't it? So they only say it in their private publications.

**In fact, various schemes were hatched within an American intelligence community regarding the arrest and detainment of troublesome citizens during times of national emergency. In particular, and under the banner of the Federal Emergency Management Agency, were plans for the building of actual detention centers and the amassing of dossiers on potential inmates for those centers. —Editor*

Their press and political infiltration is so deep, their influence so wide, their public statements and activities so different than what they print for themselves, they fully qualify as a special-interest group.

And when you examine their system of coercion and terrorism and their ceaseless political efforts to expand it, you are looking directly at an intended Totalitarianism. What's worse, they even espouse all the prophets of Totalitarianism clear back to the Comte de Saint-Simon.

Sure is ridiculous, isn't it? Sure is. But remember how at first the world laughed at Hitler?

And George Orwell's *1984* is based exclusively on what would happen if the headshrinkers took over the world.

"Such a sudden emergence into the light is not always political: The US 1932 bank takeover wherein the huge chain banks used political frontmen to smash all private banks and grab the assets of a nation. Countries have been in economic slavery ever since. It was such a sudden emergence and so well 'explained' that it took economists a quarter of a century to begin to realize there was a total revolution in economics and finance and that a new banking 'Totalitarianism' existed where not one independent banking voice could be raised successfully."

CHAPTER TWO

On Justice &
JURISPRUDENCE

On Justice & Jurisprudence | 59
Fast Justice | 63
Justice | 67
Riots | 71
The Justice Department versus Americans | 75

On Justice &
Jurisprudence

IN ADDRESSING THE STATE OF WESTERN JUSTICE AS OF 1969, L. Ron Hubbard is yet again moving onto highly significant historical ground. For example, then United States Attorney General—and thus United States Justice Department head—was none other than Watergate accomplice John N. Mitchell. Among other blatantly unjust activities conducted in the name of appointer Richard Nixon were the secret Mitchell discussions with International Telephone & Telegraph, generally known as ITT. In brief and quite frankly: in exchange for a six-figure ITT contribution to the Nixon presidential campaign, Mitchell conveniently swept aside Justice Department blockage of an ITT corporate acquisition. Then again, there was the Mitchell tenure as Coordinator of Law Enforcement Tactics, which included the directing of riot-stick-wielding National Guardsmen to break up antiwar demonstrations, the recommending of illegal wiretaps on suspected political dissidents and much else relating to what was described as "the government's right...to override the right of individuals' privacy."

Pertinent to LRH remarks on links between psychiatry and failing justice, readers should note that psychiatric encroachment into a Western judicial system effectively began with the likes of Drs. Winfred Overholser and Zigmond Lebensohn—both longtime foes of Dianetics and Scientology and longtime proponents of a larger psychiatric presence within the governing process. That is, while Overholser lobbied for a psychiatric explanation of criminality as stemming from "irresistible impulse," Lebensohn authored articles in praise of the "Symbiotic Relationship between Soviet Psychiatry and Soviet Law," wherein offenders were routinely turned over to psychiatrists for treatment. That Soviet treatment frequently involved the worst forms of psychosurgery and straitjacket medication did not, of course, figure in the Lebensohn argument.

Finally, no discussion of American justice, circa 1969, is complete without mention of

The American author, philosopher and gentleman at Saint Hill Manor, East Grinstead, England, 1960 that archetypal G-Man, J. Edgar Hoover. As LRH suggests—and once again he writes well in advance of public disclosures and well in front of later Hoover criticism—Hoover finally proved himself among the most sinister figures in American history. In addition to thirty-odd years of political blackmail—he actually compiled incriminating dossiers on United States presidents—he regularly instructed agents to violate the laws of the land. To cite another pertinent case in point, and one not even discovered until the 1990s: under a Hoover program known as COMINFIL (for *Com*munist *Infil*tration), Federal Bureau of Investigation agents regularly conducted infiltration/surveillance of several hundred United States civil and religious organizations, very much including Dianetics and Scientology. In essence, the ploy played out in this fashion: First, and generally covertly, an agent would inform a targeted organization that certain unnamed members were probably Communist infiltrators. When leaders of that organization then logically requested assistance in weeding out those alleged Communists, the Bureau would just as logically request membership lists and a free hand for a thorough investigation. Moreover, the Bureau successfully amassed files on virtually every citizen Hoover had deemed "un-American"—which essentially meant, anyone inclined to oppose what Hoover embodied as a truly fascistic power. In this way, the Bureau gradually succeeded in destroying all targeted organizations—except, of course, Dianetics and Scientology.

That Hoover himself is now known to have secretly inclined towards the donning of women's clothing (nylon stockings and all) was another matter entirely. ■

The Jefferson Memorial, Washington, DC, 1958; photograph by L. Ron Hubbard

1 March 1969

FAST JUSTICE

by L. Ron Hubbard

It is obvious that false accusations and the failure to confront a person directly with his accusers break down the social structure of a nation to a point where any internal insurgent or foreign nation with a rallying cause can overthrow it. This has happened in country after country in this century and includes the bulk of the land areas of the planet. Indeed, the hidden false accusations, corruption and injustices of Czarist Russia began our present international troubles with its successful Bolshevik revolt in 1917.

This new datum, taken from the philosophy of Scientology, gives us a rapid way to rehabilitate the West before it too goes the route.

Usually such proposed reforms carry with them ponderous administration or change.

There is a very simple way to provide fast, inexpensive justice for the entire population.

All that is necessary is APPOINT EVERY QUALIFIED ATTORNEY IN THE COUNTRY A JUDGE.

Leave all existing judges as they are, but handling only appeal cases.

Grade attorneys and judges against a scale arranged with bar associations.

Do not prevent attorneys from appearing as attorneys in courts other than their own.

Make the penalty for false accusation, whether or not under oath, commensurate to the amount of damage it would have done if it succeeded in unjustly disciplining or punishing someone.

Repeal all insanity commitment laws and replace them with the ordinary penal code. Cease to involve jurisprudence with mental expertise.

Indict any and all physical damage by reason of shock or brain surgery as a criminal offense, which it already is.

Pass legislation requiring any accused to be confronted by his or her accusers.

Prevent the seizure of property by psychiatrists or the state or a "custodian" by reason of legal proceedings.

Protect people and groups from fallacious and vexatious attacks.

Eradicate all "special privilege" categories wherein officials and others cannot be sued or disciplined for abuse of power.

Eradicate and make actionable any and all forms of police brutality.

Remove from the statute all laws calculated to "get" somebody for crimes or misdemeanors other than those of which he is suspected.

Pass legislation preventing Bills of Attainder in which groups or persons who have committed no offense can be injured.

Adhere to the principle of law that a person is innocent until he is proven guilty beyond reasonable doubt.

It is *lack* of ready, speedy, inexpensive justice that creates crime.

Justice is only taken into a person's own hands when it is nowhere else available.

The man branded by record as a criminal usually has only crime left by which to live.

This is no planned airy-fairy "Utopia." It is just the actual *application* of those principles which once existed, are often written down, but are seldom applied.

And I have seldom seen a lawyer who did not know he could solve the problem on his own if just left to it.

"It is lack of ready, speedy, inexpensive justice that creates crime. Justice is only taken into a person's own hands when it is nowhere else available."

1 March 1969

JUSTICE

by L. Ron Hubbard

THE MAJOR BREAKDOWN OF Western democracy is its habit of carelessly basing legal actions on false reports.

Anyone can say anything about anybody, and police powers and courts are liable to act on reports so false that a child could see through the lie.

This was the most odious thing about the NAZIS. And this characterizes Communist "justice."

In February 1969,* I isolated the false accusation, false report and failing to confront the accused with his accusers as the basic breakdown of justice. These undermine personal security and involve the whole judiciary in endless, needless traffic.

Innocent people are subjected to press attacks, court procedures, endless expense and ruined lives by these factors alone.

Corrupt pressure groups, such as the psychiatrists, can disrupt any possible rival or tear the social structure of a nation to pieces as long as false reports are published, accepted and acted upon.

So flagrant is this abuse that it destroys, for one and all, the value of the cause of democracy.

When justice becomes slow, when it becomes expensive and when false reports on people and groups are allowed to go unchallenged and unpunished, any ideology becomes a tyranny.

So great are these factors in the disruption of loyalty and creation of revolutionaries that no government that permits them is safe.

This is, in fact, a new philosophic breakthrough in the field of jurisprudence. The great importance of the false report in breaking down a nation's social structure and its cause has not been understood.

Most of the internal conflict in a country is caused by individuals and groups defending themselves against false reports.

*See Hubbard Communications Office Policy Letter 24 February 1969, JUSTICE. —Editor

"When justice becomes slow, when it becomes expensive and when false reports on people and groups are allowed to go unchallenged and unpunished, any ideology becomes a tyranny."

In a period where governments "seek to capture the minds of men," a great deal of reform will have to be done.

Human rights have as one of their threats the false report. Yet there is no adequate practical recourse. Suits for libel? Forget them. They cost more than anyone can afford, take forever to try and leave the public with the false reports even when they are won.

As false reports tear down the security of the individual and small group, these then have to assert themselves. They do so, in their turn, by attacking.

A nation which permits these to be acted upon will eventually find itself deserted by its populace and supporting groups, attacked by its decent people and eventually will be overthrown.

To save itself, a nation must permit direct legal action which is fast and inexpensive so that an individual or group can legally protect itself from false reports.

Only if the "free" world reforms its human rights will it have a cause worth fighting for, worth supporting. Otherwise its public and social groups will desert it to any other cause without even much examining it.

The virtues of patriotism, loyalty and devotion to the government are not dead by some strange social decay. They are dead because people feel their government no longer protects them, even attacks them, opens the door on them to easy psychiatric seizure, fantastic taxation and personal insecurity.

For instance, the black man in the US has long been saying he will not fight for the government. That isn't because he's a Communist. It's because anyone can lay a charge on them, no matter how false, get a black man jailed, beaten up, lynched. And authorities shrugged with "It's just a coon." He had no equal *respect* under law. Any false report, untested, could get him arrested, beaten or killed. So he became very insecure. And now he continually riots, loots, burns, is even closing universities. All because any false report was accepted. And he could be beaten or hung waiting on slow, expensive justice.

It isn't limited to US blacks. This was true of all US minority groups and is true of religious and racial minority groups in far too many countries. So they form a core of resistance and unrest. They are nervous and defensive.

Then, as the situation worsens, many social groups begin to react to false reports against them, again unable to obtain justice fast enough to prevent name damage.

About that time the officials better look to their foreign bank accounts and decamp. For that government, even while still functioning, is no longer the government of its people. It is their enemy. Any revolutionary movement will be joined. These are the mechanics of revolution.

People will stand for an awful lot. Then one day patriotism is dead. Because the government no longer has a cause the majority believe in or will fight for.

The principles of not accepting false reports and confronting one with his accusers and their accusations *before* punishing actions of any kind are so strong that if the West accepted them and scrupulously practiced them, IT WOULD HAVE A CAUSE GREAT ENOUGH TO SURVIVE.

It could then "out-cause" the Communist.

As it stands, Western governments have to BUY and BRIBE their defense at a cost so fantastic it will break them.

Our position is this: We are standing up and befriending Western powers, trying to get them to pull up their honor and justice before the mob gets to them and tears them to bits.

In dramatic testimony to what LRH addresses in his 1969 "Riots," readers might well consider the 1992 eruption of Los Angeles and neighboring communities following the acquittal of law enforcement officers involved in the videotaped beating of black motorist Rodney King. The point: having isolated the real Why behind civil rights, LRH had isolated the cause of all riots—no matter the time, place or circumstances. Had Los Angeles understood Ron's 1969 "Riots" prior to the Rodney King affair, Los Angeles would have known precisely what to expect. As if to prove the point, when copies of "Riots" were broadly distributed among stricken Los Angeles residents, more than a few assumed the article had specifically been written in reference to the Rodney King affair itself. In that regard, and yet again, LRH was not merely commenting on disturbing events; he was getting to their root cause.

19 March 1969

RIOTS

by L. Ron Hubbard

Riots are not always caused by economic deprivation.

The bulk of American riots are caused by injustice.

Only the wealthy can afford justice. It may say there must be justice in the Constitution, but it can only be obtained in upper courts.

The little fellow doesn't have $100,000 to fight the unjust actions of those in power.

Until there is justice for the little people, not just for the rich, there will be riots. And these riots can easily swell into complete raw, red revolution.

A black person can be innocently standing on a street corner. Can be grabbed, beaten, thrown in jail and worked at hard labor all on some imaginary charge. It may say it can't be done in the law books, but where's his $100,000 to take it high enough for action?

I have seen a Filipino university professor hauled in for nothing, his jaw broken, held without bail, all because he was a Filipino in a white US community (Port Orchard, Washington).

I have seen jails full of men who could not even say what the actual charge against them was—but they worked like dogs every day as convict labor.

As a minister, going amongst the people, I have witnessed enough injustice to overturn a state, only waiting for a spark to ignite the suppressed wrath into revolution.

Until justice applies to all, until a person is really assumed innocent until proven guilty, until it no longer costs a tenth of a million to get to an upper court, the government is at risk.

They may be very big, their sweat may have no odor, their arrogance may put them above all others, but the leaders of a nation who, for one instant, tolerate injustice to their poorest citizens today should have their heads ready for the basket. Another 1789 is boiling up, only waiting for one big spark to flash across the Western world.

Injustice is not something in which any man with power should ever trade. It is not just a sin. It is suicide.

"The little fellow doesn't have $100,000 to fight the unjust actions of those in power."

23 February 1975

THE JUSTICE DEPARTMENT VERSUS AMERICANS

by L. Ron Hubbard

EVERY NATION HAS HAD its disastrous public officials at one time or another. Russia had Stalin, Germany had Hitler, England had Cromwell and the United States had J. Edgar Hoover.

My first contact with J. Edgar began in the early '30s.

Having made a balled-up mess out of Prohibition, which had now ended, J. Edgar was in very great need of publicity.

The Justice Department ran on the theory that if they could get enough columns of print, they could get enough Congressional appropriation to expand into a National Police Force.

Accordingly they contacted writers' organizations and offered to put all writers through their "G-Man" school.

Several writers, under one pen name or another, went down and popped .357 Magnum revolvers at bobbing picture targets and examined dead dummies that had just been "murdered" to solve the "crime." But, in general, to be lectured at about how great J. Edgar was and how invincible were "G-Men" and how vital it was for the Justice Department to run a national police force and hunt down people they designated as Public Enemies by number—no. 1, no. 2, etc.

When queried as to who designated them and on what evidence, J. Edgar said his bosses did and, as to evidence, that was a secondary matter. He said that these writers should write stories about "G-Men" and the Justice Department would be glad to give them anything they wanted.

Well, it worked. Even a magazine called *G-Men* appeared.

But I began to wonder about J. Edgar and his bosses at the Justice Department.

In World War II, the Justice Department took over Counterintelligence for America and pretty well disbanded the Office of Naval Intelligence and other agencies.

As a naval officer I had only a couple of contacts with them. One had to do with another officer losing a $7.50 telephone, resulting in the ripping apart of a whole ship. (They didn't find it.) The other involved the discovery of a sodium bomb in a box of torpedo detonators. A sodium bomb soaks up water from the air and explodes when the ship is at sea. I asked that the cargo be unloaded and was refused. They said it really wasn't a sodium bomb. But when I offered to throw it in the water you never saw G-Men scatter so fast.

In 1950 it was pretty obvious that American churches were being infiltrated, a fact later confirmed by a Congressional Committee.

I dropped in to J. Edgar's office and soon was talking to the head of anti-Communist operations. And was told sorrowfully, "There is nothing you can do about Communists."

This, coming from *the* Counterintelligence agency of the US, was quite interesting, especially since J. Edgar reported in 1919 how very dangerous it was to America.

> *"Every nation has had its disastrous public officials at one time or another. Russia had Stalin, Germany had Hitler, England had Cromwell and the United States had J. Edgar Hoover."*

Such things made me interested in the Justice Department and their star, J. Edgar Hoover.

Now that time has passed and archives are beginning to leak data hitherto under heavy wraps, other people are exposing this department.

But in the main, the departmental crimes they are showing up, while serious enough, are not summarizing the depths of infamy to which this department has sunk.

Crime rates have climbed and climbed and soared and America has not prospered.

But under all this, real crimes have been done.

In the 1930s John L. Lewis was the head of the powerful labor union, CIO (Congress of Industrial Organizations), as well as the United Mine Workers. Such was his power that he almost defeated Roosevelt in his final term as President. Lewis shut off coal in the US and forced conversion of even railroads to oil (in which Lewis had a heavy personal interest). The coal upset was a heavy blow to industry and transport soon to enter World War II.

The Justice Department looked on benignly while all this was going on. Yet it was recently revealed that John L. Lewis was number C180/L of the German Intelligence Service—the *Abwehr*.

During this period, an FBI agent named Leon G. Turrou collided with and wrapped up a Nazi spy ring in America—about the only one the Justice Department ever did wrap up. MI5 of England had found out and tipped the FBI and Turrou got the assignment—and did a fine job on it. This was the Griebl-Voss-Hofman-Rumrich ring. They were all connected.

The Justice Department promptly fired Turrou!

Asked why, J. Edgar glowered, "He wrote a book about it!"

But that is *not* the reason. The story of "resigning" is *in* the book. The dismissal obviously happened before he wrote it.

Then much bigger news turned up about the Justice Department.

The shock of Pearl Harbor and the "lack of warning" was a mystery to anyone in intelligence from the day it happened until recently.

The official UK government publication *The Double-Cross System in the War of 1939 to 1945* and the recently released book *Spy/Counter Spy* by the ace British agent Dusko Popov reveal that in AUGUST of 1941, *four months* before Pearl Harbor, J. Edgar Hoover was personally, fully and officially informed of the intended Japanese attack on Pearl Harbor, how it would be done and when, AND DID NOT ADVISE HIS GOVERNMENT.

There is no need to stress how many lives this cost or how it destroyed the Pacific Fleet!

Looking a bit further at this department and their omnigod Hoover, one encounters the fact that the FBI knew all about Lee Harvey Oswald. G-Man James P. Hosty, Jr., of the seventy-five-man FBI office in Dallas, had his file, knew he was murderous, vengeful, knew he worked at the Texas School Book Depository, knew that that place was on the parade route of President John F. Kennedy and knew that Dallas was seething. But the Justice Department didn't inform Kennedy's bodyguards or even exercise their own rule book obligation to protect the President.

And on November 22, 1963, President John F. Kennedy was brutally murdered by Lee Harvey Oswald firing from his known place of work.

Then during the remaining '60s, the Justice Department even bettered their roaring crime rate by adding organized crime and drugs to the national ills.

Their antitrust and drug sections vividly ignored the chief drug pushers of America—the AMA and their APA branch psychiatrists—and stood by whistling while schoolkids were ordered onto speed and pills to form the basis of a drug culture.

No-knock raids and shooting people in the back became the order of the day.

The Justice Department had moved from catastrophe by omission to actual chaos-creation.

During the riots of the '60s, the Justice Department could be counted on to discourage or charge local police who sought to handle.

This finally built up to labeling as "dissident" any organization or church that sought to stem the avalanche of disaster engulfing the country.

Manufacturing dossiers for public leaders who had none, but whom the Justice Department did not like, they set organizations against organizations and promoted chaos wherever possible. Their list of thousands of men and groups they secretly attacked reads like *Who's Who*—and indeed is becoming a sort of honor roll.

The Justice Department had now become a carbon copy of a Nazi secret police force.

It was found that it forwarded false dossiers on Americans abroad to get them in trouble.

Its channel was Interpol, the Nazi group, that J. Edgar has joined despite objections of Congress.

Ah, well, now it all begins to make some sense.

Anger at an agent who would dare clean up German spies, permitting Pearl Harbor, protecting German psychiatrists, subjecting the country and its better-known opinion leaders to a reign of terror, even the assassination of a far-too-liberal President, all bear the stamp of just one thing: a secret love of Fascism and a knowing or unknowing patterning of its actions on Fascist lines has led the Justice Department not only to protect Hoover, but to perpetuate him.

Probably Justice Department clerks, lawyers and even "G-Men" do not consciously realize where they have been led.

A department that favors such sentiments and tactics will always *breed* crime and lawlessness.

Fascism and Secret Police do not belong in the American scene.

It is quite wonderful to see these people mouthing concern about crime and revolt.

They are breeding, starting and fostering it with their raw, naked vengefulness against the American people.

The country, one cannot help but see, would get along just fine without any Department of "Justice."

The appropriations it obtains by exhibiting the crime it does not handle and the unrest and spirit of revolt it generates should be cut off totally before it takes over all the police forces in the country and we have a Fascism complete, total and in earnest.

But anyway, one mystery is solved.

All his years, Mr. Hoover hunted relentlessly for "Public Enemy No. 1." As crime soared higher and higher during his reign, the search apparently was in vain.

But what do you know? Now after all the archives have been opened, at last we know who was Public Enemy No. 1. It was J. Edgar Hoover!

"But what do you know? Now after all the archives have been opened, at last we know who was Public Enemy No. 1...."

CHAPTER THREE

ON ECONOMICS

On Economics | 83
Economics | 85
Economics—War and Tax | 95

On Economics

While the 1960s still generally constituted the "Golden Years" of Western economic development, LRH proved quite correct in suggesting all was not as rosy as economists imagined. In point of fact, right around the fiscal corner lay all we associate with the early 1970s, including: quadrupling fuel costs, usury interest rates and—as LRH again points out—the utter collapse of a gold dollar-based world monetary system. In consequence came all we now associate with a subsequent worldwide inflationary recession, including: a steady decline of the average wage in terms of real purchasing power, double-digit unemployment across much of Western Europe, and—particularly in consequence to increasing taxation for the socialist safety net—what has been aptly described as a "growing culture of hate."

In mentioning psychiatric interests in the economic realm, LRH is touching upon most intriguing links between heavily monied interests and psychiatry. For example, close scrutiny of a World Federation for Mental Health through the 1960s and 1970s reveals many a tie to British banking interests, while similarly close scrutiny of American psychiatric funding reveals consistent Rockefeller Foundation support since the early 1920s, especially as regards what Foundation directors described as psychiatry's "potential contribution" to education, sociology and "the general business of living."

That LRH further focuses upon the failure of economists to either predict or explain what followed from the end of those Golden Years is also highly significant. For the truth is, in citing the failure of Keynesian theories—and thus the driving force of economic theory for half a century—he was citing the dramatic decline of student enrollments in economic graduate programs, the closing of economic departments in many a major corporation and even the federal abandonment of what economists themselves described as "the dismal science." ∎

Yet another vantage point from Saint Hill Manor:
"We aren't some small voice in the tumult. We are several million people, we Scientologists." —L. Ron Hubbard

17 March 1966

ECONOMICS

by L. Ron Hubbard

One of the primary barriers in this society to total freedom is economics. Suppressives have been weaving a web of economic entanglement for societies for some time using economic misinterpretations or ignorance to involve those societies which only recently struck off their chains of actual slavery. Today the chains are made of economic restrictions and, to be blunt, economic lies.

An understanding of economics is a bold step forward toward total freedom in a society. Aberrations tend to blow when their lies are exposed.

Therefore I have written this short essay on the actual *laws of economics*, as they may help you on your way to freedom.

Today almost any person has a present time problem, growing more pressing as time goes on and as our society evolves.

It is a simple question:

"How can I live?"

The answer to this question in a broad general way can be found by attaining an understanding of a subject called Economics.

Economic Theories

Economics are as simple as they are not obscured. And as confused as they are made to serve a selfish purpose.

Any child can understand—and practice—the basic principles of economics. But grown men, huge with the stature of *Government* or *Chain Banks,* find it very useful to obscure the subject beyond all comprehension.

The things that are done in the name of "economic necessity" would shame Satan. For they are done by the selfish few to deny the many.

Economics easily evolve into the science of making people miserable.

Nine-tenths of life are economic. The remaining one-tenth is social-political.

If there is this fruitful source of suppression loose upon the world and if it makes people unhappy, then it is a legitimate field for comment in Scientology as it must form a large "misunderstood" in our daily lives.

Let us see how involved it can be made. If Mankind increases in number and if property and goods increase, then money must also increase unless we are to arrive at a point where none can buy.

Yet money is pegged to a metal of which there is just so much and no more—gold. So if Man's expansion is to be checked, it will be checked simply by running out of this metal. And aside from art uses and superstition, the metal, gold, has almost no practical value. Iron is far more useful, but as it is one of the most common elements about, it would not serve the purpose of suppression of Man's growth.

MONEY IS SIMPLY A SYMBOL THAT PEOPLE ARE CONFIDENT CAN BE CONVERTED INTO GOODS.

The most virulent philosophy of the nineteenth century was not that of Dewey or Schopenhauer. It was that of a fellow named Karl Marx, a German.

In his book, *Das Kapital,* he set out to destroy the world of Capitalism by introducing the philosophy of Communism, borrowed in some part evidently from the leader Lycurgus of the ancient Greek state of Sparta.

Marx has succeeded to date (though himself dead and buried in England) in extending his philosophy over perhaps two-thirds of the world's population and upsetting the remainder most thoroughly.

Capitalism, under attack, surviving only in the West in a faint form, has borrowed so heavily from Marx in its modern "Socialism" that it cannot long survive.

Capitalism had little to recommend it to the worker. He had no hope of ever getting enough cash together to loan it at interest and so retire. By definition that was all Capitalism was—a system of living on interest by loaning money to more industrious people. As it implies, "All take and no active participation," it of course is a rather easily destroyed system. It had no vitality. It could only foreclose mortgages and seize property. It could not and did not operate cleverly. The trick was and is to loan an industrious person half of what he needed to make a go of his business and then, when he failed, to take over the business *and* the invested money loaned as well.

Governments and chain banks in the West are still at it today. They are assisted by income tax. The profits of a business are taxed each year so that it has no money to renew its machinery or expand. To keep going, it has to borrow money from the chain bank or the state. One slip and it is taken over entirely by the chain bank or state, mismanaged and knocked about.

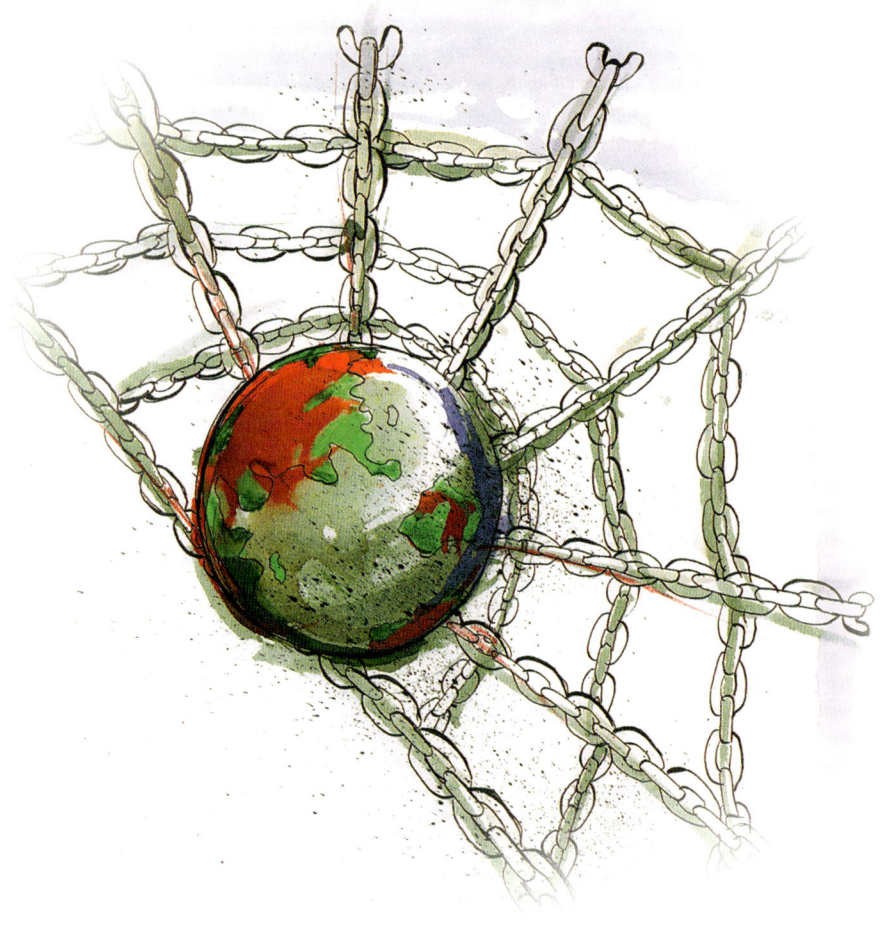

"Suppressives have been weaving a web of economic entanglement for societies for some time using economic misinterpretations or ignorance to involve those societies which only recently struck off their chains of actual slavery. Today the chains are made of economic restrictions and, to be blunt, economic lies."

Thus the world gets poorer under Capitalism.

Communism, in revolt, throws out all middlemen, simply takes the final step of Capitalism and seizes everything in the country. It fights Capitalism by becoming the Super-Capitalist.

It is not an idle comment that George Washington in the American Revolution, the Marquis de Lafayette in the French Revolution and Fidel Castro in the last Cuban Revolution were each the richest man in the country at the time.

Communism, far different from the hope of Marx, is the tool of the rich and powerful to seize everything in sight. And pay *no* wages. It is the final answer to Capitalism, not its opponent.

Socialisms, in different costumes, all tend to the same end product—total ownership by the state. And so are also the end product of Capitalism, total ownership.

So we can conclude about economics that

1. There may be a subject called economics; and
2. There is certainly a large use of economic confusion in the effort to bring about total ownership.

What you are observing, apparently, in our modern world, is an obscuring of actual economics to the somewhat ignoble end of taking everything away from everyone but the state. The state can then be a chosen few who own all. Capitalism, Communism and Socialism all wind up with Man in the same situation—owned body and soul by the state.

So if you are confused by "economic statements" by a few chosen mouthpieces of the intended few who will be the state, realize it is not the subject itself, but the intentional misuse of the subject which is causing the trouble.

Since all roads—Capitalism, Socialism, Communism—all lead to the same total ownership, none of them are in actual fact in conflict. Only those several groups who each want to own everything are in conflict—and none of them are worthy of support.

There is an answer to all this. If these -isms all tend to a total state, then the obvious rebuttal is a no-state. This alone would be an opposition to the total state.

As this is instinctive in Man—to oppose his enslaver—people manifest their personal revolt in various ways.

They cannot simply overwhelm a well-armed government. So their revolt takes the form of inaction and inefficiency.

Russia and Cuba, for two, are going on the rocks of individual inefficiency and inaction. They do not see it as a revolt as it hasn't any peaks. The grain and cane just don't come up, the trains somehow don't run and the bread doesn't get baked.

America and England, driven still by some faint remaining spark of "free enterprise," muddle along. But the economic squeeze is too great for this long to continue. Income tax, bank and state loans, all the evils are there waiting.

Sensing the coming total ownership of all, the worker even in the US and England begins to put on the brakes. A good day's work today was an hour's work a century ago. Strikes enthusiastically paralyze anything they can. Inefficiency and inaction are the order of the day.

Not clever, the Capitalist, the Commissar, the Great Socialist do not believe anyone has penetrated their actual intent and so continue to twist economics about in the hope of convincing the people—who strike, won't really work and get more inefficient.

The societies of Earth, whether East or West, are all approaching with rapidity the same end—dissolution by a personal people's revolt. The revolt has no name, no leader, no banner, no glory. It only has a common end in view—the end of all states and all economic systems.

And surely the people will win.

The Science of Economics

Any group of children will soon work out a practical economic system.

"If you are confused by 'economic statements' by a few chosen mouthpieces of the intended few who will be the state, realize it is not the subject itself, but the intentional misuse of the subject which is causing the trouble."

Recently children in a park in Russia became the subject of government horror by developing a barter system, exchanging toys for toys, an act which was duly chastised as "Capitalistic." The Russian word values are shaky, for to be Capitalistic they would have had to develop an interest system of recompense for the loan of toys, not the barter system.

So long as there is a supply and as long as a demand can be generated, some form of goods exchange system will develop.

There are innumerable combinations of supply and demand actions. There is the reluctant supply and the demand by force—a system commonly followed by troops or feudal barons or simply robbers.

There is the eager supply action aided by creating a demand by advertising, a system we know as business and at which Madison Avenue is so adept. Man finds this the most pleasant of the systems, but it has a limitation in that it demands in return money and causes people to demand pay in order to buy the advertised goods.

Then there is a system based on creating want. Governments almost uniformly believe in this system and use it. They repress supply by taxation of suppliers and increase demand by punishment of the consumer for lack of funds—i.e., income tax. The theory, in its most crudely expressed form, is the reduction of production coupled to the enforcement of demand. Fathers can be arrested for not caring for children, but the price of bread, rent and service is beyond Father's ability to pay. One is arrested as a vagrant if one does not dress well, but the price of clothing, through scarcity, puts it beyond his reach.

There are many, many variations of the same two factors, supply and demand, and these can be played on by huge industries or the state or robbers or beggars or anyone almost without number.

A great deal is made of "deflations" and "inflations" and tomes are written to interpret them, but there are only two operative laws that govern them:

1. An INFLATION exists where there is more money in circulation than there are goods.
2. A DEFLATION exists where there are more goods than there is money to buy them.

These two laws can be twisted about at will to confuse people. But that's all there is to know about either an Inflation or a Deflation—or booms or depressions either, for that matter.

Fundamentals

The economic laws break down to only one fact, or fundamental, usually never mentioned in the best suppressive circles.

This is the genus of economics, the beginning, how the whole subject comes about.

To bring about economics a being must be led to believe he needs more than he can himself produce and must be restrained from consuming his own production.

After that, one has economics, a society and rules, laws, governments and huge industrial combines.

Let us take the simple matter of a poor cow. The cow produces milk, more cows and even meat.

By being a producing animal, the cow is made to surrender the lot. She does not need her own milk, cannot use her calves and is also made to surrender her own body for meat. In return she gets a sloppy barnyard, a thistle pasture, barking dogs and abuse.

Sentient or not, intelligent or stupid, the cow yet sets us a fine example of the perfect citizen of the state.

The perfect citizen (from a suppressive governmental viewpoint) is one who demands nothing and produces everything and even surrenders her own body on demand. The ideal citizen. The perfect factory worker. The complete soldier. The praised comrade.

Life gets itself rigged this way. Those who can produce are then convinced they must produce and in production are given less and less until at last we have a slave—all work, no pay, minimum food and untenable quarters.

Economics are used to bring about this condition remorselessly.

Income Tax

If you have reservations about the end product of various state acts or the intentions behind them, consider this hitherto-hidden fact.

Income tax is designed on the Marxist principle (to be found in *Das Kapital,* the Communist text) of taxation:

"To each according to his need,

"From each according to his ability to pay."

About the turn of the century most Western nations gladly swallowed this potion and wrote income tax laws.

It looks quite innocent.

In a letter written by the Treasury of a great nation, a question as to why income tax was levied so unequally instead of on merely a set percentage of everyone's gross income, was answered with the astounding datum that taxation of one's net income and on a sliding scale was far more humanitarian.

Let us see how "humanitarian" this sliding scale income tax is.

Inflation is the order of the day. Few Western governments take any but inflationary actions—to wit, to devaluate the buying power of money by spending more money than there is produce to absorb it.

"By being a producing animal, the cow is made to surrender the lot. She does not need her own milk, cannot use her calves and is also made to surrender her own body for meat. In return she gets a sloppy barnyard, a thistle pasture, barking dogs and abuse. Sentient or not, intelligent or stupid, the cow yet sets us a fine example of the perfect citizen of the state. The perfect citizen (from a suppressive governmental viewpoint) is one who demands nothing and produces everything and even surrenders her own body on demand. The ideal citizen. The perfect factory worker. The complete soldier. The praised comrade."

Income tax is arranged so that the more one is paid, the more percentage he is taxed. For a crude example, if one makes 500 monetary units a year, his tax is 2 percent. If he makes 100,000 monetary units a year, the law is so written that his tax is about 90 percent. The more one makes, the more one has to pay in proportion.

Very well, let us use this as hours of work. In a low-income bracket on a forty-hour week, one pays the government a half-hour's work a week. In a middle-income bracket one pays the government twenty out of forty hours. And in a high-income bracket one pays perhaps thirty-nine out of forty hours as tax.

All right. Inflation willy-nilly is shoving the lowest worker toward the higher tax bracket.

The price of bread and rent and all will go up proportionate to value of money. So will his pay. But his tax will increase.

Therefore governments are very anxious to inflate their money. The more it inflates, the more workers have to be paid, but the more percentage the government gets of the work hours.

The end product is of course a total state. Industry cannot pay a worker 40,000 monetary units if tax laws take all but 5,000 monetary units.

If you will look at taxation schedules, you will see that if a loaf of bread cost ten times its current price and you had other costs rising proportionately, your pay would shrink to where you could not afford to eat because the higher tax percentage would engulf your pay, no matter what it was.

Now no one has been mentioning this. And governments defend their right to a rising percentage as income rises with a tenacity that is quite surprising.

As inflation wipes out savings also, right up ahead is the big chasm, waiting.

Every time your pay rises to take care of the "rising cost of living," you then expend more work hours for the government and less for your employer and finally he goes broke too.

Anyone trying to say that inflation is inevitable and income tax vital is simply suppressive or stupid. Surely the big wheels of government economies know as well as any other trained economist that all one needs to do to check inflation is increase production and decrease government spending.

One Western nation has a lovely one going. Export the goods! is the cry. The more goods exported, the less there is to buy. By Currency Exchange laws, one cannot also export the money. A prohibitive duty is put on all imports. Naturally, inflation! With a vengeance. And this is coupled with an income tax which is easily the highest in the world.

Citizens of that nation are traditionally determined to never, never, never be slaves. But here come the chains, one link for every penny rise in the cost of bread. When a worker has to spend £100 a week to keep himself and family, the government will take £50 of that, leaving him on half rations. And when he would have to spend £250 a week to provide food, clothing and shelter, he will get only about 25 percent of that, even if he is paid that, due to income tax sliding scale, and he will starve to death.

To be charitable it is possible that the leaders of these countries do not know these things and are being badly advised or are confused. But if so, what vicious blokes must be doing the advising!

A very proper course for the country would be to abandon the empire no citizen of that country cares about anymore, cutting off all its support and defense funds for lands that hate the British anyway. Then, or at the same time, engage upon a furious research program to discover how to

"Inflation is the order of the day. Few Western governments take any but inflationary actions—to wit, to devaluate the buying power of money by spending more money than there is produce to absorb it."

produce food enough for its people, let down all its trade barriers, cancel the projects that make income tax vital and prosper beyond all imaginings.

One can't tax nothing. And if taxes depress the producer to zero, then so goes the land.

The bright-eyes visionary (with some insanity shining through the brightness) raves about Utopia and the beautiful dreams and beautiful schemes of various political solutions.

These are supposed to open the bright new future if only we grit our teeth and starve today.

There is *no* political philosophy that ever can or ever will solve economic problems, for they are two different fields, aren't they?

When Marx married them, he gave a terrible tool to suppressive men.

Many Marxist complaints are just, many are quite factual. But he erred in trying to solve them.

For whenever he proposed a solution and whatever solution he proposed, he offered as part of it a government.

Governments are not always run by sane men.

The man in the street has no guarantee his ruler is not really "bonkers."

If we as Scientologists have anything to do with government, it would only be to guarantee that the rulers were not suppressive and insane. And there our interest ceases.

The Question

The relationship of any man to Economics is a simple one:

HOW CAN I LIVE?

To that adheres the question, how can his dependents and his community live?

Whenever a person asks this question or any version thereof in this, the complex society of today, he is asking "What is economics?"

In this article, short as it is, all the vital factors of economics are listed.

What needs to be guaranteed is that one's economic destiny is not managed by men who hate and who will not be comfortable until all other men are slaves.

The long-term solution to the question "How can I live?" is never work for a suppressive firm and do not support a suppressive government. And work to put us in a position to guarantee that leaders are sane.

ECONOMICS WAR AND TAX

by L. RON HUBBARD

ONE OF THE WAYS major Western powers will lose was once explained to me by a friend of mine, a famous US Senator.

He said that the drain of "brush wars," rising taxes and resultant inflation could be maintained for only a few years, after which, because of economic collapse, the Communists might win after all. That was several years ago—1955.

When one sees that the gold reserves of the US are at this writing at a minus 21 billion and that they have done a steep nine-year 45° dive since their zero in 1960 (American Institute for Economic Research, Boston, report of 17 Feb. 69), one can understand what he was talking about.

The uninterrupted plunge leaves the International Monetary Fund holding about $39.7 billion worth of gold demands on the US only slightly offset by US balances.

Oddly, in the same report, the 1968 US produce year of food was 3 percent higher than the record-high year of 1967.

As big bankers are also strangely found to be directors of psychiatric front groups, one begins to see that they are not always as pleasantly minded toward Man as one might be led to believe by their press officers and press chains.

Peculiarly, the economic doctrine followed by Western governments for the last quarter century is that of Lord Keynes. The germ (or bacteria) of the Keynes theory (as I was carefully taught at one of these universities they say I never attended) is simply this: "Create want!" Followed to its natural end, this means starvation would produce prosperity (for whom?).

Now, the "International Monetary Fund" was founded by Lord Keynes and the famous Communist Harry Dexter White.

"This 'tax' is really a very uneconomical method of collecting money and a serious threat to the individual citizens. Income Tax has been continually used to 'get' people against whom no charge could be proven. It cuts the money off before it can be invested or used in the country."

By paying out gold and never demanding Lend-Lease payments in gold, the US public is getting its throat cut very nicely. The US soldier shortly won't have an economically stable country to support. Inflation will have sent the dollar away with the wind.

These International Bankers are satisfied only with "increased taxes to stabilize the currency."

One of the Russian objectives is to make a US public rejection of "brush wars" by reason of the resulting oppressive taxation. So it is being accomplished very nicely.

Now, you can't have much faith in any country, be it England or France or the US, which taxes its citizens via a dossier-collecting Income Tax czar. The true ruler of every citizen, including those at the top, would be that bureau one had to report to or else. When Income Tax gets up to one collector per taxpayer and interferes with one's ability to live, and when inflation sweeps away all one's savings, the population is likely to say that it's not worth serving, not worth supporting, and that any insurgent group would furnish a better government.

Henry Cabot Lodge's one-time boast that "With modernly armed armies no citizen revolt could ever succeed." That, of course, supposes that the Army remains loyal to the politicians—and armies seldom do when the country has no cause and the pay won't buy anything anymore.

Income Tax is dead against the original US Constitution. Since its adaption in England there have been only depressions.

This "tax" is really a very uneconomical method of collecting money and a serious threat to the individual citizens.

Income Tax has been continually used to "get" people against whom no charge could be proven.

It cuts the money off before it can be invested or used in the country.

It denies expansion to commerce and inhibits trade.

If a revolutionary wanted to set a country up to antagonize its citizens, shatter pride in their government and prepare the ground, he would advise putting in Income Tax and then, year by year, insist it became more onerous.

———

So the West is getting itself into severe "economic trouble."

Yet the US just had a record produce year and England just had a record export year.

Any Commie could tell them that the real wealth of a nation is its production and natural resources. Any other economist knows this. But apparently the governments don't get the word somehow.

———

Now let us consider what really happens when money, inflated beyond use, fails to buy any longer.

That's right. Barter ensues.

What is barter? An egg for bread, a glass for a dish. People start trading actual commodity.

In other words, when money fails, it does not reduce down to gold. It reduces down to produce!

So the whole theory of money is really that it represents produce. Not gold. Not bankers. Not paper. But *produce*.

The US can't make gold, but it sure can produce wheat.

England can't produce gold, but it sure can make machinery and cheap tin trays.

So what's all this phony junk about "dollar balances," "gold reserves"?

And for that matter, what's all this bunk that if you tax a nation to death, it will be solvent?

Ah! Keynes' "Create want!" If you put money on an impossible standard, it will cease to exist and then everyone will starve very nicely.

Who do they think swallows all this "economic" hocus-pocus? Not the public.

The public mutters quietly to itself and wonders who'll give the eventual signal to mob these idiots. They dutifully vote. They still play the game just to keep up appearances, but meanwhile they hope and dream.

The French population in 1789 dreamed about Dr. Guillotine's new invention. They were quite docile—right up to the moment the National Guard went over to them and they stormed the Bastille.

Strangely enough, it doesn't seem to be emphasized in history that on that same day an enterprising fellow led mobs that emptied every "insane asylum" and tore the "sanitariums" apart. They knew what they were doing!

It never seems so quiet as just before the hurricane.

———

So how can a country go down?

By being put down by its "*best* people" through denial of real justice, oppressive taxation and unreal, unworkable money standards.

During the 1929–1939 US depression there were a lot of books written by fellows who saw clearly that a country full of produce that couldn't be bought for lack of money was a farce. These may still be on the shelves, but Lord Keynes is all they read.

It is very very plain that if barter comes in when money goes out, that the real substitute for, the real yardstick for, money is PRODUCE.

Nobody needs to deflate and hurt the people. Or inflate and collapse.

All one has to do is say that a dollar or a pound or a franc are worth so many pounds of wheat, so many tin trays, so many onions and, voilà, we're rich. Take any given day of comparable prices and say that's the comparable price day.

Gold? Forget it.

Forget also Income Tax.

One of the standard equations of economics is that Inflation occurs when money exceeds the produce, depression occurs when produce exceeds the money to buy it.

As all Western nations are heavy producers of produce, they'd issue money to the value of their total land and production. They could probably "re-fund" their debts by pushing the issue ahead in date and gradually work it back.

Gold would probably increase in value, but so what. It's just a metal. You can't eat it and today you can't even have it.

"What is barter? An egg for bread, a glass for a dish. People start trading actual commodity. In other words, when money fails, it does not reduce down to gold. It reduces down to produce! So the whole theory of money is really that it represents produce. Not gold. Not bankers. Not paper. But produce."

"When inflation, no matter how well 'controlled,' takes off, it takes off like a sudden rocket. And that's it. Curtains. Our job is to somehow keep Western powers from vanishing. They must be made to see that their cause must be strengthened before some enemy cause is espoused by their insecure and harassed populations."

A dollar or pound or franc that is guaranteed by commodity would be very acceptable indeed and would force governments to encourage production and help and protect those who produce instead of trying to sterilize people to reduce their population explosion.

This would not even wreck the banker. As he seems to have overlooked, he deals in a commodity called money and if it goes, he's gone. His "planned inflation" as recommended by Keynes is plain suicide.

Inflations go suddenly up. It is very easy to lose control. The retailer one day becomes afraid he can't replace his stock at the distributors', jumps his price. The distributor jumps his. The retailer jumps his. Then seeing that money is going up to the level of wheelbarrow per loaf of bread, he refuses to sell. Barter takes over. The nation and its existing government are finished.

Several countries, notably Nationalist China, lost the whole nation this way. Their money went into a sudden inflation. From 50 sen, a postage stamp went in two weeks to 5,000 dollars and in another three weeks went to 7 million! The civil servants' pay was not raised. That was it—Communist China.

When inflation, no matter how well "controlled," takes off, it takes off like a sudden rocket. And that's it. Curtains.

Our job is to somehow keep Western powers from vanishing. They must be made to see that their cause must be strengthened before some enemy cause is espoused by their insecure and harassed populations.

We aren't some small voice in the tumult. We are several million people, we Scientologists.

Our religion is our Truth. Our prayers will be heard. Our postulates work.

Christianity tried to make Man tolerant. We can make that goal if we also can make Man wise.

Our churches are growing in influence.

Any attacks on us are solely the signs of the degradation and injustice of our times.

We do not want the government. We do not side with revolutionaries.

As churches we have a responsibility to reform injustice and oppression and better our society.

If anyone objects to this, let him object, so long as he does not carry our world down to the decay and destruction toward which ignorance has led it for so long.

CHAPTER FOUR

On Psychiatric SUBVERSION

On Psychiatric
    Subversion | 105
A Reason Psychiatric
    Front Groups Attack
    Scientology | 109
Druidism and
    Psychiatry | 113
Today's Terrorism | 117
Pain-Drug-Hypnosis | 121
Failures | 127
Diplomas | 129
Psychology and Psychiatry, the
    Sciences of Saliva | 131
The Planned
    Revolution | 135
Sciences of Saliva | 139
Control "Sciences" | 143
The Bland Personality | 147
Quackery and Fakery | 151

How to Win an
    Argument | 155
Crime and Psychiatry | 159
Our Intentions | 163
The Unholy Stick
    Together | 167
Cultural Deficiencies | 171
The Fight for Freedom | 177
Drug Problems | 183
Tangled Terms | 185
Being Good | 189
Drug Addiction | 191
Cultural Destruction | 195
Old-Fashioned
    Holdovers | 201
Criminals and
    Psychiatry | 205
The Criminal Mind and the
    Psychs | 209
The Cause of Crime | 211

On Psychiatric Subversion

IN DISCUSSING THE ROOT SOURCE OF MODERN DECAY, LRH is touching upon a very grim and tangled story of psychiatry. To cite a few telling episodes: At the outset of the Second World War, and the psychiatric advance into Allied military circles under a banner of "combat conditioning," British Colonel and psychiatric head of the Tavistock experimentation clinic, John Rawlings Rees delivered this crucial message to colleagues:

"We have made a useful attack upon a number of professions. The two easiest of them naturally are the teaching profession and the Church: the two most difficult are law and medicine.... If we are to infiltrate the professional and social activities of other people I think we must imitate the Totalitarians and organize some kind of fifth column activity!... Let us all, therefore, very secretly be 'fifth columnists.'"

To cite the next critical move, having spent a profitable war advising on the destruction of enemy morale (and only recently returned from early biological warfare testing), Canadian Army General and cofounder of the World Federation for Mental Health, Brock Chisholm effectively added this to the Rees "Fifth Column" Plan:

"Reinterpretation and eventually eradication of the concept of right and wrong," he declared, was the key object for "practically all effective psychotherapy."

Finally, and bearing in mind the combined thrust of both the Rees and Chisholm message, we inevitably come to what had been dubbed the Alaska Mental Health Act but is best remembered today as the Siberia Bill. The final extension of a decade-long psychiatric effort to simplify commitment procedures, the bill specifically called for the establishment of a remote Alaskan mental health facility and radically streamlined means of incarcerating inmates—hence the moniker Siberia Bill to evoke precisely what the plan comprised, i.e., an American Gulag. Eventually described

Johannesburg, South Africa, where L. Ron Hubbard shall forever be remembered as that rare and original voice for the end of apartheid and its psychiatric architects

by Superior Court Judge Joseph M. Call as representing "totalitarian government at its best," the bill proposed that "any health, welfare or police officer who has reason to believe that an individual is mentally ill and therefore likely to injure himself or others if not immediately restrained" may transport that individual to a mental asylum for professional evaluation. There "the prisoner" could be detained five days or, if judged mentally incompetent, "for the rest of his natural life." No statement of probable cause was required, no issue of warrant was necessary and no hearing. Moreover, while an American press was fast asleep and a general public utterly oblivious, architects of that bill enjoyed a clean and straight road to those Alaskan wastes...or at least until LRH and fellow Scientologists received word of the matter.

Although certainly not alone in their protest, particularly in light of several thousand letters and telegrams, what Scientologists eventually mounted in the way of a broad public awareness campaign proved very fatal to that Siberia scheme. Indeed, as any general American history text bears out, the bill was soon quite forgotten...or at least by all those beyond psychiatric circles.

Those familiar with the greater history of Scientology's fight against psychiatric subversion will recall the names Drs. Winfred Overholser and Daniel Blain—American Psychiatric Association heavyweights, both linked to United States military mind-control experimentation and, following the 1956 death of their cherished Siberia Bill, bent on the destruction of what they termed the "antipsychiatric movement" and correctly spelled Scientology and L. Ron Hubbard.

But there was another consequence to the death of that bill and it has everything to do with both the shape of the world today and the world of which LRH writes in the essays to follow.

To explain: Given psychiatry's failure to cut a path directly through the social fabric with mental health legislation, the psychiatric steering committee took another page directly from Rees and launched their "attack upon medicine." In very willing partnership stood an always profit-minded pharmaceutical industry with an eye to expanding product lines well beyond children's cough drops and aspirin. And, of course, what followed from that partnership is all we now legitimately describe as a truly pandemic drug crisis.

To cite one more telling sequence relevant to what follows here from LRH, let us first bear in mind that all we remember as the psychedelic era of the late 1960s sprang directly from psychiatric experimentation of LSD on behalf of the United States Central Intelligence Agency. Then again, let us not forget that when a psychedelic generation turned to methamphetamines, barbiturates and even heroin, they were likewise turning to the psychiatric medicine cabinet originally stocked in the name of mind control. Finally, let us also consider this: Among other aims of psychiatric experimentation on behalf of the United States military and Central Intelligence Agency was the shaping of a perfect assassin—principally through conditioning under pain, drugs and hypnosis and, factually, first publicly disclosed in Ron's *Science of Survival*. Thereafter, of course, the subject became a popular topic of speculation and especially so following Richard Condon's *The Manchurian Candidate*. Not generally remarked upon, however, is this chilling footnote: although programs to shape that perfect assassin proved only marginally successful, subsequent experimentation among residents within San Francisco's Haight-Ashbury had everything to do with the shaping of such unimaginably brutal creatures as mass murderer Charles Manson.

Also following from that original psychiatric equation come the LRH discussions on psychiatric fraud, to which we might add this: although comprising the smallest faction within a United States healthcare community, bogus psychiatric claims actually accounted for some 20 percent of all fraudulent healthcare claims—or in raw terms, as much as $20 billion annually. Then again, there was all a United States Congressional Committee cited as wasted funds and extravagance regarding National Institute of Mental Health studies: the unisex behavior of the whiptail lizard, at a cost to the American taxpayer of $1.4 million; the hormonal mechanism of salt-depleted rats, at a cost of $5 million in national revenues; the electronic monitoring of pigeon jaws, at a cost of $545,000; and a five-year examination of red-winged blackbird mating habits, at an equally obscene $539,000. While if only to underscore the absurdity, one feels compelled to additionally mention Canadian psychiatric studies of "Rabbit Psychosis" and "Rats and Mice in a Swimming Pool—Some Surprising Differences." ∎

27 February 1969

A REASON PSYCHIATRIC FRONT GROUPS ATTACK SCIENTOLOGY

by L. Ron Hubbard

In Book Two, Chapter Five of *Dianetics: The Modern Science of Mental Health,* you will find a mild remonstrance against psychiatric electric shock and surgery. It described these as ways to get into trouble with mental healing.

This was in 1950. Within three months of its appearance the book was under violent, irrational attack by psychiatric frontmen and groups.

In the late '50s psychiatrists actually got a bill half through the US Congress authorizing a Siberia. Any man, woman or child could be seized and sent without trial to Alaska, deprived of human and civil rights and detained forever, all without trial or examination.

The Founding Church of Scientology of Washington, DC, caught wind of this bill and instantly mobilized US civic groups and defeated it.*

These marked Scientology for slaughter in the books of these madmen.

As recently as 1968 the same International Psychiatric group was trying to push the same Siberia Bill through the New Zealand Parliament.

Kenneth Robinson, former Minister of Health in the UK and vice-president of a branch of this psychiatric front group, is the one who began trouble for Scientology Churches in the UK.

Robinson, in his book published by this front group, advocates personally the easy seizure of anyone in the UK for despatch to death camps.

Press chains headed by men who were also directors of the psychiatric front group, Cecil King and Sir William Carr, kept pounding at Scientology, urging "official action," trying to build up an anti-Scientology public opinion and obliterate it.

*For the full story of the Scientology victory over the Siberia Bill see article "On Psychiatric Subversion." Page 105. —Editor

Any other hostile actions toward Scientology build back step by step to the same group.

Scientology has fought a consistent and winning battle for Human Rights for two decades. During that entire time, not one crime has been found in Scientology.

But during that time psychiatry has seized and killed tens of thousands of people they don't like.

It is said Scientology breaks up families. They don't. But psychiatrists call their own rape and death of men's wives "necessary treatment."

Any type of crime this psychiatric group accuses the Scientologists of has now been traced back to be standard psychiatric practice.

Being slightly more than mad, these fellows are trying to put public attention on an innocent group to distract attention from their own brutal and perverted activities. By saying someone *else* does these things, they think the public will believe the psychiatrist is a lofty public-spirited paragon of virtue.

The public is not fooled. They detest psychiatry. Forty-seven percent of people with mental trouble go to their clergymen. Twenty-eight percent go to their general practitioner. The psychologist and psychiatrist, between them, only get sixteen percent of the "trade."

To enlarge their sphere, the psychiatrist (United Nations World Health Organization Technical Report Series No. 98) plans to knock out all churches in the field of Mental Healing.

Scientology is their first target. If they win there, they will take on other churches and so build their empire.

The only puzzle in all this is how does the psychiatrist influence governments?

As a terror symbol? By blackmail of politicians using confession data of wives? Holding politicians' family members hostage? By bribery?

The psychiatrist, handling almost none of the "trade," yet obtains hundreds of millions from governments annually over the world. For this he gives no service, injures or kills his patients, seeks to seize anyone and everyone at a whim, yet is strangely immune from the correct murder charges. Not even a medical doctor is allowed to kill people.

How could the allied nations hang Germans at Nuremberg for these crimes and yet award heavy appropriations at home to run their own death camps?

Scientology continues to demand Human Rights for all men and continues to defy these psychiatric front groups.

The world today will not stand for such flagrant rights violations as the psychiatrist demands. The world today will not stand for death camps, human experiments, torture and murder.

The Scientologists are fighting this and will fight it down to a final and complete victory over the powers of evil.

Someday even the press, even politicians will wake up and say, "Hey! These are the guys in the good hats!"

Or else the press and politicians were the bad hats all the time.

The century has a long way to run.

The public has already realized the Scientologists are good people.

"The world today will not stand for such flagrant rights violations as the psychiatrist demands. The world today will not stand for death camps, human experiments, torture and murder."

27 FEBRUARY 1969

DRUIDISM AND PSYCHIATRY

by L. Ron Hubbard

SOME YEARS AGO I asked a psychiatrist, who came to a Scientology meeting, why he did not personally refuse to electric shock and refuse to do brain "operations" on people if he knew it often killed them.

He gave me an astonishing answer. He said, "I *have* to do it. If I didn't, I would be dismissed from the hospital for refusing to take part in the sacrifice."

This puzzled me. But recently my attention was recalled to the work of Jung, one of the three major psychiatric authorities, who are Freud, Jung and Adler.

As you can find in Jung's work, he laid tremendous stress on DRUIDISM and wrote a great deal about it.

Druidism was a Celtic inner circle of priests and lawgivers who seem to have practiced human sacrifice. Their cruel and inhuman rites led to their direct suppression by Rome.

In modern times, Druidism has revived and they are said to meet annually at Stonehenge, possibly their ancient stronghold in England.

This is the first clue I have ever had as to why psychiatrists think they have to kill and injure people.

Many psychiatrists have told me, when I interviewed them or when they tried to get me to take themselves or their wives for treatment, that electric shock *retards* a mental patient's recovery by about six weeks on the average, that when it does not kill them it usually breaks their teeth and often their spines. Over 1,200 were killed outright by electric machines in the US in one year. As to "operations" on the brain, they die either at once or within two to five years according to psychiatric official tables.

Psychiatrists freely admit these treatments do no good and are murderous or damaging, the evidence appearing in their own publications or in public media such as *Time* magazine.

This has never ceased to astonish informed observers: That torture, injury and murder were practiced in the full knowledge of no benefit, much less cure.

Their authority Jung, Druidism and human sacrifice offer for the first time some clue as to what it is all about.

Psychiatric front groups act frantically against any group who might discover their crimes.

Druidism in its day was the senior body above Celtic governments and dictated their actions.

The Profumo scandal laid bare wild, fantastic orgies by high officials.

I wonder if, when all the evidence is in, some fantastic explanation of why some UK Labour officials back up the psychiatrist and why the psychiatrist kills might not come to life.

Like human sacrifice or ritual murders such as those of Britain's recent colonies.

This enigma of unpunished official murder is one of the biggest social puzzles of our times, to say nothing of seizure violations of human rights.

"Druidism was a Celtic inner circle of priests and lawgivers who seem to have practiced human sacrifice. Their cruel and inhuman rites led to their direct suppression by Rome."

Given the weight of that word "terrorism" in the twenty-first century, here is yet another LRH statement proving all too true today. For while billions are indeed now spent on fighting terrorist activities, little heed is paid to the telltale links between such activities and psychiatry. In point of fact, psychiatric coercion tactics / drugging is often attendant to shaping the terrorist mind-set. While in the wake of terrorist attacks—most especially the tragedy of 9/11—there again were psychiatrists doling out drugs to survivors and lobbying for appropriations to "further study the matter."

1 March 1969

TODAY'S TERRORISM

by L. Ron Hubbard

While Western countries are spending billions fighting terrorist activities abroad, they are neglecting the one they have at home.

The psychiatrist and his front groups operate straight out of the terrorist textbooks. The Mafia looks like a convention of Sunday-school teachers compared to these terrorist groups.

Setting himself up as a terror symbol, the psychiatrist kidnaps, tortures and murders without any slightest police interference or action by Western security forces.

Instead these forces attack churches and peaceful, decent social groups under the direct orders of these terrorists.

Rape is rape, torture is torture, murder is murder. There are no laws that let even a medical doctor do these things.

The men who directed the attacks on Scientology in the press and parliaments were also directors of the main psychiatric front group.

A Scientology preclear has an aunt who says she doesn't like Scientology. Instant parliamentary investigation! Laws banning Scientology! Police raids with drawn guns.

A psychiatrist kills a young girl for sexual kicks, murders a dozen patients with an ice pick, castrates a hundred men. And they give him another million appropriation.

One can only conclude that psychiatric terrorism is not limited to the families of mental patients. It must extend all the way to the top.

Extortion, kidnapping, murder—these are crimes. Yet where are the security forces? Thousands of miles away tending to other people's business.

Very few people can be brought to testify against psychiatry. Yet four out of five contacted in a recent US survey had family or friends who had been ruined by psychiatry! They said, in general, "If I spoke up or complained, they'd take it out on my (son, friend, relative)."

I well recall a conversation I had with a Dr. Center in Savannah, Georgia, in 1949.* It well expresses the arrogance and complete contempt for law and order of the psychiatrist.

A man had just called to inquire after his wife, who was "under treatment" in Center's hospital. Center asked him, "Do you have the money.... That's right, thirty thousand.... Well, you better get it or I'll have to send your dear wife to the state institution and you know what will happen then!"

I was there doing work on charity patients the local psychiatrists wouldn't touch. Center had forgotten I was in the room.

He looked at me and shrugged, "He's sold his house, car and business already and he isn't good for any more. So over she goes to the operating room. It's just as well. The attendants got her pregnant and we'll have to abort her anyway. So we may as well wash her out. Hell of a business to be in for some quick bucks and a few kicks."

Thousands and thousands are seized without process of law every week over the "free" world, tortured, castrated, killed. All in the name of "mental health."

Terrorists never operated more effectively in any land with less interference and less outcry.

The evil is so great the public won't confront it. 1984 here we come!

LRH is specifically referencing Dr. Abraham Center of the Savannah, Georgia, mental asylum where much early Dianetics research was conducted in the late 1940s. Center was also noted for his utterly dismayed response to the miracles Dianetics worked on Savannah patients. In point of fact, the whole of the Savannah "charity list," some twenty men and women in all, were eventually discharged from the asylum following LRH employment of Dianetics procedures. —Editor

"Thousands and thousands are seized without process of law every week over the 'free' world, tortured, castrated, killed. All in the name of 'mental health.'"

2 March 1969

PAIN-DRUG-HYPNOSIS*

by L. Ron Hubbard

THERE IS A VERY dangerous and not publicly known technique used by psychiatrists to install compulsive behavior in a person.

Hypnotism is that act of fixating a person so that he or she will react only to exterior orders. POST-HYPNOTIC-SUGGESTION consists of installing, below the level of conscious awareness, an order, command or suggestion which the person, when again awake, will obey. These are well-known actions.

However, when it is realized that there are people who say they "don't believe in hypnotism" when it has been a common activity for about two centuries, there should be no wonder that the public and even some hypnotists are unaware of a far more sinister mental phenomenon known as PAIN-DRUG-HYPNOSIS.

Only about 22 percent of the population, according to some hypnotists, are susceptible to hypnotism. The rest are more or less immune to it.

Pain-drug-hypnosis on the other hand is effective on 100 percent of the population. It often leaves a person mentally deranged.

Hypnosis is a process, in effect, which works on a person already quite overwhelmed. One action of the hypnotist is to fixate such a person's attention and cause the person to react only to the orders of the hypnotist. The mechanism, not well understood before *Dianetics,* is really quite simple. A "suggestible person" (one who can be hypnotized) is already one whose insecurity readily causes him

---

*Initially described in L. Ron Hubbard's Science of Survival, LRH revelations concerning PDH, or pain-drug-hypnosis, constituted the first public disclosure of psychiatric-intelligence mind-control techniques. In fact, not until the mid-1970s, and United States Congressional hearings under Senator Frank Church, would pertinent Central Intelligence Agency documents come to light. —Editor

to desert, when fixated, his own self-determinism and accept the other-determinism of a hypnotist. Even body sensations will "transfer," as Mesmer discovered in 1775.

Any person placed in an emotional condition of terror, the most common emotion elicited in patients by psychiatrists, with understandable reason, is fixated. He knows the psychiatrist in an institution will probably injure him severely or ruin him physically, sterilize him or depersonalize him.

Such a person readily responds to orders subconsciously. He or she is in a frenzy to agree to anything in a frantic effort to escape some part of the agony of "treatment."

In the Nazi death camps, Jewish inmates even killed other Jews on the mere suggestion of it, such was the degree of fixation on the Nazi terror symbol.

When, to this, one adds drugs to open the subconscious and deepen the impact of commands, greater and more lasting effects occur. Commands given to a person in this state, even when unreasonable or against his interests or safety, can be made effective.

When, to drugs, one then adds pain of high intensity and accompanies it with commands, a person afterwards will continue to follow the order. This is true even when the order will bring death.

To restate this—a person under the usual hypnotic influence will not execute orders contrary to his moral code. A person under drug hypnosis will afterwards obey orders even contrary to his interests. Under pain and drugs, a person will accept orders which even bring about his death and afterwards execute them.

It is a matter of the amount of effect upon him physically. He identifies the pain with the strength of the order. The drugs lessen his will to resist.

Psychiatrists use pain-drug-hypnosis as an ordinary activity in institutions. They speak to drugged people during or after 50,000-volt shocks. They often lay in a posthypnotic suggestion.

The trouble with all this is not only its immorality. Hypnotism *lessens* the ability of the individual to become aware of the mental block oppressing him. The route to sanity is becoming aware of the root of the trouble. Even if ordered to be sane or get well, the effect is a dazed, agreeing person who, under a thin layer, is madder than ever. And the "treatment" wears off in under six months, leaving a sick and damaged being.

This type of duress hypnotism has, however, much more deadly uses. The psychiatrist is quite well aware of these.

A person drugged and shocked can be ordered to kill and who to kill and how to do it and what to say afterwards. And depending upon the expertise with which the "treatment" is given, the person, now depersonalized and only a robot, will do just that.

Thus you see why Scientologists, being technically superior to psychiatrists and about a hundred light-years above him morally, object seriously to the official indifference to drug–electric shock treatments.

The Scientologist is feared by the psychiatrist because a Scientologist can FIND AND RECOVER THESE PSYCHIATRIC ACTIONS IN PSYCHIATRIC MENTAL PATIENTS.

We find orders to give the psychiatrist a huge fee, to commit adultery, all sorts of things which, when revealed by the mild and nonphysical techniques of Scientology, make the person well again. The psychiatric "treatment" made him ill and kept him that way until the Scientologist came along and dug it up for the patient.

"Psychiatrists use pain-drug-hypnosis as an ordinary activity in institutions. They speak to drugged people during or after 50,000-volt shocks. They often lay in a posthypnotic suggestion."

Scientologists do not treat the insane. Why? Because the increasing statistics of insanity are directly attributable to the brutality of the psychiatrist. Ninety percent of the "insane" would get well in a week or two if left alone.

Inmates of sanitariums would get out six weeks earlier on the average if they were not electric shocked, according to the psychiatrists' own statistics. But at $2,000 a month in the US or £60 a week in the UK, that wouldn't be economical, would it?

Scientology is fought by the psychiatrist not only for economic reasons. A superior technology is always a threat to the old school.

In this case it is a threat to the life and liberty of the psychiatrist personally.

Scientology auditors find in these mental patients rape, perversion, sexual orgies, orders to pay huge fees, to commit crimes, a lot of unpleasant things.

The psychiatrist screams, "It's just delusion." If it is, then why does the patient recover? And why do the dates and personalities check out?

A person who is insane is in pretty agonizing shape to begin with. To then hurt him or her brutally, to use the patient as a sexual toy (as Frieda Fromm-Reichmann attests in her book of warnings to psychiatrists), to use a healing technology for extortion are all crimes.

Someday the police will have to take the psychiatrist in hand. That is the main reason the psychiatrist fights Scientology with such terror. The psychiatrist is being found out.

But that any official would defend psychiatry or fight its enemies for it is stupidity. Such an official has too little knowledge to live. Here is why:

Two mental patients attacked Dr. Verwoerd, late Prime Minister of South Africa.

He was no more than well-recovered from the first assassination attempt by a mental patient than he was successfully attacked and killed by another.

Nearly every major political assassination found psychiatrists quickly on the job getting the person off or out of sight.

The famous defection of Burgess and Maclean came shortly after a psychiatric treatment.

It just isn't politically safe to let electric shock, brutality and surgery be used on mental patients.

Let us grant that the humanitarian angle, the destruction of human beings, rape, kidnapping and violations of human rights do not interest some officials.

The political threat of the psychiatric technique of pain-drug-hypnosis cannot be overlooked.

"A person drugged and shocked can be ordered to kill and who to kill and how to do it and what to say afterwards. And depending upon the expertise with which the 'treatment' is given, the person, now depersonalized and only a robot, will do just that."

Although much of what LRH references as regards the consequences of a psychiatric partnership with governments is obvious enough, his 1969 "Failures" touches upon a then relatively unknown subject: the psychiatric barbarity and the death camp. That is, prior to the formation of the Citizens Commission on Human Rights in 1969, word of actual psychiatric murder was largely confined to Iron Curtain nations, particularly a Gulag-ridden Soviet Union. Through the energetic work of Scientologists, however, international attention was soon focused elsewhere—especially on what amounted to psychiatric torture chambers in the United States, the United Kingdom, Hungary, South Africa, Australia and New Zealand.

1 April 1969

FAILURES

by L. Ron Hubbard

THE PSYCHOLOGISTS AND PSYCHIATRISTS depended upon utterly by Western governments use only the technology of failed areas.

From Poland, Germany, Austria and Russia we get the arrogant psychologist and psychiatrist whose animal and death-camp practices come from the work of PAVLOV and WUNDT.

After these and their colleagues' work was accepted in these countries and used by their governments, total revolution and catastrophe followed.

The mental technology being used today by the Western governments gave Germany a Hitler, Russia a Stalin. Poland, Austria, Germany and Russia have been the scene of death camps, mass slaughter, wars and total defeat. The ruling heads who bought and used this work are long-since dead, execrated and condemned by Mankind.

Yet Western governments now pantingly beg for the faintest opinions of the current exponents of these technologies.

With their crime rate soaring in England since they began to use this degraded technology, yet even the police are forced to study it.

It is taught even to schoolchildren in America and American mothers raised the generation on it who are now deserting in hordes from the army.

Not only do Western governments now use this mental technology, but also use the advice of the very men, nationals of those countries, who were part of the downfall.

A list of these "experts" in the work of Wundt and Pavlov and other Eastern authorities shows in New York alone as 62 percent imported from those countries.

Further, the public wants *nothing* to do with them and their "Man is an animal" death-camp orientation. The public will not support them financially or willingly go to them.

These men exist on government handouts and appropriations.

So they are doubly a failure.

Further, these people attack every new Western development in the field of the mind by slamming against one the full control they now have over governments.

These men, operating from a headquarters close to the Russian-German border, control the entire field of "mental health" in the West.

Scientology, the only new Western development in the mind and spirit, is fought by these men with demoniac fury.

AND WESTERN GOVERNMENTS OBEY THEM.

Anyone in the public who disagrees with this new Fascism is slated for their stockades, torture by ingenious shocks and murder. All avidly agreed to by the "very best people."

In my humble opinion these very best people had better remember the fate of the Czar of Russia, of Adolf Hitler, of the crowned heads of Austria and the rest. *These* were the "best people" of their day too. They died very horribly after using the work of these psychiatrists and psychologists.

Western crime is soaring, violence stamps Western cities, students are in total revolt, armies of men are deserting. And the Western leaders listen raptly to the same technology that made dust of its own world.

Either Western leaders are being stupid beyond belief or they are themselves criminal. Take your choice. There are no other possible explanations.

To scorn and attack all Western developments in the field of the humanities and engage in a death-kiss orgy with the Wundt, Pavlov rantings against Man is not a "symptom of the times." It is a planned destruction of the West by the use of its own heads of state and should be regarded as such.

Watch carefully wherever the leaders of a country shrug off these death camps that are now being brought to view; you have men whose hatred of their own people is deep and bitter and will not end until the population is shattered and destroyed.

There is no possible sane excuse, pretext or explanation for planned and "lawful" seizure, torture and murder of innocent human beings.

Why import failed technology?

CIRCA JUNE 1969

DIPLOMAS

by L. Ron Hubbard

THE USUAL REQUIREMENT FOR a diploma in a subject is that the holder be able to accomplish a result with the subject.

Psychiatrists obtain their "diplomas" without ever demonstrating any cure of anything.

Psychologists obtained "diplomas" in the mind for a subject which in all their textbooks insisted Man could *not* be changed, that intelligence and personality could not be altered.

In that the psychiatrist bragged that it took twelve years of training to be one and a psychologist boasted it took six years to be a psychologist, one can assume that they certainly took long enough to learn nothing.

Other criminals require no diplomas to become competent murderers.

It is in keeping with the rest of the fakery of psychiatry and psychology that this "training" also doesn't take place.

Institutional psychiatrists spend a few years as a yardman beating up patients and that's "training."

Both of these activities are sponsored by private groups who pretend to be officials of the state. The word "National" is a fake.

The only expertise one can be sure of in psychiatry and psychology is fakery. They are without doubt the world's most accomplished fakes.

A diploma in a subject which can accomplish nothing is all part of the facade that is used to extort billions annually from the government.

It would be far cheaper if governments just hired the Mafia to drug and kill their citizens and have done with it.

One is sure the Mafia could also furnish very good diplomas, earned, most of them, with many years in prison. Or, like those of psychiatry, outright counterfeits.

CIRCA JUNE 1969

PSYCHOLOGY AND PSYCHIATRY
THE SCIENCES OF SALIVA

by L. RON HUBBARD

SOME RECENT RESEARCH HAS disclosed that the much advertised and heavily government-financed control sciences of psychology and psychiatry are based on a single discovery.

Karl Friedrich Wilhelm LUDWIG (1816–1895), the head of the Dept of Physiology of the University of Leipzig (Germany), was the first to demonstrate that human digestive glands might be under the influence of the secretory nerve. This was a sort of breakthrough, that nerves controlled physical reactions.

Another German, Wilhelm Max WUNDT (1832–1920), teaching at the same university (Leipzig, Germany), promptly, in 1879, declared all men just animals, as nerves controlled saliva, and became the father of psychology. This was the first institute of psychology.

Ivan Petrovich PAVLOV (1849–1936), a veterinarian, promptly came over from Russia and studied up on this and went back home to show that dogs salivate when you ring bells and stop when you electric shock them.

Pavlov was part of the violent university revolution in nineteenth-century Russia and emerged in the 1917 revolution that murdered the Czar as the head of the new Communist experimental laboratories.

In 1928, at the same time Stalin was having Pavlov write a 400-page book on how to nervously control human beings, the UK Royal Society made him a fellow.

John Dewey (1859–1952), the "great" US educator who revolutionized teaching in America (and brought revolution into *its* universities), was a follower of Wundt's theories. In Dewey's time US psychologists were sent to Leipzig to study under Wundt.

Pavlov and the "great" US educator John Dewey had the same teachers.

The entire rationale of psychology and psychiatry trace to Ludwig and to Wundt. It is based entirely on the following data.

A nerve, if cut or torn or shocked, can cause the physical body to react.

As the nerve can control saliva, the nerves must control food demand and sex demand.

Therefore men are animals. They can be trained like sheep or dancing bears.

This is *all* the psychiatrist is trying to do with shock and surgery—sever the "right" nerve.

It has NEVER been proven anywhere by anyone that there is any right nerve.

The politicians of Germany, Russia, the US and England became very fascinated with the *promise* of being able to control men utterly.

Unfortunately the basic premise of psychology and psychiatry is a limited and partial truth. And as it has been applied, it has rolled up the following records:

Czarist Russia—perished through the university activities of revolting students.

The Kaiser's Germany—gone by 1918.

Hitler's Germany—gone by 1945.

Austria, Czechoslovakia and Poland absorbed into Russia.

The Russian people enslaved.

US universities in total, uncontrolled riot.

UK universities going out of control.

The total dominance exerted by these Leipzig-indoctrinated "psychologists," educators and psychiatrists has been very marked since the last half of the nineteenth century.

The tenets of this school are:

1. There is no God.
2. Man is an animal.
3. Man can be totally controlled.
4. Man cannot be changed.
5. Man has no will, he is just a stimulus-response mechanism and therefore totally irresponsible for his actions.

These fellows—Wundt, Pavlov, Dewey, the lot—took universities out from under the Church where they had prospered for over a thousand years, taught Man that he was a soulless wild animal and presented us on a flaming platter with what is laughingly called modern civilization.

On their heels came cultural oblivion and national destruction.

Control of Man?

Look at the riots.

Isn't it about time somebody booted out these arrogant pretenders and let somebody do who can?

Dianetics and Scientology have been fought bitterly by these priests of revolution and decay. Yet Dianetics and Scientology can make in hours students who can study, men who can think and well, happy human beings. It's time the old school was buried with its dead and let those who *can* try to bring some order out of the past century of lies.

"The entire rationale of psychology and psychiatry trace to Ludwig and to Wundt. It is based entirely on the following data. A nerve, if cut or torn or shocked, can cause the physical body to react. As the nerve can control saliva, the nerves must control food demand and sex demand. Therefore men are animals."

In suggesting psychiatry's "Planned Revolution" is doomed to failure in the face of Scientology, LRH is alluding to the long and consistently victorious efforts of Scientologists to stem the psychiatric tide. To cite but a few landmark victories beyond 1956: With the 1969 formation of the Citizens Commission on Human Rights to expose and eradicate psychiatric abuses, Scientologists did just that—first and most notably in South Africa, where native African "patients" were held in literal slave-labor camps until a CCHR-sparked ministerial investigation. In consequence to that investigation came the recommendation for a charter of patients' rights and actual prosecution of psychiatric crimes. Following exposure of similarly grim psychiatric crimes in Italy, Scientologists once more stood at the forefront of parliamentary investigations and the recommended closure of some ninety psychiatric asylums. Then again, Scientologists led the crusade against psychiatric abuse in Greece and New Zealand, while inspiring the banning of electroconvulsive treatment on children in Texas and California.

In highly dramatic emphasis of that phrase ending psychiatric abuse, Scientologists descended on the Chelmsford facility in Sydney, Australia. As internationally reported, and yet again under the CCHR banner, Scientologists uncovered the now infamous "deep-sleep" experimentation wherein patients were rendered unconscious for weeks on end and subjected to as much as twenty-four shock treatments a week—and naturally told nothing of what they suffered when eventually awoke from their drug-induced sleep. These discoveries ultimately led to a Royal Commission Inquiry of the matter—the highest level of government inquiry in Australia. While just to cap it: On the eve of hearings wherein Chelmsford's chief psychiatrist, Dr. Harry Bailey, faced professional extinction and certain deregistration, he literally "took his own medicine." That is, he intentionally swallowed a fatal dose of Tuinal—the very same drug he had fed his patients. It seems he did have much to fear, as inquiry findings and recommendations eventually led to sweeping reforms across the whole Australian mental health establishment. Moreover, and likewise through CCHR efforts, some two hundred Chelmsford victims finally received compensation.

As a final word on these matters, one should also note that at the time of LRH's article it was unheard of for any psychiatrist to be held accountable for atrocities committed in the name of "treatment." Today, however, and directly following from the work of Scientologists, psychiatrists prosecuted under criminal statutes and serving out sentences number in the thousands. Then, too, Scientologists have successfully secured the passage of more than a hundred bills to safeguard patient rights worldwide. While just for good measure, it was none other than Scientologists who spearheaded the 1991 United Nations mental health "Bill of Rights" unanimously issued for the protection of patients everywhere.

THE PLANNED REVOLUTION

by L. Ron Hubbard

THAT THE PSYCHIATRIST AND psychologist knowingly intend to supplant the politician and present rulers of state through their "National" Mental "Health" organizations is not an idle statement.

The ambition is plain in their literature.

As early as 1938, Harold D. Lasswell, a psychiatric spokesman, wrote in *Psychiatry* an article entitled "What Psychiatrists and Political Scientists Can Learn From One Another."

He stated, "...The most far-reaching way to reduce disease is for the psychiatrist to cultivate closer contact with the rulers of society....

"So the psychiatrist may decide to become rulers of the 'King.' Now the history of the 'King' and his philosophers shows that the 'King' is prone to stray from the path of wisdom as wisdom is understood by the King's philosophers. Must the psychiatrist, then, unseat the 'King' and actualize in the realm of fact the philosopher-King of Plato's imagination? By the grace of his psychiatry, of course, the modern philosopher who would be king knows that he may lose his philosophy on the way to the throne and arrive there empty of all that would distinguish him from the king he has overthrown. But, if sufficiently secure in his knowledge of himself and his field, he may dare where others dared and lost before."

Lasswell also preached, "Power corrupts and absolute power corrupts absolutely—except psychiatrists."

The psychiatric bid for total power is well progressed.

Like the early ambitions of Hitlers and Napoleons, it is looked on as too incredible to be believed—until millions died for their ambitions.

Since 1938, the psychiatrist and psychologist have advanced a long way toward their goal of power seizure.

They employ terrorism, corruption and blackmail to cow political henchmen.

They have taken over education not only in universities, but even in the lesser schools and are producing a submissive, degraded generation over which to rule.

A state-financed secret police seize anyone they do not like.

The state finances their death camps for dissenters.

They have nearly paralyzed Christianity.

They control total "respect" in the press through pressures on newspaper owners.

They strike down any promise of real help or freedom for the people.

Russia, Poland, Czechoslovakia, Germany and other countries have already bowed and use them absolutely to control whole populations.

They have earned the "right" to be above the law utterly and to seize, torture or murder whomever they wish. They operate totally beyond human law and defy utterly every progress ever made in human freedom.

The psychiatric revolution is not only planned. It is well on the way to actual accomplishment.

These outlaws have only made two serious mistakes:

1. They are running directly counter to the desires, mores and customs of the huge majority of world populations.
2. They attacked Dianetics and Scientology without provocation or reason and demonstrated fully that they oppose any real mental technology that would help.

Only madmen seek to rule the world. Only completely insane degenerates would try to rule a world wholly opposed to their activities.

But madness encourages rather than discourages mad ambitions.

One of these days even their political puppets will wake up and realize that murderers are murderers. If they don't alert in time, they too will accompany the political psychiatrist and psychologist up the fateful thirteen steps.

You can fool some of the people some of the time, the old saw goes. But it will be found impossible to oppress and tyrannize all the planet without fantastic and painful retribution.

They'll never make it. For one can't make a police state if one is wholly detested by the police and security branches.

The criminal and outlaw is an arrogant fellow. He goes right on being arrogant until the end.

The psychiatrist and psychologist have been so arrogant that they have openly stated in writing many times what they fully intend to do. It seems incredible. That is its only protection.

Due to the public-spirited efforts of Scientologists, you will see an end of this within your time.

"Since 1938, the psychiatrist and psychologist have advanced a long way toward their goal of power seizure. They employ terrorism, corruption and blackmail to cow political henchmen."

13 June 1969

SCIENCES OF SALIVA

by L. Ron Hubbard

Pity the poor psychiatrist and psychologist.

He has no tech to back him up.

A lot of bombast and salesmanship with nothing to sell.

He couldn't cure a pimple, yet has boasted he is able to run the world.

His sociology and all his other ologies are a basket of empty bottles.

He can't even make a dog salivate on schedule.

His whole skill is confined to hoodwinking politicians into total appropriation.

He cannot deliver what he promises.

The Utopian society he is supposed to be setting up at vast expense is just one long mass of riots and civil commotion.

Whatever he touches revolts, whether it is a university or a country.

One could safely offer a million pounds' reward for any person cured of anything or any group controlled.

Pavlov "spit theories" are false. Only about two out of a hundred dog subjects can ever be made to salivate when a bell is rung. The psychologist is quiet about the other ninety-eight. They didn't salivate. They did almost everything else. The most common reaction was to bite! Not food, but the psychologist.

Out of hundreds of captives brainwashed by Pavlovian techniques in Korea only about twenty-two were "converted to Communism" and most of them relapsed.

In rat mazes, some rats insist upon entering the shock route to get at the cheese and few ever use the nonshock door. They get mad about it.

"Pavlov 'spit theories' are false. Only about two out of a hundred dog subjects can ever be made to salivate when a bell is rung.... The most common reaction was to bite!"

Pity the poor psychiatrist and psychologist. They promised the politicians to cure all social ills. They promised to set up a total Utopia for only a few billion quid.

All they set up was *revolt!*

It has not dawned on them that they will be "for it" shortly. They cannot deliver.

The first generation they raised in American schools using Pavlovian techniques and bloated promises has revolted en masse, is deserting the US Armed Forces in droves and is destroying the whole US school system.

God help a technician who can only promote and can never deliver.

Pity the poor psychiatrist and psychologist.

The most horrible thing that could happen to them has happened.

Somebody came along and developed a real mental technology that *works*.

For nineteen years psychiatrists and psychologists have fought to destroy Dianetics and Scientology.

Even in this they failed.

There is only one reaction in common in all the psychiatric and psychological experiments and efforts at control. Whether rats or dogs or men, their victims demonstrate revulsion and rage at these charlatans.

But pity the psychologist and psychiatrist. Unmasked for what they are, they are dying.

15 JUNE 1969

CONTROL "SCIENCES"

by L. RON HUBBARD

IT IS NOT WELL known to the public that psychiatry and psychology, as taught in schools and lavishly financed by governments, are NOT intended to cure anything. The idea of CURE is the furthest from both the government and scholastic intention.

The idea that a science could be developed to CONTROL populations sprang up to counter the Liberty, Fraternity and Equality demands of the French Revolution. The Comte de Saint-Simon (1760–1825) advocated reorganizing all society. In association with Auguste Comte (1798–1857) the theory was put forward that one could control the entirety of the population by isolating certain principles.

These men were violently opposed to a free society and neither were personally successful in life.

Comte, as a student, was part of the mutiny which destroyed the École Polytechnique, beginning the trend of university mutinies, which extended through the nineteenth century in Europe and Russia and in our own times, everywhere that these totalitarian principles were advocated.

At Leipzig University, Ludwig and Wundt were to further this movement by advancing the idea that nerve conditioning could be done.

In Russia, Pavlov conceived the idea that men's former social responses could be altered and, after the university mutinies, the Communist Totalitarian State was brought into being with psychiatry and psychology in charge in the background.

Using the same principles, German doctors pushed Nazi Totalitarian Germany into existence and extended "conditioning" to mean outright murder of all dissenters.

The Russian Totalitarian State, using its KGB and psychiatric agents, and assisted by the "very best people," has pushed the British Empire to extermination and is currently working on America.

The pattern is invariable. The questionable joys of the totalitarian state are pushed into the textbooks of schools, called "psychology" or "sociology," and the new generation rises, with trained-in disloyalty and treason to their country.

The "very best people" and the most corruptible politicians are engineered into compliance and *voilà!* as Comte would say, we have our totally controlled society where Liberty, Fraternity and Equality are the nastiest words one can utter.

These harebrained visionaries are listened to by feebleminded politicians and by snobs who actively detest "the mob." It seems so convincing—a system by which one can CONTROL the entire population by the natural laws these "experts" pretend to know (but which are too learned to possibly be communicated).*

It is a strange dream wherein everybody likes strawberries, everybody is tame, all is calm. And the very best people sit on a knoll and play a shepherd's pipe while the sheep quietly graze.

However, it doesn't work out that way. Mainly because the exponents of the total social state know nothing of the mind, people or government. Any policeman knows more about crime than the most learned "criminal psychiatrist." Any hospital nurse knows more about the society than the best-trained "sociologist" in the world.

What happens when D-day arrives is a bit more unpleasant. The "very best people" are slaughtered, very painfully. The population, decimated, begins to starve. A violent and cruel secret police has to be active everywhere to continually prevent counterrevolution. A gruesome constant reign of terror crushes the population for decades.

It has never occurred to any of these totalitarians that the whole detestation of Mankind becomes focused upon them in these Totalitarian monstrosities. And when they blow up, they spatter their organizers in fragments.

This half-witted dream to control society for its own sake has so far slaughtered more than a hundred million human beings in this century alone.

I would say that the control philosophies called psychiatry, psychology and sociology were a failure. Probably the biggest human failure of the last two centuries.

Isn't it time we got rid of them?

In particular, and specifically in the name of societal control, were Psychological Strategy Board discussions regarding the use of national radio broadcasts to manipulate popular morale and bolster support of United States foreign objectives. Also discussed among psychiatric participants to Board meetings—including, incidentally, vehement Dianetics foe Dr. Daniel Blain—was the enlistment of newspaper editors willing to play upon popular fears of a Soviet nuclear threat. —Editor

"The pattern is invariable. The questionable joys of the totalitarian state are pushed into the textbooks of schools, called 'psychology' or 'sociology,' and the new generation rises, with trained-in disloyalty and treason to their country."

15 June 1969

THE BLAND PERSONALITY

by L. Ron Hubbard

The "social engineer" bent on producing a totalitarian Utopia is anxiously trying to redesign "acceptable personality" into a submissive, emotionless state.

People who become annoyed, angry, excited, exhilarated are alike in his bad books.

Yet it is a fact that the primary complaint of psychotics in institutions is that they can't "feel" anything anymore. They can no longer be happy or sad or "feel" in response to life. They are just numb.

The psychiatrist and psychologist pronounce as abnormal any departure from a single monotonous "good dog" mental state. They have resounding Latin curse words for any personality reaction or behavioral difference in men. All these states are "crazy." We look in vain for any approval of anyone being happy. Instead we find the curse word "euphoric," which means "psychotically cheerful."

Restaurant food today is mostly "bland," which is to say, "inoffensively tasteless." One looks in vain on Hilton menus for peppery dishes or strong flavors. Since an occasional patron complains of strong flavors, EVERYONE must be subjected to tasteless dishes.

So it is with the totalitarian social "expert." Employed by the state, hopeful even of running the state, he conceives his job as a sort of dog boy who punishes anything but the unnoticeable personality. "Good" dogs are easy to keep in line. So therefore all dogs who show any signs of becoming happy or leaping about or not feeling up to it today are promptly stigmatized as having "psychotic" tendencies. This gets the dog boy off the hook in case anything goes wrong. As this particular dog boy doesn't like dogs anyway, it saves him a lot of work if he only has dogs with negative personalities.

The question of who is going to remain sufficiently alive and interested to run anything has never entered the head of the social tyrant.

"The 'social engineer' bent on producing a totalitarian Utopia is anxiously trying to redesign 'acceptable personality' into a submissive, emotionless state."

And the other question of who is going to remain interested enough in life to want to live it poses a very high future suicide rate.

The Bland Personality—no joys, no sorrows, submissive, obedient and dull—is the obvious target of the government's social experts.

Behold tomorrow's Man—a being never interested in anything.

He probably won't even talk—bark is more like it.

16 June 1969

QUACKERY AND FAKERY

by L. Ron Hubbard

THESE "MENTAL HEALTH" ORGANIZATIONS that seek to create a totalitarian state superior to the police, the courts and the people are very fond of stating in their literature, to the press and to governments that they oppose "quackery" and that all "quacks" must be eradicated.

Historically a "Quack" was someone who sold *quick*silver or mercury at English fairs as a cure for disease. Specifically a "Quack" is one who sells ointments or patent medicines and refuses to refund the fee of ointment or treatment if no cure is effected. The old English-fair "Quack" of course passed on to the next fair before his clients found that the ointments didn't work.

Strangely, the full-fledged DOCTOR of that period and the psychiatrist of this current period could not and do not cure anything either.

Politicians, social departments are always being harassed by these fake "mental health" groups to round up "Quacks," abolish "Quacks" and leave the entire field open to men who can't cure anything.

The psychiatrist and psychologist do not ever refund any fees. If they did, they would owe every penny of every collection ever made from public individuals and the state.

A survey across five countries failed utterly to find ONE person who had ever been cured of anything by psychiatrists and psychologists. The survey found thousands who had been permanently disabled or killed. And in at least one mental prison, the admission total and the death total were found to be equal. So nobody there ever lived long enough to reclaim his fee.

So we have the interesting question of who are the "Quacks"?

To offer the politician the promise of controlling the whole population is a promise of cure.

The politician appropriates hundreds of millions for institutions and Community Psychiatry.

Promptly, universities revolt, agitators flourish, crime shoots into statistics not even policemen can graph, insanity soars.

This is nondelivery. The psychiatrist, psychologist and their clerk the sociologist point out how bad things are getting and demand even *more* money.

The patients who live get crazier, the state itself becomes imperiled and yet no psychiatrist or psychologist or sociologist or their "mental health" cliques ever pay back a penny of their unearned fees.

So what is this label "Quack"?

We have to have a more solid term.

It is hypocrisy to accuse others of doing what one is himself secretly doing.

It is arrant fakery to pretend to cure all social ills and control populations and then produce only riots.

These men, their appropriations, their tortures and murders are all in vain.

They have produced only chaos.

They are the quacks.

Sometimes a family has to prevent one of its members from associating with bad companions.

It is time the public forbade its politicians to associate further with these bad advisers, the psychiatrist and psychologist.

"These men, their appropriations, their tortures and murders are all in vain. They have produced only chaos. They are the quacks."

16 June 1969

HOW TO WIN AN ARGUMENT

by L. Ron Hubbard

It is not entirely just to say that psychiatrists and psychologists have *no* technology.

True, they can cure nothing and cannot change anyone for better or worse and as a result have to kill "difficult patients."

But they *do* have one piece of technology.

This is concerned with winning arguments.

Anyone who disagrees with their planned totalitarian rule is pronounced "insane." He is seized quietly, conveyed to a prison, tortured and usually permanently injured or killed.

People they cannot get their hands on, but who exist in literature or legend, they also pronounce "insane."

Barry Goldwater was labeled a "paranoid schizophrenic" by psychiatrists employed by the opposing party. Whittaker Chambers was dubbed a "psychopathic personality." Woodrow Wilson was declared a "megalomaniac," and even Jesus Christ, when the psychiatrists decided religion barred their way to world control, was called a "born regenerate" with a "fixed delusional system" manifesting a "paranoid clinical picture (so typical) it is hardly conceivable people can even question the accuracy of the diagnosis."

In other words, psychologists and psychiatrists *do* have a piece of technology. Anyone who has any other idea than total social control is labeled "crazy." This at once disposes of the fellow, of course. It invalidates his views and so gets them out of the road of "psychiatric progress" toward the Total State.

There are only two things odd about this technology.

One is that it is only used on people who speak of freedom or whose views oppose psychiatric ambitions.

"...psychologists and psychiatrists do have a piece of technology. Anyone who has any other idea than total social control is labeled 'crazy.'"

The other is that it cannot be called new. Even though a lot of Latin is employed to make the point, it is very difficult to find any difference between this technology and that employed by little boys.

As almost anyone has always known, devoid of all Latin terms, when two little boys can't agree on some vague point little boys disagree about, one or the other since caveman times has always tried to end the argument by saying:

"You're crazy!"

Could it be their whole technology has never really advanced beyond that of the neighborhood bully?

23 JUNE 1969

CRIME AND PSYCHIATRY

by L. RON HUBBARD

WHEN YOU PUT CRIMINALS in charge of crime, the crime rate rises.

The soaring crime statistics which the police are battling began to rise when the psychiatrist and psychologist moved into the field of education and law.

It used to be that a crime was a crime. When a police officer did his duty, his duty was done.

Now all that has changed. Criminals are "maladjusted" and it is "all society's fault that they are" and the police officer is a beast for daring to interfere with the poor fellows.

The psychiatrist and psychologist have carefully developed a lawless and irresponsible public attitude toward crime.

First and foremost is that Man is just a soulless animal who is not answerable for his own acts. They advertise Man as a push-button stimulus-response robot and claim that only *they* know where the buttons are.

"Underprivileged" people always become criminals, according to these "experts," so the thing to do is make the criminal a privileged being with far more rights than ordinary people.

But the main fault to be found with this psychiatric and psychological influence is that these people only escape the hangman's noose by a fanfare of being above the law themselves.

Crimes of extortion, mayhem and murder are done daily by these men in the name of "practice" and "treatment." There is not one institutional psychiatrist alive who, by ordinary criminal law, could not be arraigned and convicted of extortion, mayhem and murder. Our files are full of evidence on them.

By a mental trick they have hypnotized some politicians into actually believing they are working in "science" and are above the law in that it is necessary that they commit these crimes.

"By a mental trick they have hypnotized some politicians into actually believing they are working in 'science' and are above the law in that it is necessary that they commit these crimes."

The brutal truth is that these people have not a clue as to what makes the mind work. If they did, they could cure somebody, couldn't they? But they can't and don't. It is obvious, for crime stats have soared since these archcriminals wormed their way into the field of crime.

If you put a complete fake in an engine room to run it, your engine room would soon be a shambles.

This is what has happened in society. Instead of letting the police go about their business, a whole new hierarchy of fake experts has been superimposed on the field.

Thus there is chaos.

If these psychiatrists and psychologists and their "National" Mental Health groups knew their business, then crime statistics would be falling. Naturally. But they are not. Crime statistics, ever since these men have taken over in courts, prisons, education and social welfare, have soared to a point where the honest policeman is near despair.

ANY EXPERIENCED LAW ENFORCEMENT OFFICER KNOWS MORE ABOUT THE CRIMINAL MIND THAN ANY "TWELVE-YEAR-EDUCATED PSYCHIATRIST" OR "SIX-YEAR-EDUCATED PSYCHOLOGIST."

Not the smallest of their crimes is that they absorb all appropriations to rehabilitate people and actively campaign against every church and civic group that used to help with the problem.

But then real top-level criminals wouldn't want the problem of crime to be handled. Would they?

It remains historical fact that one can always tell a totalitarian regime from the fearful voice with which it responds to Scientology's popular dream of freedom. Case in point, the terrified J. Edgar Hoover and Richard Nixon responses to LRH and Scientology. But the greater point, as LRH explains in his definitive statement on Scientology objectives, is simply this: any government, agency or official opposing Scientology is finally opposed to both what Scientologists represent as honest and responsible citizens and what their religion embodies in the way of still greater freedom.

28 June 1969

OUR INTENTIONS

by L. Ron Hubbard

ONE OF OUR MINISTERS calling at the United Nations was suddenly confronted by a delegation which, recognizing him as a Scientologist, rushed up to him and said, "What are you going to do with the United Nations?"

There was real fear in the voice tone.

The actual intentions and beingness of Scientology, its organizations and groups, therefore, should be factually stated.

In 1949 a friendly and highly workable mental technology was developed. It handled mental problems without duress or hypnotism.

It was offered to the medical and psychiatric professions, but they refused the gift.

A popular book was written, became an instant bestseller.

Grass-roots organizations sprang up over the world, supported by the public.

Seeing an immediate economic threat from a more workable technology, psychiatric front groups instantly began to fight the new knowledge using *agent provocateur* and intelligence tactics.

Many lies and threats were spread about by these hostile elements.

Politicians who were under blackmail by these psychiatric front groups tried to stir up police interest and failed. They then resorted to "government inquiries" to obtain bans.

The Scientology organizations continued to grow. Public support became stronger.

The political henchmen of psychiatry began to lose their seats and prestige.

Scientology discovered that psychiatry ran death camps and existed as a new form of population oppression.

Scientology groups and organizations continued to grow.

The new subject was even further developed even though hampered by psychiatry's dog-in-the-manger absorption of all public mental funds.

It began to be proven that "governments" had no evidence of any kind against Scientology, its founder or its organizations and the psychiatric front groups lost prestige and they themselves began to be subjected to scrutiny on the not-mild charges of public sabotage, *agent provocateur* actions, misappropriation and murder.

That, in short, is the history of nineteen years.

Because Scientology did what it said, had no evil intent and tried with integrity to do its job, it was much too strong to be eradicated, despite a worldwide conspiracy which spent millions to destroy it.

The actual intentions of the founder, Scientologists and Scientology organizations are easily stated, easily proven:

1. To make well, happy human beings by individual processing.
2. To be friendly and always willing to help.
3. To create a safe environment by protesting the use of hypnotism, violent treatment and illegal seizure of people.
4. To make a better world by making more able individuals.
5. To work toward spiritual freedom.
6. To support the legal government of the country in which each organization is situated.
7. To make its organizational technology and other discoveries generally and freely available.
8. Not to interfere with the mores and customs of any people.
9. To refuse no one help by reason of race, color or creed.
10. To conduct activities, as good citizens, working in the interest of the country.

Those are the full intentions of Scientology, its organizations and people.

Anything stated by the enemy to the contrary is an effort to discredit a development which would cost them their godlike pretensions and illegally obtained power and finance.

Scientology organizations are composed of good, sound citizens of their countries who work for the organization because they believe there is hope.

Not one scrap of actual evidence exists anywhere in the world that would refute any of the above.

Thousands of papers, daily deeds and decent actions exist to prove the above.

The world was hit by a breakthrough in mental technology.

All new things have a hard time.

The only charge that could be successfully leveled at Scientology is that it is fast, workable and does exactly what it says it can do. And this being the case, there's no room left for men who use a pretense of curing mental illness to become oppressors of humanity and enemies of the state.

> "The only charge that could be successfully leveled at Scientology is that it is fast, workable and does exactly what it says it can do."

One could say with truth to that frightened UN delegation, "What are we going to do with the UN? Why, help make the individuals in it bright enough and competent enough to do their jobs and so bring peace, perhaps, to the world."

Diogenes had a very bad time finding an honest man, it is said. But any honest organization in a world with as much unrest and suffering as this one is going to have a very hard time of it until people realize at last that its sole threat is that it makes honest men.

2 AUGUST 1969

THE UNHOLY STICK TOGETHER

by L. RON HUBBARD

THERE IS PROBABLY NO organization on Earth that operates as illegally as the WORLD FEDERATION OF MENTAL HEALTH.

This psychiatric front group, advocating injury and death for the insane and anyone they wish to seize and pronounce "insane," is a fly-by-night corporation, registered to do business in Delaware, the US state where corporations are given with no questions asked.

But it does not do any business in Delaware.

It used to operate illegally in Switzerland. It was not registered to do business there. Yet it engaged in moneymaking activities for twenty years.

When reproached for overlooking its illegal status, the Health Minister for Switzerland (all these "Health Ministers" are connected to the WFMH ring) said it was all right for it to be illegal, but it wasn't all right for anyone else to be illegal. Wonderful.

It is presently in Scotland, where it isn't registered either. It has no right to do business there and if the crime were discovered it would entail very heavy fines.

In fact, it isn't a legal organization.

Although it is heavily engaged in politics and appoints most of the Health Ministers in the world and influences elections, it makes no report of campaign contributions.

Its "directors" have some dizzy personal retirement scheme in addition to a fantastic salary of £7,000 a year. All this is paid for by local contributions to "help the starving insane."

This group's members are other groups, making a secret network over the world.

The member groups call themselves "National," whereas this is illegal as they are not part of any government, they just falsely state they are. They are private profit-making groups.

There is only one National mental health activity in the world that is part of a government. This is the National *Institute* of Mental Health in Bethesda, Maryland, USA.

Through this one official agency, these false groups and their secret center, the WFMH, are supported by government graft funds.

The US government hands out vast sums to organize the WFMH "Congresses." These are attended by Russian and Iron Curtain country delegates.

The man who keeps up the WFMH front in the United Nations is financed by a huge munitions combine.

This international network pushes dope, advocates death and easy seizure.

Their couriers fly over the world continually arranging new ways to influence legislation and keep their resident directors informed.

Their activities in the US are unconstitutional.

The reason government agencies do not act against them is that they control, by holding wives and daughters as hostages, many political figures.

This is the group and network which spreads the lies and instigates actions against Scientology and its people.

This group is seeking to suppress every beneficial treatment of the insane, to eradicate all boundaries and constitutions, to spread dope and seize anyone who disagrees.

The Intelligence service of the Third Reich was composed mainly of doctors, if you care to look up the list of Hitler's agencies.

The technology they advocate is Russian in origin, but is forbidden to be used in Russia.

There probably is no more illegal group on the planet.

If their program of "Mental Health" is closely examined, it will be found to be curiously like the plans of Stalin and Hitler, complete with seizures in the night, weird experimental surgery and death camps.

The only organization that is making any progress against these people is Scientology.

Scientologists have exposed them, have made them afraid. Seven out of twelve of their top leaders are now no longer functioning. Their income has fallen to a point where representatives in charge of the fund collection drives are whining that the WFMH is going bankrupt.

There is probably no more hated figure in the world today than the psychiatrist.

When this illegal and preposterous network set as its target the eradication of the only new Western development in the field of the mind, they made a fatal mistake.

Politicians who still bow to their will are also making a mistake.

Organizations like the WFMH went out of style the day the world learned of Dachau and other Nazi death camps.

The public is wholly on the side of Scientology.

This has been a fight to the death.

The WFMH is dying.

"There is probably no organization on Earth that operates as illegally as the WORLD FEDERATION OF MENTAL HEALTH."

As a further word on Ron's 1969 "Cultural Deficiencies," when alluding to his study of political science at Princeton University, he was indeed citing what appeared as an introductory note to this publication, i.e., his attendance at the United States School of Military Government in November of 1944. While as a word on what he describes as the sheer "scope" of political science, it just so happens that his Princeton papers draw from some two thousand years of geopolitical history—quite literally from Mongolian military maneuvers under Genghis Khan to Allied operations in Sicily.

9 September 1969

CULTURAL DEFICIENCIES

by L. Ron Hubbard

Everyone knows that physical sciences have outstripped the "humanities" today and that the planet is endangered by incautious application of science without humanitarian restraint.

The H-bomb, which could give electrical power cheaply to all the world, is used instead as a threat to "deter" war.

Poisons flood the streams and eradicate fish. Industry and other actions sweep away game. Yet the cry is up that the population must be reduced because food will be short.

A thousand thousand such idiocies tell us that material knowledge has run away with good sense and that the "humanities" are deficient in technology.

Yet no one has said just which of the humanities are deficient.

The zones of ignorance in the humanities are in fact very few.

First and most flagrant is a lack of political science. A great deal of this technology actually exists, but it is hidden in the back halls of learning. Smothering it are political ambitions.

There *is* a subject called political science. It is in a crude form, but many of the rules of this technology have been isolated. Lessons learned from past civilizations have been codified into political must-nots and should-dos.

Although political science exists, it is not used. Having studied the actual subject at Princeton University, I had some idea of its scope and exactness. Imagine my surprise when I found by questioning them—some were my personal friends—that politicians in the US were:

    a. Completely unaware that the subject of political science existed, and
    b. Saw no reason for such a science.

These men were governing the millions. Their everyday problems in office stemmed from mistakes in the past. Actions taken contrary to political science natural law had involved them in difficulties beyond their depth and ignorance of the technology was giving them their failures.

They did not even know the simple axiom "Laws which are not generated by the mores and customs of a people cannot be enforced even if passed."

US Prohibition was an example. A dozen years, millions spent in enforcement, huge revenues lost, countless lives sacrificed, crime financed, all came about because the law was contrary to the mores and customs of the people. It could not be enforced. It eventually had to be repealed.

Those who proposed it and voted for it and tried to enforce nonalcoholism on the people were ignorant of political science.

When fascists and totalitarians try to force their ideas on a democratically minded population (or vice versa), catastrophe occurs.

Wars, mass murders, raw red revolutions, overthrown governments and vanished civilizations all come from an ignorance of political science.

Those with the name of government have some clever knack of handling an office or party or the press, but have no command of their basic trade. If a plumber was that ignorant of the technology of laying pipes, we would laugh at him. But these ignorant tinkerers in a field which does have natural law are looked up to, honored, overpaid and revered. That so many of them get buried and that there is so much trouble in the world seems to be looked on as "inevitable." Trying to fix TV sets with no knowledge of or training in electronics is exactly comparable to political leaders governing without even ten minutes spent studying political science. Yet no state on the planet requires their leaders to take at least a cram course in their trade before they take office.

So that is one area of the humanities which is ignored and where physical science has outstripped over vital knowledge.

Another major area of neglect is economics.

This subject is far from lacking in developed technology.

There *is* a real subject called economics. Yet in its place is injected a thousand alterations in order to "make a quick quid" or a "fast buck."

The men who should know and use the subject have found it very profitable to obscure it. In this way they can sell a "bill of goods" to ignorant government leaders and oppress whole populations.

Inflation, balance of payments, crashes, deflating currencies, recessions, all come from ignorance of or willful refusals to apply known, sound, natural economic laws.

By fiddling the subject, the men who advise governments and their monetary systems can fiddle the books.

> *"These men were governing the millions. Their everyday problems in office stemmed from mistakes in the past. Actions taken contrary to political science natural law had involved them in difficulties beyond their depth and ignorance of the technology was giving them their failures."*

Such men, by altering natural laws to their own benefit, degrade and impoverish every citizen. They shrink one's paycheck, swell one's taxes to the explosion point and are primary factors behind every public revolt.

For instance, of late years, each time a nation's currency trembled, the monarchs of money have demanded increased personal taxation. In fact it is the country's exported funds that are causing the trouble. How reducing funds internally solves too many funds overseas is a point that hasn't been explained.

Following Lord Keynes' alterations of natural economic laws, Western governments are all devoted today to the Keynes perversion of the law of supply and demand. The Keynes formula to make it all go right is "Create want!" If you follow that through, you will see that the Keynes Utopia will wind up with the ultimate in "created want" which is, of course, starvation. So one is given the whole plan—to be economically sound, a population must be starved to death.

The grim joke is, however, at the expense of the money moguls. They are enriched by pushing false economic theory. But what they are playing with is the thing on which all their power depends—money. The worse off money gets, the more endangered are the fiddling financiers. If it's any satisfaction, when one stares out of the economic ruins they have made, one will see *their* former empire in the worst ruin of all. When madmen assert apples always fall upwards and pretend there is no law of gravity, one expects they will sooner or later step off the roof of a ten-story building expecting to fly.

The absence or misuse of the real technology of economics is a serious hole in all nations today and inevitably will spell the doom of this society—unless the H-bomb gets there first.

The third glaring outness in modern civilization was the technology of the mind.

This had never been developed or even approached. The insane could not be made sane, the criminals could not be made honest, the IQ necessary to run things well could not be developed.

Mental technology was so bad off that murder was being sold for mercy.

A group of confidence tricksters had entered the field. Calling themselves "psychiatrists" and "psychologists," they actually sought by brutality, blackmail and pretense to dominate the courts, to extort huge sums from governments and to crush savagely any technology of the mind which might be developed.

Political science being disregarded, no one noticed the public hatred which these pretenders were generating.

Like the witch doctors, the jujus of South Africa, these men were a festering sore in the culture. Yet states sought to use them to control the population.

Seizing, imprisoning and disabling and murdering members of the society who were antagonistic in any way to the system, these "psychiatrists" and "psychologists" were primary in building up a question in men's minds of the integrity of the state.

It went largely unnoticed that this "technology" preceded every major revolution in the last century. Russia, Germany, the Balkans, Poland and many more were heavy work scenes of these people just before the populace boiled over.

The university revolts of this decade stem directly from the ignorance or direct action of the departments of psychiatry and psychology in those same universities. They teach that Man is an animal, governable by force alone, that training is entirely a matter of teaching bears to skate using hot skates, or dogs to obey using starvation. They have perverted the entire field of training and education as well as that of health and sanity. They have yet to make one man better. But they have inspired a million murders.

So adroit is their public relations and so covert their sway that the government itself is the last to find out that, of all subversives, they are the most determined and the best organized. They advocate the overthrow of all constitutions and the destruction of all boundaries, the release of criminals on the society and adultery and drug addiction.

Yet governments finance them lavishly. It is sort of like paying one's own executioner to be sure one gets executed.

But their worst crime is making very sure that any successful real mental technology developed by Man is discredited, hounded, legislated against and left unused.

When Scientology entered on the scene, these men, in the executive committee of their international front group, resolved that it was a threat to their criminal interests. They spent millions, money given to them to "make people well," to engage in a secret and vicious war against Scientologists. One of their key men has now confessed to this.

It took Scientologists years to run down and identify its attackers. And since this was done, the most unsavory stench has begun to arise from the institutions of these criminals. Dead bodies dug up in their grounds, political prisoners held a decade without trial, death camps comparable to Belsen being run with a mortuary and crematorium just across the road, selling women inmates as prostitutes, knowing and willful political murders are only a few of the crimes of psychiatry and psychology.

So when we speak of the humanities not having kept up with the physical sciences, it is an understatement.

There can be no human sciences at all unless the nature and mind of Man can be understood and improved.

Mental science is the most basic human science of all.

Without it, political science and economics will not be used even if further developed than they are. For who can say whether or not the men in charge are mad or sane?

And if mental science has turned back into the Dark Ages and all new discoveries are to be crushed, what hope is there for any of the lesser humanities?

None.

Not until the society and its governments rid themselves of yesterday's superstition, cease to support madmen in charge and decide to give freedom and a chance to new developments in the field of the mind.

The picture is not all black.

Scientology is letting more than a little light into a formerly dismal scene.

With some active help and public support, we can see the way out of this and bring at last some sanity to the world.

At this moment, the physical sciences do not need to be feared, providing human sciences are allowed to get ahead.

The data to resolve this is already known and in practice in Scientology.

The end is not yet.

With several hundred chapters of the Citizens Commission on Human Rights at work across six continents, what LRH proposes here has indeed come to pass: Scientology's Fight for Freedom now engenders support from every corner of the world. To cite but a few examples: While Scientologists work with Danish and Italian ministers to outlaw indiscriminate electroconvulsive treatment, they similarly work with Japanese officials to free psychiatric patients from physical restraints. Then there is the long and determined alliance between CCHR volunteers and US authorities in Texas, California, New Jersey and Virginia—specifically and relentlessly to expose and prosecute fraudulent psychiatric insurance claims. Meanwhile, in the federal arena, Scientologists regularly liaise with United States Department of Justice officials to expose psychiatry's bogus Medicare claims. While in consequence to all such alliances, the beginning of psychiatry's end is at hand, psychiatrists are increasingly held accountable and no longer stand above the law.

24 September 1969

THE FIGHT FOR FREEDOM

by L. Ron Hubbard

Scientology's battle against psychiatry is receiving more and more support across the world.

Largely unchallenged in the century after psychiatry's origin in Leipzig, Germany, and its steady and brutal campaign against the dignity and freedom of Man, psychiatry hit its only major dissent in the early 1950s.

Brock Chisholm with his friends, which included Harry Dexter White and Alger Hiss, were very alarmed at Scientology's threat to their sweeping plans.

Secretly, from cover which was not fully exposed until last year, they used every press and government channel they could hoodwink and control to discredit Scientology, its principles and its organizations.

Up until then, the groups of psychology and psychiatry had worked undetected for nearly eighty years in establishing an above-law dominance.

There was some challenge in the late nineteenth century when authors occasionally exposed this psychiatric group as acting to put away the rich relative so that some unprincipled family member would benefit and give the asylum keeper his cut.

In the first quarter of the twentieth century the movies often portrayed their mad experimentations as inhuman and the "Mad Russian doctor" was a prime horror movie villain.

With tactics which would have filled a confidence trickster with awe, the psychiatric front groups successfully wiped out all important criticism and by 1950 were secretly and successfully engaged upon a two-pronged campaign.

    a. The degradation and dominance of Man, and
    b. The harvesting of government millions.

In 1948 when "Dr." Brock Chisholm and a dozen other fellow conspirators in the World Federation of Mental Health and the World Health Organization took over the grass-roots international organization of Clifford Beers and perverted it to their own planning, they had no real powerful enemy in the world.

The nineteenth century ridicule of their kind had died out. By vast pretensions and lies, they had worked themselves into a towering position of power and authority.

They authored easy seizure laws in every land; they were in a position to kidnap and kill any human being on the planet. Their word was accepted without question as the only authority on sanity and insanity, crime and criminality and life and death. The money was rolling in, in avalanches.

This was no mean trick as it was done without *any* demonstration of any kind that they could cure or change insanity or make even one man consistently well. It was a trick done without any helpful technology. It was done totally by "PRO" skills—public relations, press, pomp, brag, "the best people."

Then Dianetics and Scientology appeared. Here was a real, an actual, working technology. They worried about it and considered it was a direct threat to psychiatry.

And they made a very ghastly mistake.

Secretly they spent time and money all over the world to discredit and suppress Dianetics and Scientology.

Working through heads of press chains they controlled, working through Ministers of Health they had appointed, with lies and false alarm they continuously, secretly fought Dianetics and Scientology.

Enduring these attacks and alert, Dianetics and Scientology people somehow kept going and kept watching.

In the autumn of 1968 the cat was out of the bag. The source of all these attacks all these years was identified.

Helped by allies among medical doctors and the psychiatrists themselves, helped quietly by police agencies and national intelligence forces, Scientologists were at length able to name names and furnish proof.

Now it was the psychiatrists' turn to take it on the chin.

Because Scientologists broke no laws, committed no crimes and had a factual, effective mental technology, they could not be destroyed. The public was on their side.

But this was not the case with psychiatry.

The most basic laws of humanity had been broken by them. Mayhem, rape, torture, murder were commonplace crimes among them. Decaying bodies, dead by violent torture, were exhumed in the grounds of psychiatric asylums. Vicious political connections, misappropriated funds, incarceration of patients for political reasons, these with a parade of social, sexual, drug and unnatural offenses began to fall out of the skeleton-filled closets of psychiatry.

Their laws of easy seizure began to be challenged and thrown out. Funds began to be cut off. Man again began to raise his head.

The Scientologists were the only roadblock on the psychiatric joyride to degradation.

The story as it unfolds, as it has become documented, reveals psychiatric ambitions so bizarre as to be as incredible as Hitler's mad delusions.

"The nineteenth century ridicule of their kind had died out. By vast pretensions and lies, they had worked themselves into a towering position of power and authority."

"Vicious political connections, misappropriated funds, incarceration of patients for political reasons, these with a parade of social, sexual, drug and unnatural offenses began to fall out of the skeleton-filled closets of psychiatry."

They dreamed of being the philosopher-kings of Plato with the power of life and death over every man, woman and child on the planet. They had been fantastically successful as far as they went. They had infiltrated and influenced every law-making body and government in the world. They had effected legislation entitling them to seize, injure or kill any person anywhere. They dominated education and had intimidated medicine. And they had almost wiped out all influence of Christianity and the churches.

To withstand the brutal, covert attacks of psychiatry and still survive was no small trick for the Scientologists. Yet they not only did that, but actually located and documented the enemy. And the Scientologists are turning the tide.

Easy seizure laws are being challenged and cancelled in high courts. The death camps are being exposed.

The fight for the Dignity and Decency of Man is still in progress.

This battle is not finished. It will not be done until all psychiatrists and psychologists are brought back under law, deprived of their unearned millions in appropriations and the world made safe.

There must not be men above the law. There must not be any influential group dedicated to Man's degradation. Governments must prevent their domination by men who could never pass the first requisites of decent citizens.

The whole problem of "insanity" could be cleaned up in a few years by technology tried and proven in medicine, Dianetics and Scientology. The soaring statistic of insanity under psychiatric management could not only be halted, but reduced sharply.

That the breakthrough of technology in Dianetics and Scientology could be denied Man is a serious thing in itself.

Man's wars, his revolutions, his suffering all stem from his lack of data on the mind and Man. With psychiatric dominance of this field, we have had a century of untold suffering and violence.

Isn't it time to support the Scientologists, the people who can get the job done?

The next time you hear Scientology being discredited, trace the source. And give the Scientologists a hand in their successful fight to bring some order into the treachery, confidence trickery and crime which has been, up to now, the field of mental "healing."

It is only wisdom to bet on the winner. Scientology is plainly winning. It is your world too.

Following the writing of this essay, LRH continued his researches into both drug addiction and the long-term effects of drugs in the body. From this research came both the Detoxification Program to rid the body of harmful drug deposits as well as an entire regimen to address drug addiction and the prevention of recidivism. Today, the LRH method is employed by Narconon centers across every continent. Declared the benchmark of all drug rehabilitation centers, Narconon not only works to rehabilitate the "casual" drug user, it is also the only program that caters to and successfully rehabilitates the hard-core addict. Or as one expert in the field explained, "If I can't help them in my clinic, I've got nowhere else to send them anymore except Narconon."

Essentially expressing the same are the courts and social-service offices regularly referring addicts to Narconon centers across Europe and the Americas, and the numerous government agencies now broadly funding the program.

25 SEPTEMBER 1969

DRUG PROBLEMS

by L. Ron Hubbard

IN AT LEAST TWO countries, Scientology is closely cooperating with the government in programs to handle the drug addiction problem now becoming chronic in society.

Drug addicts have been found to have begun drug taking because of physical suffering or hopelessness.

In one country a Scientology pilot project has been in progress for about a year and has produced data of great value. Even without processing, but by education, some 50 percent of the committed addicts have recovered and have not been recommitted.

By eradicating in the addict the cause of the original suffering or hopelessness, the need of drugs is voluntarily dispensed with by the former addict.

These Scientology projects are pilot in nature and were undertaken to develop the programs for larger applications. At present the number of unselected cases number only a few hundred.

So far it has been found that the cost per case, exclusive of food and bed, is about £35 a person when done on a mass basis using individual practitioners. The time is between seven and ten weeks, the first six of which are spent "drying out" under medical care. The actual processing takes less than fifty hours to permanent full rehabilitation. If only the drug factor is handled, the time is under ten hours.

A pilot project has just been begun in a state prison where the addicts will be trained to handle one another's cases. If successful, this could greatly reduce costs and facilitate the handling of very large numbers.

The addict has been found not to want to be an addict, but is driven by pain and environmental hopelessness.

As soon as an addict can feel healthier and more competent mentally and physically without drugs than he does on drugs, he ceases to require drugs.

Drug addiction has been shrugged off by psychiatry as "unimportant" and the social problem of drug taking has received no attention from psychiatrists—rather the contrary, since they themselves introduced and popularized LSD. And many of them are pushers.

Government agencies have failed markedly to halt the increase in drug taking and there has been no real or widespread cure.

The political implications of increasing addiction in a country are great. All nations under heavy attack by foreign intelligence agencies have experienced increased drug traffic and addiction.

Japanese intelligence forces before World War II conquered by carefully making addicts out of every potential leader they could reach, particularly bright children, in a target country.

The last dynasty (the Manchu) of China was overthrown by a country that imported opium into the kingdom and got it into widespread use.

There are many historical precedents.

The liability of the drug user, even after he has ceased to use drugs, is that he "goes blank" at unexpected times, has periods of irresponsibility and tends to sicken easily.

Dianetics and Scientology processing has been able to eradicate the major damage in those cases tested as well as make further addiction unnecessary and unwanted.

Scientology has no interest in the political or social aspects of the various types of drugs or even drug taking as such. The whole interest of Scientology is concentrated on those who want to "get unhooked" and "stay unhooked."

In one Scientology organization at least half of those coming in for processing have been on drugs and this figure is less than that in the surrounding public, where it evidently goes to an even higher percentage. Therefore in 1968 and 1969 research on this as a specialized subject was completed successfully.

Scientologists do not stand ready to punish drug takers or reform a whole society on the subject. But they do stand ready and are active in helping anyone or any government to handle the problem.

Like the Flaming Youth era of the Prohibition 20s, drug taking will probably also come to pass away as a national pastime. But it will leave a lot of people who wish they hadn't. The Scientologists can help those. And are helping them right now as a routine duty to the community.

Governments need the Scientologist a lot more than they think.

25 September 1969

TANGLED TERMS

by L. Ron Hubbard

IN THEIR ANXIETY TO keep their failures explained while they ask congresses, parliaments and legislatures for more millions to put in their pockets, psychiatry continually redefines key words relating to the mind.

Their "diseases" have become entirely different diseases over the last quarter of a century—and none of them have come any closer to being cured.

The German, Kraepelin, had a scale of mental diseases that became so long and involved (once said to number 1,500), and on which there was so little agreement, that it was largely abandoned.

Freud had a number of "mental diseases," but these terms are not in extensive use today.

What is amazing is the psychiatric tendency to try to describe rather than to cure.

Schizophrenia and paranoia seem to be the modern favorite terms. But paranoia today becomes schizophrenia!

To these tangled terms today is added "incurable." If one *can't* cure something, the only way to maintain an authoritative pose about it is to say it *can't* be cured. This also excuses absorbing all those funds with nothing to show. But if all these "diseases" are *known* to be incurable, then why spend money researching them?

The main point of all these tangled terms today is that anyone can be said to have some form of insanity just by saying a big word. As no one has agreed what the word means or what the symptoms are, this leaves the psychiatrist as an "authority." In court and sanitarium, all he has to do is say, "Hm, er, hurumph, he's a—ahem—borderline catatonic with—er—ahem—symptoms of paranoia—hm, hurumph."

It sounds so impressive, and the fact he is about to be disabled for life so frightening to the person in question, that even jurisprudence is swayed. And some poor guy is sent to a living hell.

Confidence tricksters, bamboozlers, flimflam artists and psychiatrists have all mastered the same tricks. To say long words impressively is three-quarters of the game in "taking a mark."

At least one world dictionary, unable to find psychiatric texts to quote, uses phrases from the *New York Times* and from the *New Yorker* magazine to define psychiatric terms. Maybe it is or isn't intentional, but the *New Yorker* is world-renowned as a humor magazine.

Lord Dunsany's famous story about the day the temple fell is a wonderful example. Somebody walked into the temple one day and pulled back the curtain on the holy of holies, the all-powerful and mysterious shrine that had overawed the world. There was nothing there!

That is what is happening to psychiatry today. The outpoured government millions bought no cures, but only a lot of tangled terms and how they were all incurable.

When the curtain was pulled back, all that was behind it was PRO, public relations brag, and an empty hole.

If society wants insanity handled as a social problem, don't go to the boys who have increased the insanity statistics for a century and who have only tangled terms to show for it. Go get the people who know what they are doing—the Scientologists.

"The main point of all these tangled terms today is that anyone can be said to have some form of insanity just by saying a big word. As no one has agreed what the word means or what the symptoms are, this leaves the psychiatrist as an 'authority.'"

26 September 1969

BEING GOOD

by L. Ron Hubbard

WE IN SCIENTOLOGY ARE evidently expected to be paragons of virtue in a very messy world.

Scientologists are evidently expected to control absolutely anyone in the movement or on its fringes.

Meanwhile psychiatrists can advise adultery, sexually pervert their patients, cause 30 percent to commit suicide, maim or injure anyone who comes near them, beat up, murder and bury in the grounds anyone they please. The conduct of psychiatry is so criminal that only blackmail or influence in high places could account for their strange immunity from ordinary criminal law.

Among Scientologists, investigations by the most competent agencies in the world have failed to find any broken laws or social misconduct.

So what is this?

It is unreasonable to expect anyone in the field of mental healing to be totally simon-pure, yet the most sweeping investigations have revealed that Scientologists are just that.

Slandered, lied about, unjustly accused by a pack of murderers—the psychiatric front groups—Scientology still survives and even makes headway.

But what kind of world is this? What kind of governments do we really have where the criminal practices of psychiatry are financed and supported and the decent actions of Scientologists attacked?

Beware of a state which neglects its criminals and only attacks its decent citizens.

Scientologists will go on being decent, will go on doing their jobs and will go on being the only effective group in the field of mental healing. But it is a long way from just to make life so hard for them.

It is an old truism that one gets what he pays for. If governments pay for psychiatry, they will reap social chaos and crime.

If the millions now handed to psychiatry—and which buy only civil disorder and more insanity—were given to church groups instead, the society would improve enormously.

All facts, all figures, all statistics and all documents declare the incompetence and criminal conduct of psychiatry. They reek like a Roman arena.

And all facts, all figures, all statistics, all documents and even the "evidence" of the state inquiries into Scientology support the character and integrity, helpfulness and value of Scientology.

Evidence is evidence.

Justice is justice.

Isn't there anyone in charge up there in the stratosphere of government?

Or is it just a big muddle with only madmen at the top?

> *"If the millions now handed to psychiatry—and which buy only civil disorder and more insanity—were given to church groups instead, the society would improve enormously."*

19 October 1969

DRUG ADDICTION

by L. Ron Hubbard

In the absence of workable psychotherapy, wide drug addiction is inevitable.

When a person is depressed or in pain and where he finds no physical relief from treatment, he will eventually discover for himself that drugs remove his symptoms.

In almost all cases of psychosomatic pain, malaise or discomfort, the person has sought some cure for the upset.

When he at last finds that only drugs give him relief, he will surrender to them and become dependent upon them, often to the point of addiction.

Years before, had there been any other way out, most people would have taken it. But when they are told there is no cure, that their pains are "imaginary," life tends to become insupportable. They then can become chronic drug takers and are in danger of addiction.

The time required to make an addict varies, of course. The complaint itself may only be "sadness" or "weariness." The ability to confront life, in any case, is reduced.

Any substance that brings relief or makes life less a burden physically or mentally will then be welcome.

In an unsettled and insecure environment, psychosomatic illness is very widespread.

So before any government strikes too heavily at spreading drug use, it should recognize that it is a symptom of failed psychotherapy. The social scientist, the psychologist and psychiatrist and health ministries have failed to handle spreading psychosomatic illness.

It is too easy to blame it all on "social unrest" or "the pace of modern society."

The hard, solid fact is that there has been no effective psychotherapy in broad practice. The result is a drug-addicted population.

Dianetics was designed as broadly applicable low-cost mental health. It is the only mental technology fully validated by actual test. It is fast. It is effective.

Health services should assist it into wide general use.

It can handle the problem.

"In the absence of workable psychotherapy, wide drug addiction is inevitable."

To what LRH provides as a broad but incisive word on "Cultural Destruction" from foreign intelligence, let us add a few specifics. As regards the employment of mass media for the disruption of enemy populations, *Operation Mind Control* author Walter Bowart informs us: "…electronic propaganda became the staple weapon for waging the Cold War" and the weapon was by no means one-sided. In opposition to the Central Intelligence Agency's Voice of America radio network beaming Western propaganda across the Iron Curtain, much evidence suggests a continuous Soviet effort to covertly foster American racial and labor strife through militant black and leftist organizations.

Moreover, and even more in keeping with what LRH warns of here, among the weapons apparently falling into terrorist hands after the dismemberment of Eastern Bloc intelligence services was a whole array of psychological warfare tactics ready to be unleashed in this twenty-first century.

30 October 1969

CULTURAL DESTRUCTION

by L. Ron Hubbard

Since World War II, Eastern intelligence services have developed a new weapon.

The security forces of Western countries are too fond of tracing the history of intelligence to show there is nothing new.

There have been new intelligence technologies developed in every decade for the last century or more. The extent and literature on the subject are so vast that the superficial student or the nonspecialized government executive is as outdistanced as he would be in the field of Chinese literature.

Intelligence is highly specialized and intricately sophisticated in the East. A founder of the extremely efficient German services, the most vast the West had known, spent seventeen years studying the intelligence technology of the Japanese and, even then, only scratched the surface.

It is no wonder, then, that a new intelligence technology has been in use against the West since 1948 without detection or understanding.

The basic idea of weakening or corrupting a population has been in use since before the Persian attacks on Greece. Naturally the degradation of a population is possible on a long-term basis if actual war is unsuccessful or impossible as a method of removing a natural enemy.

A sufficiently degraded or weakened people are in effect demilitarized.

Where direct combat confrontation is undesirable or considered too dangerous, the weakening of an enemy's trade or economics and the contraction of his sphere of influence by covert means becomes the next solution available. That is textbook.

The degradation and weakening of the enemy population itself is more difficult and requires a longer timespan. Although this is considered desirable by potential attackers, no feasible technology to fully accomplish it had been worked out and employed on any scale before 1948.

The advent of fast transport and mass communication media and the internationalization of finance controls offered an opportunity to design and use technology which could destroy the enemy's population totally as an effective nation.

The atomic bomb made direct combat confrontation between major powers too dangerous and thereby opened the door to any program which would promise successful destruction of a considered enemy even on a long-term basis.

The techniques of Cultural Destruction were developed, financed and pressed into action.

The West, naive and traditional in the field of security, has failed utterly to detect and handle Cultural Destruction—the major weapon now in full use against Western nations.

Espionage to Western security forces and politicians still means enemy efforts to steal the plans of the battleship. Even where Western security officers confusedly suspect what is going on, their political seniors are not likely to permit action, since they have been carefully coached to believe in the inevitable deterioration of Man in modern society.

The essence of the campaign is to make it all seem internal and inevitable with a ready social explanation for each new decline.

Spies, as enemy agents are called by those who know very little about it, are generally caught at the point they relay information after citizens, whom they have persuaded to steal plans, have turned them in to the national security service.

A new feature in Cultural Destruction is that *these* "spies" are agents who do not report. They merely *act*.

Briefed at some period long ago, they need no further detailed briefing. They just go on working.

These agents need no funds from their masters as they are financed internally and most often by the government they seek to subvert.

Three things mask their activities: (a) they assume identities ("cover" in intelligence argot) which are considered above the law, (b) they seem essential to handle the disorder which they themselves are actually creating, (c) the extent and coordination of their actions are too incredible to be grasped by people who take a "reasonable view of things."

All the evidence of their successes is in plain view. Yet they pose as the authorities vital to handling these conditions.

Soaring crime rates and widespread drug addiction are hallmarks of intelligence subversion and always have been. To these more common signs of attack on the population, Cultural Destruction has added "miseducation," soaring insanity totals, sexual perversion, racial warfare and the sabotage of sound economics.

The somewhat natural impulse of rather barbaric societies to go astray and become hectic is being exaggerated to such a degree and with such swiftness that almost anyone with a little help could see that natural turbulence is being enormously assisted.

The exact technology by which it is done makes a fascinating and revealing study. All the inventiveness that commonly emerges only during actual warfare has been redirected into the resolution of the problem: "How to destroy a nation which cannot be directly fought."

"The West, naive and traditional in the field of security, has failed utterly to detect and handle Cultural Destruction—the major weapon now in full use against Western nations."

England has watched her whole empire contract to the possession of Scotland, Wales and Northern Ireland as her only undisputed external terrain. An event usually requiring centuries of decline happened within two decades.

The US, conquering hero of World War II, is reduced to bargaining at a Conference table while her postage-stamp enemy confreres direct public campaigns to end the war *within US borders*.

Any voice raised in protest against national decay is silenced and vilified, such has become the strength of the external enemy.

Security forces in the West see in all this only an effort to bring about an internal revolt where they observe it all. It is not an attempted revolt. It is Cultural Destruction on a grand scale.

It took the originators half a century to smash utterly the basic educational standards of Western people and substitute new values (or lack of them) which opened the door to total subversion. An examination of the changing textbooks and the connections of the authors of those which then crept into use and the political color and background of the "educators" who recommended them is an interesting search.

The source area of the training skills used by "social scientists" is traceable directly to enemy terrain.

The basic cultural institutions normally relied upon to uphold the standards of Western society have been infiltrated, discredited and swept out of power. The motif of the destruction of churches springs directly from the enemy.

In place of these institutions have sprung up a horde of "unimpeachably respectable" societies run by suave, glib and enemy-connected confidence tricksters to whose deadly advice congresses and parliaments listen with an awe usually reserved in barbaric societies for fathers.

In two countries recently, the governments paid all the expenses of meetings of the enemy agents who, in their posh hotels carefully protected by the internal security forces, carefully planned and put into effect the next steps of the Cultural Destruction of those countries—and in the bargain, discussed behind carefully closed doors the abolishment of their hosts' constitutions and cancellation of their boundaries. A large percentage of those who attended were direct from enemy territory.

Another member of this group, a card-carrying enemy, was listened to attentively by a Congressional Committee who were already acting on her advice not to oppose so strenuously the widespread drug addiction being pushed by her infinitely "respectable" friends.

Nearly half a hundred of these wholly "respectable social scientists" recently entered a Western nation straight from satellite countries and set up in business there at once, marvelously financed, entirely above the law because they were "authorities" and "scientists" and "vouched for" by "eminently respectable professional societies." The security forces there were restless about it, but evidently could do nothing because of "pressure from above."

It has gone so far that anyone who mentions it is at once accused of "seeing a Red under every bush." The last political figure in the US who refused to believe it was "natural" was stopped and killed as surely as though he had been poisoned.

"The source area of the training skills used by 'social scientists' is traceable directly to enemy terrain. The basic cultural institutions normally relied upon to uphold the standards of Western society have been infiltrated, discredited and swept out of power. The motif of the destruction of churches springs directly from the enemy."

There are many ways to win in competition between nations. Where outright war is impossible or covert military operatives unprofitable, there is now Cultural Destruction, a complex and highly skilled tool which not only destroys the national will to fight, but also morally reduces and destroys the social and economic fiber of the enemy.

If action is not taken, if the trend is not halted, the West will be dead within a decade.

15 November 1969

OLD-FASHIONED HOLDOVERS

by L. Ron Hubbard

PSYCHIATRISTS AND THEIR FRONT associations are as far back in the past as some of their insane patients.

They belong to the bad old days of about 1450.

Every hill had its robber-baron castle ruled by the very, very, very best people only from the very, very, very best families.

Underground beneath each castle fortress were dungeons with chain-studded walls and torture rooms complete with racks, lead boots and a very thorough technology of maiming and murdering with the greatest possible agony in the longest possible time.

At any passing whim any peasant, soldier, merchant or passing traveler could be seized without any slightest process of law, his possessions confiscated, and thrust away for years without any charge whatever, to emerge, in those rare instances when they did, broken in health and limb and completely mad.

Any writer or pamphleteer who dared breathe a breath of caution to these arrogant "lords" and their "ladies" was hunted like a rat, torn to bits by the rack or hanged, drawn and quartered.

The countryside lay in ruins, the people cowered in filthy hovels and the spirit of Man lay crushed and nearly dead.

Such was 1450 in the "civilized world."

Up through the decades as time crept on, Man won, bit by bit, small points of rights and freedom. But only over mountains of "rebels" slain, only over a roadway paved with the bones of fearless champions of Mankind whose courage almost always carried them to their death.

Now we have arrived in the twentieth century. We have laws and due process of law and at least some rights and freedom.

Here sit these psychiatric front groups, representing only a handful of "specialists." Here they sit with their "lords" and "ladies" and their very, very, very best people.

They have their mental "hospitals" where any torture, any crime can be done.

Here are mental "laws" by which anybody can be seized without any process of law and held without any charge.

Using "shock" and surgery and water "cures" and violent drugs, men are released, when they are released at all, shattered and incompetent wrecks.

By the full evidence recently unearthed, the majority of the inmates of these "institutions" are not and never were insane. Only the minority are mad and how many of these have gone mad through these gruesome tortures or beatings?

So these psychiatric front groups are badly stuck in 1450.

They are only composed of the very, very, very best people at the top.

Democracy, decency, processes of law are all regarded by them with sneering arrogance.

All this is becoming well known. It is fully documented.

But what of politicians and legislators who bow slavishly and give them easy seizure laws and millions of taxpayers' money to spend?

What of writers who toady to them in the press and literature and strike at anyone or any group like the Scientologists who seek to expose such crimes?

Why, mate, I'd say such politicians and scribblers were a lot of bloody traitors to the human race. That's what I'd say.

It's not 1450, you know. It's the twentieth century.

Come up to present time, that's what I'd say.

"Here sit these psychiatric front groups, representing only a handful of 'specialists.' Here they sit with their 'lords' and 'ladies' and their very, very, very best people. They have their mental 'hospitals' where any torture, any crime can be done."

With increasing frequency of violent crime through the latter 1970s, and LRH research on evil purposes and the criminal mind, come three articles from the early 1980s. As a word on what LRH so correctly predicted regarding the unparalleled and senseless violence from psychiatric patients, one need only consider the 1981 shooting of President Ronald Reagan and crippling of White House press secretary James Brady by psychiatrically treated John Hinckley, Jr.

Then again, and if only to underscore the point, it just so happens that a third of all schoolyard shootings are committed by adolescents prescribed psychotropic drugs, while those on psychiatric stimulants are twelve times more likely to use heroin, fifteen times more likely to use Ecstasy and twenty-one times more likely to use cocaine than unmedicated classmates.

29 July 1980

CRIMINALS AND PSYCHIATRY

by L. Ron Hubbard

ALMOST EVERY MODERN HORROR crime was committed by a known criminal who had been in and out of the hands of psychiatrists and psychologists, often many times.

There is no particular reason to enumerate endless case histories of this: they occur too frequently in news accounts and the newspaper morgues are thick with them. And as such stories develop, it is found that the perpetrator had a long history, some even from childhood, of psychiatric and psychological treatment.

Such a record of failure does not seem to come to the attention of legislators and these continue to pour floods of money into the coffers of the psychiatrists, psychologists and their organizations. The public at large, by survey, seems to be aware of this state of affairs, if not the whole facts: the only real customers the psychiatrist and psychologist have are the governments—the public does not of its own volition go to them.

The most charitable look at this would be that the psychologists and psychiatrists are simply incompetent. But other, more sinister, implications can be drawn.

Developed in the latter part of the nineteenth century, they appeared on the militaristic scene of a re-arming and conquest-minded Germany. At that time, the archcriminal Bismarck was laying the groundwork for the slaughters of World War I and World War II. It fitted with the philosophy of militarism that Man was an animal and that there was neither soul nor morality standing in the way of the wholesale murder of war.

Up until that time the Church had some influence upon the state and possibly some power in restraining bestiality and savagely insane conduct but, small as it might have been, it was incompatible with the unholy ambitions of the militarists. That Man was only an animal after all, soulless and entitled to no decency, was bound to be a popular doctrine. That insanity consisted of urges to harm others would have been a very unpopular idea to government heads who had nothing else in mind. And so the notion that insanity was a physical disease was taken up avidly.

The basic tenet of psychology is that Man is just an animal. The basic tenet of psychiatry is that insanity is a physical disease. Neither has any proof that these tenets are correct. That Man can be reduced to animalistic behavior does not prove that that is his true basic nature. That some physical diseases also produce mental aberration does not prove that any "mental illness" has bacteria or virus and indeed none have ever been isolated.

The instigators, patrons and supporters of these two subjects classify fully and demonstrably as criminals.

If the crimes committed by a government in one single day were committed by an individual, that individual would be promptly put in a cell and probably even a padded cell.

Unfortunately, positions of power and authority attract to themselves beings who, all too often, need that altitude to exercise their lust for covertly or overtly harming others. Government positions are well suited to this use; they are also all too often held to be above any law. Some of the most notorious criminals in history have operated from government positions. This becomes statistically impressive when one counts the strewn corpses.

Looking this over (and it is amply documented in any history book or newspaper), one can begin to make some kind of sense out of it. Spawned by an insanely militaristic government, psychiatry and psychology find avid support from oppressive and domineering governments. The employer of these people classifies, even in the most generous view, as criminal. Thus it cannot be much wondered at that these subjects have no real success or even interest in detecting and handling criminals.

One cannot go so far as to say that psychiatry and psychology knowingly create criminals or actively plan and implant their patients to commit crimes, even though it might look this way in some cases. Rather, these subjects are false subjects, based on false principles which are well suited to the demands and ambitions of their employers. Their technology is incapable of detecting, much less helping, the criminal. It is even doubtful if their employers, the governments, would tolerate a subject which could detect and resolve criminality—for who would be the first ones detected? Some among the governments, of course. No, the wolf would only favor a jury of wolves to judge the crime of killing sheep. That is why you see governments flooding out money for psychologists in schools and psychiatrists in government departments.

With a complete, government-supported monopoly in the field of the mind, potential criminals will go right on remaining undetected until they injure or slaughter citizens and, having done so, become unrelieved or even confirmed in their habit patterns in the hands of psychiatrists and psychologists and rereleased upon the world to further injure and slaughter citizens.

The credence and power of psychiatry and psychology are waning. It hit its zenith about 1960: then it seemed their word was law and that they could harm, injure and kill patients without restraint. The appearance of an actual technology of the mind—Dianetics and Scientology—has played no small part in acting as a restraint. At one time they were well on their way to turning every baby into a future robot for the manipulation of the state and every society into a madhouse of crime and immorality. The world is still suffering from the effects of that domination.

There is no real reason why, using the proper technology, the criminal cannot be detected and also reformed. One might also, by the use of False Data Stripping, redeem a psychologist or psychiatrist—though this would be made difficult by the fact that he achieves all his power and money from the state, which might have quite different purposes for him.

The world is turning, things change. And there may come a day when the mad dogs of the world are not given over to the charge of mad dogs. But that will be to the degree that you successfully carry forward Dianetics and Scientology.

To what LRH further provides on the telltale link between psychiatry and criminality, we might bear in mind it was none other than psychiatric strategist Brock Chisholm who originally described morality as a "psychological distortion." Whereupon he exhorted his fellows to utterly eradicate "the concept of right and wrong" from public thinking. In utter contrast, then, stands L. Ron Hubbard's common sense moral code, *The Way to Happiness*—not only providing the moral compass to some 100 million world over, but serving as the basis for L. Ron Hubbard's acclaimed criminal reform program, credited with entirely eradicating prison-yard violence and reducing 80 percent recidivism rates to virtually zero.

26 April 1982

THE CRIMINAL MIND AND THE PSYCHS

by L. Ron Hubbard

It has often been noted (and reported routinely in the papers) that criminals "treated" by psychologists and psychiatrists go out and commit crimes.

It could be suspected that these "practitioners" used pain-drug-hypnosis and other means (under the guise of treatment) to induce the criminal to go out and commit more crimes. And possibly they do.

But I have just made a discovery that sheds some light on this scene.

Morality and good conduct are sensible. That is the theme of *The Way to Happiness*. It follows (and can be proven) that immorality and bad conduct are stupid.

This bears out under further investigation. One could lay aside the ancient Greek speculations of "Good and Bad" and go on an easier and less contentious logic of "Bright and Stupid."

Anything that a criminal seeks to obtain can be obtained without crime if one is bright enough. Criminals, as police can tell you, are usually very, very stupid. The things they do and clues they leave around are hallmarks of very low IQ. The "bright" criminal is found only in fiction. Now and then a Hitler comes along and begins a myth that the highly positioned are criminal—but Hitler (and Napoleon and all their ilk) were stupid beyond belief. Hitler destroyed himself and Germany, didn't he? And Napoleon destroyed himself and France. So not even the highly placed criminals are bright. Had they really been bright they could have accomplished a successful reign without crime.

The bones of old civilizations are signboards of stupidity. The jails are bursting with people so stupid they did bad things and even did those uncleverly.

So let us look at psychs again—what they call "treatment" is a suppression (by shocks, drugs, etc.) of the ability to think. They are not honest enough, these psychs, being just dramatizing psychotics themselves for the most part, to publish the fact that all their "treatments" (mayhem, really, when it is not murder) make people more stupid.

These actions of shock and crazy evaluative counseling, etc., lower IQ like an express elevator going down to the basement.

They do not tell legislators this or put it in their books. This is why they say, "No one can change IQ." They are hiding the fact that they ruin it.

So the psych in prisons is engaging in an action (shocking or whatever) that makes people who are already criminal even stupider.

Although they obviously tell their victims to go out and commit more crimes (the psychoanalysts urge wives to commit adultery, for instance), they would not have to do this at all to manufacture more crime.

Their "treatments" make the criminals more stupid. The stupid commit more crimes.

It is pretty simple, really, when you look at it.

Why does the state support psychiatrists and psychologists?

Because the state is stupid? Or does it want more citizens robbed and killed? It's one or the other. Take your choice.

One is bright and is moral and honest and does well or one is stupid and does badly.

The answer to crime is raising IQ. But only the Scientologist can do that.

6 May 1982

THE CAUSE OF CRIME

by L. Ron Hubbard

THEY SAY POVERTY MAKES crime. They say if one improved education there would be less crime. They say if one cured the lot of the underprivileged one would have solved crime.

All these "remedies" have proven blatantly false.

In very poor countries there is little crime. In "improving" education, it was tailored to "social reform," not teaching skills. And it is a total failure. Rewarding the underprivileged has simply wrecked schools and neighborhoods and cost billions in misery.

So who is "they"?

The psychologist and psychiatrist, of course. These were *their* crackpot remedies for crime. And it's wrecked a civilization.

So what IS the cause of crime? The treatment, of course! Electric shocks, behavior modification, abuse of the soul. *These* are the causes of crime. There would be no criminals at all if the psychs had not begun to oppress beings into vengeance against society.

There's only one remedy for crime—get rid of the psychs! They're causing it!

Oh yes, it's true. Cases and cases of research on criminals. And what's it all go back to? The psychs! Their brutality and heartlessness is renowned.

The data is rolling in. Any more you pick up off a criminal or anyone, send it in.

On crime we have an epidemic running on this planet. The wrong causes psychs assign for crime plus their own "treatments" make them a deadly virus.

The psychs should not be let to get away with "treatments" which amount to criminal acts, mayhem and murder. They are not above the law. In fact there are no laws at all which protect them, for what sane society would sanction crimes against its citizens even as "science"? They should be handled like any other criminals. They are at best dramatizing psychotics and dangerous, but more dangerous to society at large than the psychotics they keep in their offices and loony bins because they lie and are treacherous. Why the government funds them I do not know. They are the last ones that should be let loose to handle children.

"The psychs should not be let to get away with 'treatments' which amount to criminal acts, mayhem and murder. They are not above the law. In fact there are no laws at all which protect them, for what sane society would sanction crimes against its citizens even as 'science'? They should be handled like any other criminals."

CHAPTER FIVE

On Researching the
HUMANITIES

On Researching the Humanities

AS AN ALL-ENCOMPASSING WORD ON HIS GREATER TRAIL of discovery to the founding of Dianetics and Scientology comes L. Ron Hubbard's "A Summary on Scientology for Scientists." Originally intended for the scientific community, the paper raises issues crucial to any methodical examination of existence—namely, the traditional rift between material sciences and questions of the spiritual. Today, of course, and generally following from a closer look at the subatomic realm, one finds the hard sciences finally wrestling with precisely what LRH discusses here, i.e., the failure of a purely physical equation to explain observable phenomena. Hence, the increasing speculation within a New Physics community regarding some inherently nonmaterial force at work in this universe. Also highly significant are LRH references to his 1938 cytological experimentation wherein he demonstrated how purely chemical equations could not possibly account for the physical behavior of cellular colonies. Although not until the early 1990s, and duplicative research at the French National Institute of Health and Medical Research, did hard-science circles conclude the same, i.e., as one biologist described it, an apparently nonmaterial force "which lets things move and grow in ways that give them meaning." ∎

"The data was very hardly won. It has been a lonely road." —L. Ron Hubbard

29 January 1969

A SUMMARY ON SCIENTOLOGY FOR SCIENTISTS

A Paper on the Difficulties of Researching in the Humanities

by L. Ron Hubbard

For about thirty-eight years at this writing (1969), I have been engaged upon basic research into life and the humanities. This is basic or pure research and has the same genus as the effort of the early philosophers—to attempt to establish the identity of life as independent from matter and as associated with the material world and forms, which subjects are embraced by basic and developed sciences. The difference is that the research has been done from the viewpoint of scientific methodology in which I am trained.

The subject was, in fact, sufficiently unknown and insufficiently nomenclatured to have a clear-cut name. I say it was unknown because it has so markedly failed to keep pace with the natural or physical sciences and is in fact threatened by physical science. For example, we find physical scientist protests are based on life violations or the misuse or abuse of life by incautious physical applications (*Science and Survival* by Barry Commoner).

To protect something one has to know what it is. Scientifically know what it is. The DNA biological theories apply to life plus matter and all efforts to cause matter to produce life have, so far, failed.

This common denominator to all interests, to all efforts to protect, to all "scientific benefits" had not been studied and had no name connected with any rationale which led to a pure and predictable identification or result. Bergson's "élan vital" and other philosophic hazarding was not in keeping with what we think of in this century as orderly, controlled scientific methodology. Supposition and Authority is a poor rock on which to base all predictions.

Not having any real name embracing the study itself, it was of course impossible to take courses in it. It could not have its answers in known fields, since it itself was unknown in not only its identity, but its characteristics.

I took whatever mathematics and physics were offered at a university. But then was stopped largely by lack of further academic subjects to study. I recall that my mind crystallized on the project when I found that the psychology and philosophy courses taught were inadequate to the research task I had in mind, as in neither one could I find any students or professors who had studied modern mathematics or physics or who used what I had been trained to regard as scientific methodology and who, as far as I could find, would admit to the errors in logic (mathematics) I found in them. In his own orderly world, the physical scientist would not credit the confusion which existed in the humanities.

So I went off on an expedition and began to study Life. Primitive Cultures seemed to be a place to start.

Never was any modern researcher confronted with so many conflicting data or subjects and so little *result* among them.

Yet obviously the past century of sprint by the physical sciences, which was even then speeding up, would overreach what were known as the humanities and even overwhelm them. And so it has proven.

Burdened by researching during the prewar period's utter lack of research grants and funds, I had to solve the economics of it all. I did so mainly by writing and movies and did very well at it, at least enough to finance what else I was doing.

I wrote a book in the late 1930s after a breakthrough on the subject, but the book was never published.

Eventually I had gone back through all the mirror mazes and plain fog of the humanities and worked with cytology. I had to study the subject in the fleeting moments left in a life overworked and overstressed. I found some clues to cellular memory and retention of patterns and originated and abandoned as impossible a theory you still see around about memory storage in molecules.

Rumors of the book and some papers brought me to the attention of Russia (via Amtorg), which made me a research offer. As it unfortunately was conditional upon going to Russia (which was still fashionable) and required of me a system of measuring the work potential of workers there, I had to decline. This was fortunate, as the date was 1939.

Ideological considerations and requirements of better control or subservience of people was not on my work schedule.

The Second World War and service was a long interruption. But in 1945 I was back at research again, using the library and facilities of Oak Knoll Naval Hospital.

In under a year, by use of endocrine experiments, on the basis that the endocrines are a switchboard of stimulus-response, I found that function seemed to monitor structure in living forms.

As the reverse had been held to be true (and had not provided a breakthrough), I was therefore able to proceed now in a new direction.

I found eventually that Life increased in potential by the stripping away of additives. This meant I could possibly be on the road to isolating *life* as a pure force.

Working with small energies, I eventually found the mental energy seemed to be a band between life and emotion and what might be a pure life essence.

In handling this I found the mental energy was made up of mental image pictures and that these became jammed together into masses until the commodity known as life became nearly extinguished.

By unburdening these (by a method of erasure), I found life potential increased.

This became Dianetics (*Dia*—through, *nous*—mind).

As it had a connection with psychosomatic illness, I offered the discoveries and papers on them to leading healing societies and was rebuffed! They had nothing to do with basic research!

A medical associate and a psychiatric publisher told me I had only the public left, so I wrote a book and it became surprisingly popular.

Just before this publication the US Navy's Office of Naval Research approached me and made a threatening offer that I must go to work for them as a civilian or be recalled to active duty. The project was to make people more suggestible. I was able to resign before they could complete the threat. While I had no complaint about real active service, I had already done a prewar tour of duty in Washington offices and knew I could get little done there and I had no ambition to make people more suggestible.

This was the second and last contact regarding any research aid.

I had applied earlier for funds to foundations and none were available for basic research. Few understood at that time that basic research had any value. Only specific projects for specific products qualified.

A group formed to handle the popularity of the book, *Dianetics*. Yet it provided no research assistance beyond testing vitamins.

I had been willing to leave the project at that time. In fact I had another expedition scheduled. But the impact of the book carried along with it one of those savage parallel attacks sometimes experienced by researchers which threw my life into chaos. An attempt was made on my life, I narrowly escaped kidnapping and I was loudly berated for misdeeds I had never committed. Seldom has there ever been such a heavy change in a man's life. I was a well-liked writer on Monday and on Tuesday was a horrible beast. Same man.

A scientist releasing his material to the public or seeking to advise his fellows of some discovery sometimes finds a poor ally in the press.

For years the most unusual and imaginary charges were hurled at me. Reporters never came near me. They just wrote about me.

It was hardly an atmosphere in which to continue research, but at great stress and out of responsibility to a public who supported me, I did so.

Fifteen years after that first public release I was able to develop the full technology that would isolate a being as a pure life force. It was the person himself. And far stronger and more capable.

In the following two years, despite the heavy stresses of administration and the same unseen force that kept striking at me on public lines, I was able to stably attain the result uniformly for people in technology known as Scientology processing.

Slightly less than nineteen years after the First Book, I found the what and why of the attacks.

"So I went off on an expedition and began to study Life. Primitive Cultures seemed to be a place to start."

While they could have been motivated and financed by a Church or the state, they were not.

The hidden secret of the attacks of nineteen years was *Research Funds*.

None had been available in my day. But after the war the psychologist and psychiatrist groups, in 1948, organized a research fund activity through international organizations. Governments contributed unbelievable sums to them with incredibly small and even illegal or dishonest results of human experimentation.

My work, as I now patch it together, was considered, I do not know how, a threat to such fund appropriation. It was also considered a threat to healing income. For years I supposed the latter predominated. But this is not true. I have seen the appropriations and the lists of those to whom such funds were given.

There was nothing wrong with granting research funds. But to do this as a *scientific activity,* to men untrained in any scientific methodology or mores, has been a serious mistake. Unlike the biologist, the chemist and other scientists, the psychologist and psychiatrist know nothing of the scientific method, know little or no mathematics and share none of the basic discipline which holds scientists together. They are trained in authoritarian subjects and their approach is entirely authoritarian.

The funds are not used for actual research, but are simply paid out to their friends. I have the documents on this.

For nineteen years this multimillion dollar river over the world has been used to attack any independent researcher and to forward the most mad plans for political control I have ever perused. I would not make such a statement without the documents being close to hand, sent to me by medical doctors who also do not like them.

Therefore I conclude it is a serious mistake to finance untrained and unskilled persons with unlimited research finance, which in itself can become a small, individuated area ferociously self-defensive and very fatal to have around.

The humanities have not tracked along with physical science because there were no real scientists in the humanities. The basic rules and mores of physical scientists were missing.

Yet the entire social order, for progress, depends upon the humanities catching up their lost time. Yet the atmosphere in which the research must be done has not changed much from Hegel's time.

I have been working seriously and productively in this field, denied any funds and combating fantastically overfinanced opposition.

The society at large does not oppose advance in this field. The Churches do not. But governments at the urgings of the incompetent "authority" have attacked all advance by serious basic researchers.

Few have the courage or stamina to stand up to such opposition and still carry on their work.

The campaign of discrediting any such work discredits as well its possibility and discourages actual scientists.

In my time I have seen Dr. Wilhelm Reich, MD, who was researching in small energies in the mind, killed by the FDA of the US at the urgings of overfinanced interests. I have seen others viciously attacked for attempts to advance knowledge of the humanities.

I am not requesting and have not needed research funds for some time.

I have made a breakthrough in this field. It has taken thirty-eight years of hard work. It is successful. It can be subjected to the usual scientific proofs and controls. It has been tested over and over by competent persons. There are fifty-five axioms, there is a considerable body of application data, there are over sixteen million words of gathered materials.

I am sometimes accused of keeping the data back. It is there for public and professional use. But in offering it to the US to increase scientist IQ and halve pilot reaction time, our Washington office was raided by longshoremen with drawn guns, posing as Federal Marshals, and a Wheatstone Bridge we use was seized along with books.

"The humanities have not tracked along with physical science because there were no real scientists in the humanities. The basic rules and mores of physical scientists were missing."

I have been pressed to the most unusual means of forwarding research.

This is a short case history of why there had not been any real scientific activity in the field of the humanities. A scientist in the physical sciences would not believe the chaos, incompetence, dishonesty and opposition to be found in these subjects.

There was no field before Scientology for basic, pure scientific research into the humanities. There were no university subjects beyond mathematics and the physical sciences which also contained a scientific approach. The literature of philosophy is interesting and can be brought into a sensible alignment, however, only if not approached in the authoritarian manner it is offered. I once resigned a doctorate in protest of this atmosphere.

Authoritarianism, professionalism and dogma obscure the humanities to such a marked degree that it requires extraordinary resolution to research in them. The recoil on the individual researcher is financed by research funds which are looked upon as profit, are not gainfully applied to the subject and are granted to persons insufficiently grounded in science to embrace its ethics or methodology.

If most actual scientists are trying to safeguard, improve or protect life, then it is time that they give heed to the field of the humanities.

This field has been completely unorganized. There has been no place to publish or discuss or exchange actual data without colliding with the lines of overfinanced research interests which have said to me regarding a graph of improvement, "If you published that in our journal, it would revolutionize psychology." "All right, publish it." "Oh we couldn't do that. We have finance coming from Congress to explore that area."

Thus, you have the story of how Scientology had to develop, some of the reasons it was released as it was and is as it is.

No journals, no society, no other contacts—these were its hazards. Alone in the humanities it produces uniformly a predicted *result* in many areas.

It is now well known and used in aerospace programs by hundreds of its people, I am told by one of their leaders. Bits of it (earlier bits) are being released from time to time as new discoveries by others.

Man needs this subject. He needs, with his wars and pollutions and growing dominance of the physical sciences, a grasp of the humanities not perverted by greed, professionalism and authoritarian but untested nonsense.

Man is a spiritual being, not a vegetable or animal. And that is susceptible to scientific proof.

The data of Scientology was derived by and stands up to scientific methodology. It contains a workable system regarding life.

It has not yet begun to be applied broadly to any of the fields where the humanities are losing out. It probably has good application in biology. It can shed, possibly, some small light in physics and chemistry.

The data was very hardly won. Whole governments have crushed down on me to halt it. I do not exaggerate. It would be a great shame and possibly a great loss in knowledge if it were not reviewed by other fields in the humanities and physical sciences. It has been a lonely road.

> *"The data of Scientology was derived by and stands up to scientific methodology. It contains a workable system regarding life."*

"Thus, you have the story of how Scientology had to develop, some of the reasons it was released as it was and is as it is." —L. Ron Hubbard, Saint Hill Manor, 1959

CHAPTER SIX

Citizens Commission on
HUMAN RIGHTS

International headquarters for Citizens Commission on
Human Rights, Los Angeles, California

Citizens Commission on Human Rights

"THE WORLD TODAY WILL NOT STAND FOR SUCH FLAGRANT rights violations as the psychiatrist demands. The world today will not stand for death camps, human experiments, torture and murder. The Scientologists are fighting this and will fight it down to a final and complete victory over the powers of evil." —L. Ron Hubbard

Therefore Scientologists founded the Citizens Commission on Human Rights (CCHR). It was expressly charged with investigating and exposing psychiatric violations of human rights and cleaning up the field of mental healing. It was further charged to stand as a watchdog over psychiatric activities far and wide. Accordingly, and from a single office, it soon comprised a global network with hundreds of chapters in dozens of nations. Those chapters are coordinated from an international headquarters in Los Angeles, California, which serves as a clearinghouse for incoming reports of psychiatric abuse and a central emanation point for CCHR information. All told, then, CCHR is rightly regarded as devastating to psychiatric plans and intentions—and all as borne out by even this bare-bones account of their story.

In an era when psychiatric victims were all but forgotten or woefully neglected, fledgling chapters of the Citizens Commission on Human Rights issued public notices to elicit reports of psychiatric abuse. Among the first to reply were witnesses of psychiatric exploitation in South Africa—specifically through an aforementioned network of slave-labor camps where several thousand black patients were warehoused in disused mining

Left
The Grand Opening of CCHR's headquarters in Los Angeles

Psychiatry: An Industry of Death Museum: the definitive and unforgettable statement on psychiatric horror in our time

Above
Awarded to the Citizens Commission on Human Rights for "outstanding and invaluable service to the community" from the United States Congress

compounds. Approximately four years later, and notwithstanding concerted resistance from apartheid ministries, CCHR succeeded in producing a document entitled, "Let the Whistle Blow." Detailed therein were all previously referenced atrocities and more: the fact some ten thousand black Africans were held in captivity and farmed out to manufacture coat hangers and carrier bags; the fact that while inmates were excessively drugged to keep them tractable, punitive electroconvulsive shock was administered without anesthetics because, as a chief state psychiatrist explained, "It is too expensive."

Response from a white-supremacist South African government was stock. Scientology publications carrying the story were summarily banned and amendments to a national Mental Health Act made it a criminal offense to report on, photograph or even sketch conditions in psychiatric facilities. Undeterred, CCHR next submitted findings to United Nations and Red Cross offices. The United Nations, in turn, requested a World Health Organization investigation. Whereupon CCHR findings were entirely confirmed—and then some:

"Although psychiatry is expected to be a medical discipline which deals with the human being as a whole, in no other medical field in South Africa is the contempt of the person cultivated by racism, more precisely portrayed than in psychiatry." World Health Organization Report, 1983.

There is altogether more. Among the first case files from a CCHR investigation of improper commitment procedures came the tale of a Hungarian refugee committed to a Philadelphia mental asylum as "schizophrenic with paranoid tendencies." In fact, the patient simply could not speak English and his "gibberish" was mistaken for the ranting of a madman. Nevertheless, only after pressing legally did CCHR secure the patient's release. Latterly, CCHR pressed on with a Freedom of Information suit to break the veil of secrecy within French health ministries and so obtain evidence of similarly outlandish commitments. In fact, evidence revealed a 186 percent increase in forced commitments to French psychiatric facilities and no evidence those so committed suffered from any real mental disorder. Whereupon CCHR continued pressing legally (as well as publicly and very vocally) until patients faced with commitment were provided with recourse to legal counsel and other basic rights.

There is more. Despite American psychiatric claims that patients are physically restrained to beds for their own protection, CCHR investigation revealed as many as 150 annual deaths from restraints, more than a dozen of which were children. All of which, in turn, led to eventual federal regulations prohibiting physical and chemical restraints for coercion or discipline as well as a national reporting system to monitor hospital compliance. Similarly grim cases of patients under psychiatric restraint were unearthed in Australia, Japan, Hungary, the Czech Republic and Greece. Then, too, so inhuman were conditions in Italy—patients confined to concentration camp cells—the CCHR investigation sparked five years of Italian government raids and the closure of some ninety asylums.

Equally compelling are the stories of CCHR efforts in bringing psychiatric criminals to justice and assisting criminally abused patients to report such abuse to authorities. Included in the annals: the New Zealand psychiatrist who slowly poisoned his wife with psychiatric pharmaceuticals, the conviction of a Georgia psychologist for ninety-nine counts of child molestation and felony exploitation of minors, the Massachusetts psychiatrist imprisoned for similarly perverted exploitation of three adolescent boys and the Canadian psychiatrist likewise jailed for sexual assault. In reply—and what with sexual abuse of psychiatric patients running upwards of 50 percent, one could name many another—CCHR successfully campaigned for the enactment of some two dozen laws/regulations prohibiting psychiatric rape.

Likewise proven rampant through CCHR investigations were psychiatric financial irregularities and outright insurance fraud. The cases are legion, egregious and have thus far totaled more than a billion dollars in criminal/civil fines as well as restitution. Moreover, the cases are especially noteworthy for the fact CCHR is now universally regarded as expert in such matters and thus consulted by state and federal enforcement officials. Included in the case files are psychiatric institutions enlisting "bounty hunters" to actually kidnap patients. Victims were then held captive until their insurance ran dry (at which point they were suddenly declared "miraculously" sane). Also among records of now convicted psychiatrists: billing insurance companies for therapy sessions that never took place, inflating rosters of hospital staff to qualify for increased government funding and bilking federal institutions.

Top right
The Citizens Commission on Human Rights headquarters: coordination point for hundreds of chapters charged with investigating and exposing psychiatric abuse on six continents

Bottom right
The CCHR Accomplishments Room, presenting an array of documentary films on the whole panorama of psychiatric atrocities—from rampant drugging of adolescent populations to the wholesale slaughter of marginal peoples. This is where the *horror is revealed.*

The upshot here: closures of entire psychiatric hospital networks—most notably the Charter Behavioral Health Systems, among the largest private psychiatric chain facilities in America. Additionally following from CCHR efforts to root out psychiatric criminality are the psychiatric and psychological practitioners now regularly prosecuted somewhere in the world—actually better than one a week.

Then there is all CCHR has brought to bear on psychiatry's "technically legal" atrocities, most notably electroshock and lobotomies. In a word, and once more following from L. Ron Hubbard's original condemnation of the practice, CCHR has relentlessly fought to expose the myths inherent in those words electroconvulsive *therapy* and psycho*surgery*. Partnering with a United States Congressional Black Caucus (representing constituents particularly victim to such practices), CCHR spearheaded the defeat of a federal proposal to fund experimental psychosurgery. Also following CCHR information campaigns and legislative testimony are the extant psychosurgery bans and prohibitions across Europe and Australia.

As one might imagine, CCHR is additionally at the vanguard of popular efforts to stop psychiatric drugging, particularly that of children. As noted, psychotropic drugs are the mainstay of psychiatry's global empire. Nevertheless, and with extraordinary tenacity, the Citizens Commission on Human Rights now spearheads a worldwide grass-roots movement to stem the dark tide. In no small consequence are hundreds of federal regulatory warnings and "black box" labels now gracing psychotropic prescription bottles. Indeed, there is nary a psychiatric drug on any market that does not bear the stamp of CCHR pressure on regulatory agencies to issue incisive warnings. In even greater consequence are hundreds of thousands saved from fatal side effects / overdose. That CCHR further partners with legislators to prohibit schools from requiring students to medicate is yet another chapter in the same saga. While in consequence to that one, dozens of prohibitive bills are either on the books or in the works. Of special note are landmark Child Medication Safety Amendments as originally enacted in 2004 and an equivalent law severely curtailing child drugging in Mexico.

Again, one could cite substantially more. The Citizens Commission on Human Rights has ultimately sparked, inspired and otherwise brought into being more than a hundred bills and amendments in defense of psychiatric victims worldwide. Meanwhile,

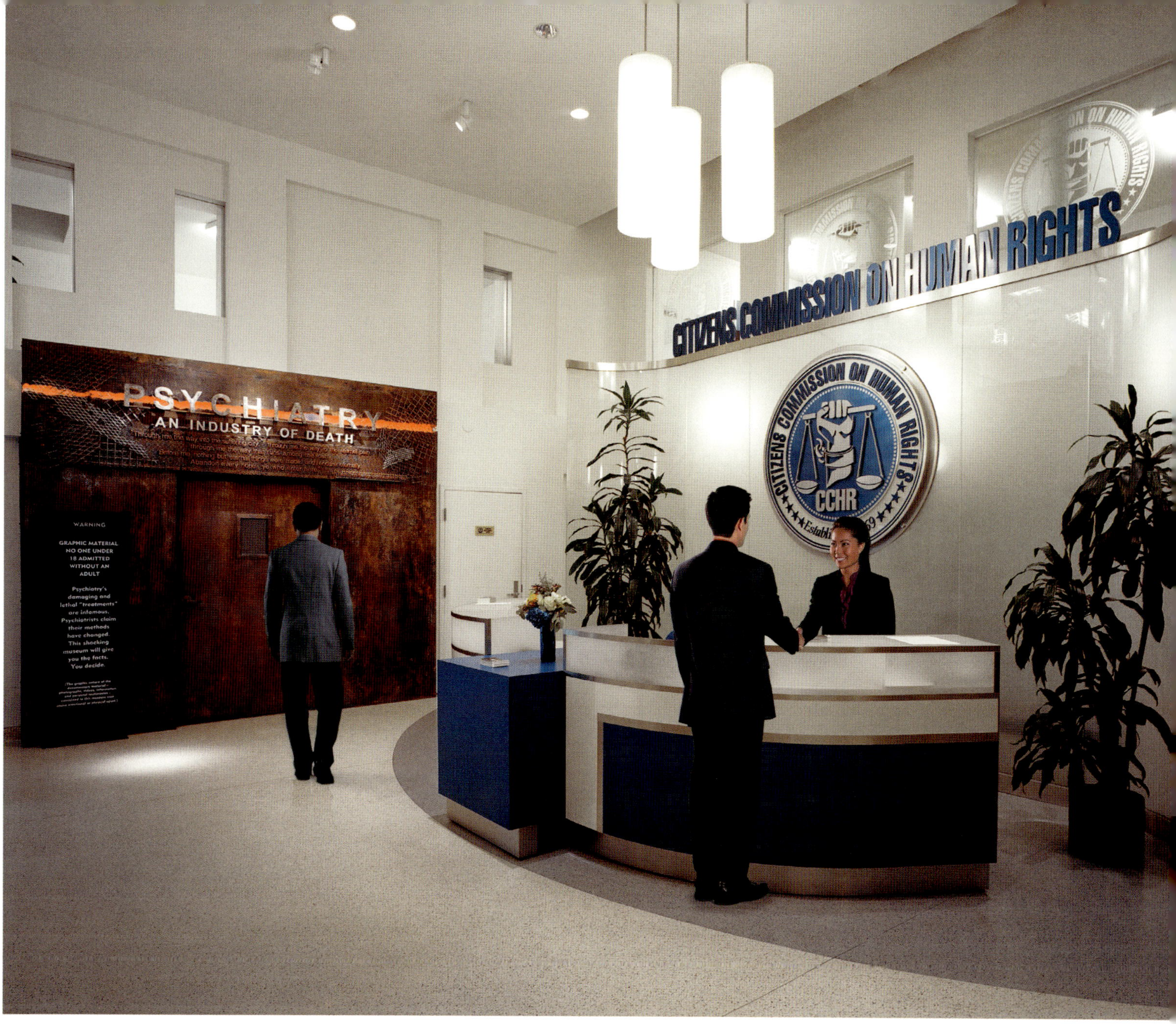
PSYCHIATRY
AN INDUSTRY OF DEATH
WARNING
GRAPHIC MATERIAL NO ONE UNDER 18 ADMITTED WITHOUT AN ADULT
Psychiatry's damaging and lethal "treatments" are infamous. Psychiatrists claim their methods have changed. This shocking museum will give you the facts. You decide.
CITIZENS COMMISSION ON HUMAN RIGHTS
CITIZENS COMMISSION ON HUMAN RIGHTS
CCHR

MAKING HUMAN RIGHTS A FACT
You are safe so long as we are here.
MAKING HUMAN RIGHTS A FACT
CITIZENS COMMISSION ON HUMAN RIGHTS
CCHR
Established 1969

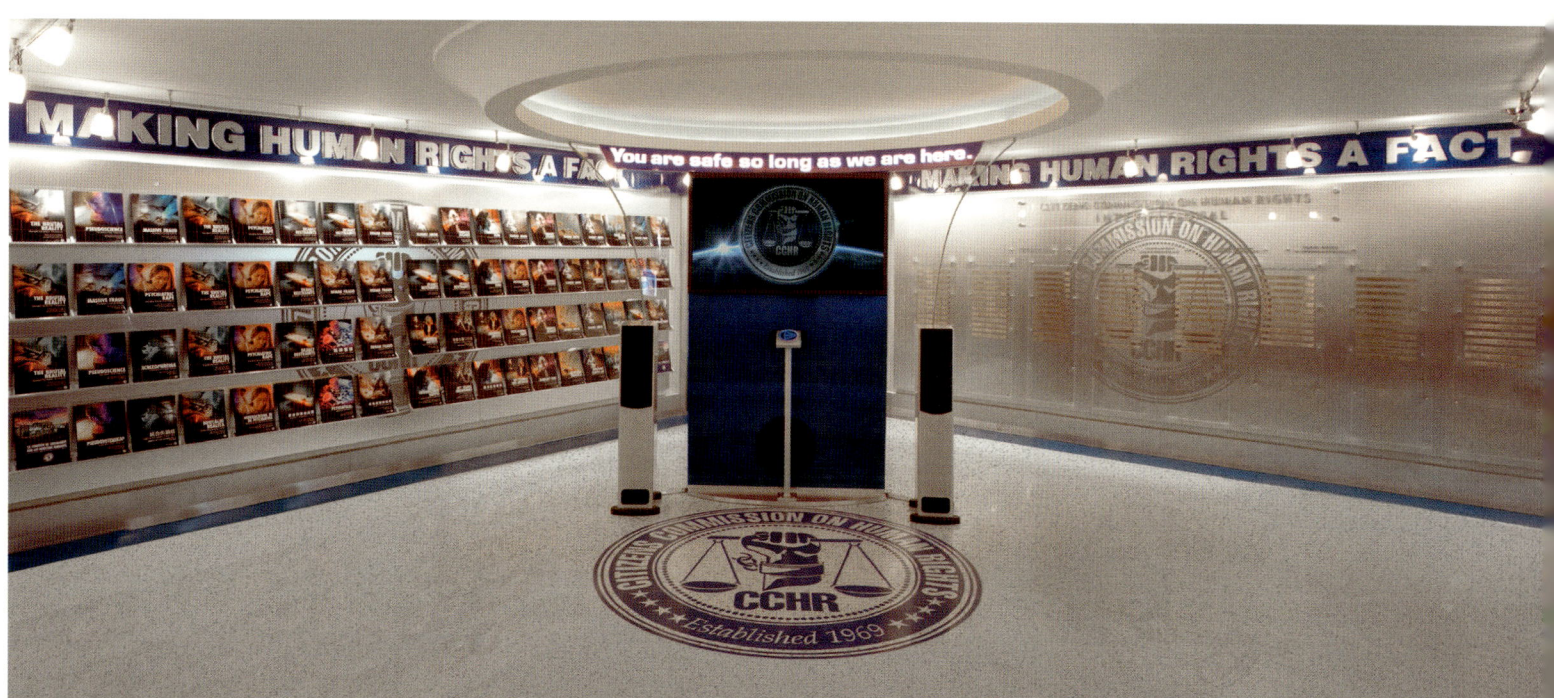

Left
The Origins of Psychiatry as graphically depicted, with actual implements of torture employed to keep patients tractable through the eighteenth century

recommendations from its own declaration of patient rights are now found in "Principles, Guidelines and Guarantees for the Protection of Persons Detained on Grounds of Mental Ill-Health or Suffering from Mental Disorder" as adopted by the United Nations General Assembly. Included therein are statements prescribing protection from all psychiatric abuses we have considered through this publication, and all as additionally described in the more than ten million copies of CCHR publications. In a word, those publications document psychiatric corruption wherever psychiatrists foray: into our homes, churches, schools, courts, among women, children, the elderly and ethnic minorities.

Simultaneously to document the larger history of psychiatric horror, there now stands the Industry of Death Museum adjacent to CCHR headquarters in Los Angeles. In another word, it is designed to awaken visitors to the horror of psychiatry and so presents all else we have considered through these pages—and in the most graphic terms imaginable, with actual artifacts of psychiatric torture and documentary footage of abuse. Psychiatry's pathetic beginnings as spawned in hellholes of seventeenth-century bedlam; the redefining of human beings as soulless animals to be coerced, manipulated and managed like so

Citizens Commission on Human Rights 235

Right
Effectively comprising a mobile version of the Industry of Death Museum, CCHR Traveling Exhibits present the shocking truth about psychiatry in a dozen languages and scores of cities internationally. Indeed, wherever dwells a significant psychiatric presence, a CCHR Traveling Exhibit is soon to visit. Pictured here is a CCHR Exhibit at the National Chamber of Deputies in Mexico City.

many sheep; the psychiatric roots of the holocaust and incipient racism; the obscene profits from psychotropic drugs; and the invention of mental illness to fuel those profits unto perpetuity—all this and more is *Psychiatry: An Industry of Death Museum*.

What amounts to a mobile version of the museum is the Industry of Death Traveling Exhibit. It is designed to replicate the Death Museum experience wherever psychiatrists prey on populations and so open the eyes of millions to psychiatric subversion. In any given year, Industry of Death Traveling Exhibits crisscross scores of cities in dozens of nations to become what is rightfully described a "mobile bulwark against psychiatric abuse" and a catalyst for popular resistance to psychiatric horror.

Presenting still another incisive view of psychiatry is the CCHR documentary series. Every aspect and angle of psychiatric subversion is chronicled. *The Untold Story of Psychotropic Drugging, How Psychiatric Drugs Can Kill Your Child, The Marketing of Madness, Diagnostic & Statistical Manual: Psychiatry's Deadliest Scam* and *An Industry of Death* itself—all is compellingly detailed in award-winning documentaries sponsored and distributed by the Citizens Commission on Human Rights.

Included in the panorama are all pertinent statistics. By way of example: over 500 million people have been prescribed psychotropic drugs for conditions with no scientific basis whatsoever and which no medical test can verify. Also included are all facts and figures of usage: psychiatric drugs now kill some three thousand patients a month while simultaneously netting psychiatry a third of a trillion dollars annually.

By the same token—and this date coincident with CCHR inception—some 30 billion dollars that would have otherwise fueled psychiatric plans and subterfuge have now been slashed from their coffers...*and so be it*.

In the final analysis, L. Ron Hubbard once remarked, psychiatry made only two serious mistakes: they ran counter to the mores, desires and customs of world populations; and they attacked Scientologists without provocation. In reply, he brought his pen to bear on behalf of those populations and rallied Scientologists under the banner of the Citizens Commission on Human Rights. In consequence, and while the world still suffers from half a century of psychiatric domination, their credence and power has dramatically waned since L. Ron Hubbard first exposed this incredible subversion of human rights. ∎

Following from L. Ron Hubbard's pioneering work in combating psychiatric abuse, the Citizens Commission on Human Rights continues to carry the torch against injustice. In consequence comes the myriad of public service awards and recognitions from government bodies world over.

A Closing Note

The Scientology movement is not pushed by one man, it is pushed by millions.

If you champion the dignity and Freedom of Mankind, you are a Scientologist at heart if not by name.

We are the most able technicians in the field of the mind on the planet and are the only skilled experts in this field who can produce uniformly beneficial and permanent good results. We now outnumber psychiatry by about 100 to 1.

We believe in Mankind. We can and are helping Man, our countries and society.

We are not "one man."
We are millions and we are everywhere.

L. RON HUBBARD

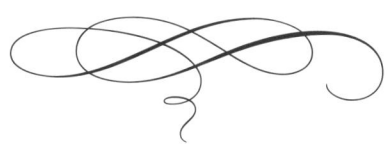

APPENDIX

**Alphabetical Listing of L. Ron Hubbard
   Articles | 245
**Chronological Listing of L. Ron Hubbard
   Articles | 247
**Glossary | 249
**Index | 317

ALPHABETICAL
Listing of L. Ron Hubbard Articles

Being Good *26 September 1969* | 189
Bland Personality, The *15 June 1969* | 147
Cause of Crime, The *6 May 1982* | 211
Closing Note, A *24 September 1969* | 241
Constitutional Destruction *9 June 1969* | 33
Constitutions *28 June 1969* | 45
Control "Sciences" *15 June 1969* | 143
Crime and Psychiatry *23 June 1969* | 159
Criminal Mind and the Psychs, The *26 April 1982* | 209
Criminals and Psychiatry *29 July 1980* | 205
Cultural Deficiencies *9 September 1969* | 171
Cultural Destruction *30 October 1969* | 195
Diplomas *Circa June 1969* | 129
Drug Addiction *19 October 1969* | 191
Drug Problems *25 September 1969* | 183
Druidism and Psychiatry *27 February 1969* | 113
Economics *17 March 1966* | 85
Economics—War and Tax *1 March 1969* | 95
Evolution of Totalitarianism, The *25 November 1969* | 49
Failures *1 April 1969* | 127
Fast Justice *1 March 1969* | 63
Fight for Freedom, The *24 September 1969* | 177
Government and Revolt *12 March 1969* | 29

How to Win an Argument *16 June 1969* | 155

Justice *1 March 1969* | 67

Justice Department versus Americans, The *23 February 1975* | 75

Old-Fashioned Holdovers *15 November 1969* | 201

On Writing to Governments *2 March 1969* | 25

Our Intentions *28 June 1969* | 163

Pain-Drug-Hypnosis *2 March 1969* | 121

Patriotism *1 March 1969* | 19

Planned Revolution, The *12 June 1969* | 135

Psychology and Psychiatry, the Sciences of Saliva *Circa June 1969* | 131

Quackery and Fakery *16 June 1969* | 151

Reason Psychiatric Front Groups Attack Scientology, A *27 February 1969* | 109

Riots *19 March 1969* | 71

Sciences of Saliva *13 June 1969* | 139

Strong Voices in the Land *Circa August 1972* | 9

Summary on Scientology for Scientists, A *29 January 1969* | 219

Tangled Terms *25 September 1969* | 185

Today's Terrorism *1 March 1969* | 117

Unconstitutional Government *27 June 1969* | 41

Unholy Stick Together, The *2 August 1969* | 167

Unite and Win *13 June 1969* | 37

CHRONOLOGICAL
Listing of L. Ron Hubbard Articles

17 March 1966 Economics | 85
29 January 1969 A Summary on Scientology for Scientists | 219
27 February 1969 A Reason Psychiatric Front Groups Attack Scientology | 109
27 February 1969 Druidism and Psychiatry | 113
1 March 1969 Economics—War and Tax | 95
1 March 1969 Fast Justice | 63
1 March 1969 Justice | 67
1 March 1969 Patriotism | 19
1 March 1969 Today's Terrorism | 117
2 March 1969 On Writing to Governments | 25
2 March 1969 Pain-Drug-Hypnosis | 121
12 March 1969 Government and Revolt | 29
19 March 1969 Riots | 71
1 April 1969 Failures | 127
Circa June 1969 Diplomas | 129
Circa June 1969 Psychology and Psychiatry, the Sciences of Saliva | 131
9 June 1969 Constitutional Destruction | 33
12 June 1969 The Planned Revolution | 135
13 June 1969 Sciences of Saliva | 139
13 June 1969 Unite and Win | 37
15 June 1969 Control "Sciences" | 143
15 June 1969 The Bland Personality | 147
16 June 1969 How to Win an Argument | 155

16 June 1969 Quackery and Fakery | **151**
23 June 1969 Crime and Psychiatry | **159**
27 June 1969 Unconstitutional Government | **41**
28 June 1969 Constitutions | **45**
28 June 1969 Our Intentions | **163**
2 August 1969 The Unholy Stick Together | **167**
9 September 1969 Cultural Deficiencies | **171**
24 September 1969 A Closing Note | **241**
24 September 1969 The Fight for Freedom | **177**
25 September 1969 Drug Problems | **183**
25 September 1969 Tangled Terms | **185**
26 September 1969 Being Good | **189**
19 October 1969 Drug Addiction | **191**
30 October 1969 Cultural Destruction | **195**
15 November 1969 Old-Fashioned Holdovers | **201**
25 November 1969 The Evolution of Totalitarianism | **49**
Circa August 1972 Strong Voices in the Land | **9**
23 February 1975 The Justice Department versus Americans | **75**
29 July 1980 Criminals and Psychiatry | **205**
26 April 1982 The Criminal Mind and the Psychs | **209**
6 May 1982 The Cause of Crime | **211**

GLOSSARY

A

aberration(s): a departure from rational thought or behavior. From the Latin, *aberrare,* to wander from; Latin, *ab,* away, and *errare,* to wander. It means basically to err, to make mistakes, or more specifically to have fixed ideas which are not true. The word is also used in its scientific sense. It means departure from a straight line. If a line should go from A to B, then if it is "aberrated" it would go from A to some other point, to some other point, to some other point, to some other point, to some other point and finally arrive at B. Taken in its scientific sense, it would also mean the lack of straightness or to see crookedly, as an example, a man sees a horse but thinks he sees an elephant. Aberrated conduct would be wrong conduct, or conduct not supported by reason. Page 85.

abhors: dislikes or rejects (something or someone) very strongly. Page 51.

abreast of: figuratively, up-to-date with something. From the literal meaning of in a position parallel to something else. Page 31.

abstractly: in a manner that is separate from concrete realities or actual instances; theoretically as opposed to practically. Page 4.

Abwehr: a German military intelligence and counterintelligence organization originally established in 1920. *Abwehr* means defense in German and the organization's original purpose was to serve as Germany's defense against foreign espionage. During World War II (1939–1945) its functions expanded and it conducted espionage operations in foreign countries. Page 76.

ace: of first or high rank or quality. Page 77.

acquittal: the clearing (of a person) of a charge, as by declaring not guilty. Page 70.

actualize: make actual or real; turn into action or fact. Page 135.

acumen: sharpness and quickness of mind. Page 4.

adaption: the act of taking up or of changing a plan, idea, cause or practice to suit particular conditions or a particular purpose. Page 97.

ad hoc: formed or set up for a particular purpose only. Literally, a Latin phrase meaning "to this." Page 15.

Adler: Alfred Adler (1870–1937), Austrian psychologist and psychiatrist; he broke with Freud (1911) by stressing that a sense of inferiority, rather than sexual drive, is the motivating force in human life. Page 113.

advent: an important arrival, especially one that marks the beginning of a new era in the history of a people. Page 1.

agent provocateur: a person employed to associate himself with members of a group and, by pretended sympathy with their aims or attitudes, to incite them to some illegal or harmful action, making them liable to capture or arrest and punishment; secret agent or undercover man. Page 163.

agitators: people who try to stir up people in support of a social or political cause, often used in an unfavorable sense. Page 9.

airy-fairy: not based on reality; unrealistic. Page 64.

Alaska: a state of the United States in northwestern North America, separated from the other mainland states by part of Canada. Page 105.

alien: hostile or opposed (to someone or something). Page 41.

all but: almost; very nearly. Page 1.

Allies: the twenty-six nations that fought in World War II (1939–1945) against Germany and those countries fighting with Germany (Japan, Italy and often Bulgaria, Hungary and Romania). Page 19.

all out: with all available means or effort; using or involving all one's resources. Page 26.

AMA: an abbreviation for *American Medical Association.* Page 77.

amassed: gathered or brought together; assembled. Page 60.

American Psychiatric Association: national society of psychiatrists founded in 1844 as the Association of Medical Superintendents of American Institutions for the Insane. Page 6.

American Psychological Association: an American association of psychologists founded in 1892. Page 6.

American Revolution: the war between Great Britain and its American colonies (1775–1783) by which the colonies won their independence. Page 88.

Amtorg: a company organized by the Soviet Union in 1924, located in New York City, to serve as the exclusive import and export agency for trade between the Soviet Union and the United States. The name is short for *Amerikanskaja torgovlja* (American trade). Active particularly before and during World War II (1939–1945), Amtorg was sometimes used as a cover for Russian espionage agents operating in the United States. Page 220.

and then some: and much more in addition. Page 230.

annals: a record of events. Page 231.

anointed: chosen or ruling as if by a God-given right and hence considered unable to do wrong. From a religious ceremony of rubbing (anointing) a ruler with oil as a sign of his holy right to rule. Page 31.

antitrust: opposing or intended to restrain trusts, monopolies or other large combinations of business and capital, especially with a view to maintaining and promoting competition. A *trust* is a combination of corporations with the purpose of reducing competition and controlling prices. Page 77.

APA: an abbreviation for *American Psychiatric Association*. Page 77.

apartheid: (in the Republic of South Africa) a rigid policy of political and economic discrimination and segregation of the nonwhite population, in effect from 1948 to 1991. Page 15.

apathy: a complete lack of emotion for or interest in things generally; an inability to respond emotionally. An individual in apathy has no energy. Page 9.

appearances, keep up: maintain an outward show of acceptable behavior, well-being or the like. Page 98.

appropriations: sums of money that have been set aside from a budget, especially a government budget, for a particular purpose. Page 26.

archcriminal: the top or leading criminal. *Arch* means chief, most important or most extreme. Page 161.

archetypal: of, relating to or resembling an *archetype,* the original pattern or model from which all things of the same kind are copied or on which they are based. Page 60.

argot: the special vocabulary and slang used by a particular profession or group of people. Page 196.

aristocracy: government by a few with special privileges, ranks or positions; rule by an elite few who are above the general law; a group who by birth or position are "superior to everybody else" and who can make or apply laws to others but consider they themselves are not affected by the laws. Page 10.

aristos: an abbreviation for *aristocrats,* members of a privileged upper class or ruling group considered to be superior and holding positions of high rank and status. Page 29.

armament: the weapons and military equipment used in an army. Page 49.

arraigned: called before a court to answer a criminal charge. Page 159.

arrant: that is plainly such; downright; thorough; complete. Page 152.

Aryanism: the doctrine spread by the Nazis that so-called Aryans (Caucasians of non-Jewish descent) possessed superior capacities for government, social organization and civilization. Page 31.

as often as not: frequently; more than or at least one-half of the time. Page 50.

Athens: chief city of ancient Greece. From the 500s B.C., Athens functioned under a democratic constitution, with all citizens allowed to freely participate in the government of the city, debating important issues in open assemblies. Page 51.

atrocities: acts that are extremely or shockingly wicked, cruel or brutal. Page 134.

Attorney General: the chief law officer of the United States, appointed by the president with approval of the US Senate. The post is the head of the Justice Department and a member of the president's cabinet, responsible for handling legal matters that involve the government and providing legal advice to the president. Page 59.

auditor(s): a Dianetics or Scientology practitioner. The word *auditor* means one who listens; a listener. Page 53.

authoritarian: characterized by or favoring complete obedience to authority, without question and without reference to facts or results. Page 222.

authoritarianism: the system or practice of an *authority* (or *authorities*), one who is a supposed expert or one whose opinion on a subject is likely to be accepted without question and without reference to facts or results. Under authoritarianism individual freedom of judgment and action are neglected in favor of absolute obedience to "experts." Page 223.

axioms: statements of natural laws on the order of those of the physical sciences. Page 223.

B

bad hats: corrupt, worthless or good-for-nothing persons; people who are morally lax or who frequently engage in improper conduct. Page 110.

Bailey, Harry: Harry Richard Bailey (1922–1985), chief psychiatrist at Chelmsford Hospital in Sydney, Australia. His use of drugs, electroshock and "deep-sleep" comas resulted in patient deaths, suicides and physical and mental complications. Following his suicide in 1985, a Royal Commission Inquiry condemned Bailey's actions, and the parliament of New South Wales banned the use of "deep sleep." Page 134.

bail, without: without setting *bail,* a sum of money deposited to secure an accused person's temporary release from custody and to guarantee that person's appearance in court at a later date. *Without bail* means the person must remain in jail and is not permitted even a temporary release. Page 71.

Balkans: a reference to the *Balkan Peninsula,* a primarily mountainous peninsula in southeastern Europe that includes the countries of Bulgaria, Romania and Croatia, among others. Balkan history has been characterized by military and political strife, including a number of revolutions, revolts and wars in the late nineteenth and twentieth centuries. Page 174.

balled-up: totally confused. Page 75.

bamboozler: someone who deceives or gets the better of (someone) by tricks, flattery or the like. Page 186.

banner: a guiding principle, cause or philosophy, from the literal meaning of *banner,* a flag on a pole, such as one used in battle by a country or a king. Page 6.

bar association: an organization of lawyers established to promote professional competence, enforce standards of ethical conduct and encourage a spirit of public service among members of the legal profession. Page 63.

barbiturate: any of a group of drugs used in medicine that act as a depressant and are used as sedatives or hypnotics. Page 107.

bare-bones: indicating the essential elements or structure of something, without any elaboration. Page 229.

baron(s), feudal: a lord or nobleman during the Middle Ages who held land in exchange for military and other services given, as laid out in the *feudal system,* a social and political system in which the land, worked by peasants who were bound to it, was held by low-ranking nobles in exchange for military and other services given to high-ranking nobles. Page 89.

base: basic; fundamental; essential. Page 4.

basket, heads ready for the: a reference to the executions that occurred during the French Revolution (1789–1799), when thousands of people were beheaded under the guillotine, with a basket made ready to receive the severed heads. Page 72.

Bastille: a fortress and prison in Paris, France, known as a symbol of tyranny, where many political and other offenders were held and tortured. On 14 July 1789, the populace attacked the Bastille, freed the prisoners and destroyed the building, an event that marked the beginning of the French Revolution (1789–1799). July 14, Bastille Day, is a national holiday in France, in celebration of the fall of the Bastille. Page 98.

bearings, lost (one's): became uncertain about where one was and in which direction one should proceed; became unable to react in a normal manner. Literally, *one's bearings* means awareness of one's position relative to the surroundings. Page 5.

bears out: shows to be true; supports or confirms. Page 106.

bears to skate using hot skates, teaching: a reference to the Russian practice of training bears to use ice skates or even play ice hockey for exhibition and shows in circuses. *Hot skates* alludes to harsh conditions of training. Page 174.

bedlam: an insane asylum, from the original Bedlam (in full, *St. Mary of Bethlehem*) in London, an insane asylum known for its inhumane treatment and filthy environment. Inmates were chained to the walls or floor. If they became restless or violent, they were beaten, whipped or dunked in water. Page 235.

Beers, Clifford: Clifford Whittingham Beers (1876–1943), American humanitarian who devoted himself to the study and advancement of mental hygiene. Between 1900 and 1903, Beers was confined in an asylum. He achieved wide recognition with the book he wrote of his experience (1908) and the organization he founded, the National Committee for Mental Hygiene (1909).

In 1950 this group was taken over by the World Federation of Mental Health and renamed the National Mental Health Association. Page 178.

beingness: condition or state of being; existence. Page 163.

Belch, Senator: a made-up name for a politician, characterized as belching (emitting wind noisily from the stomach through the mouth). Page 49.

Belsen: the name of one of the many concentration camps run by the Nazis during World War II (1939–1945). Belsen was established in 1943 in northern Germany for holding prisoners of war as well as Jews. Although built to accommodate only ten thousand prisoners, by the end of the war it was housing more than forty thousand. The camp had some of the most horrific living conditions of any, with tens of thousands of prisoners dying from starvation, disease and overwork. It was the first camp to be liberated by the British army in April 1945 and was burned down shortly thereafter. Page 174.

benchmark: a standard of excellence or achievement by which similar things can be measured or judged. Page 182.

benignly: in a way that is *benign,* showing or expressing gentleness or kindness. Page 76.

bent: strongly inclined; determined to take a course of action, usually with the word *on* or *upon*. Page 106.

berated: criticized or scolded angrily and at length. Page 221.

Bergson: Henri Bergson (1859–1941), French philosopher who advanced a theory of evolution, based on the spiritual dimension of human life (élan vital). Page 219.

bestiality: beastlike quality, character or behavior. Page 205.

best-laid plans of rats and men: a humorous variation of "the best-laid plans of mice and men often go awry," from a line in the poem "To a Mouse" by Scottish poet Robert Burns (1759–1796). After disturbing a mouse's winter nest with his plow, the poet tells the mouse that the most carefully arranged plans both of mice and men often go wrong or fail, no matter how carefully arranged or thought out. (The use of rats instead of mice alludes to the laboratory rats of psychologists and psychiatrists.) Page 26.

Bethesda: a suburb of the state of Maryland, located northwest of Washington, DC. It is the location of the National Naval Medical Center (a large government hospital founded in 1942 and run by the US Navy) and the National Institute of Mental Health. Page 168.

big wheels: influential or important persons. Page 92.

bilking: cheating out of what is due; defrauding. Page 231.

bill of goods, sell (someone) a: deceive a person, usually by persuading him to accept something untrue or undesirable. A *bill of goods* is a quantity of merchandise that can be sold or delivered. Page 172.

Bill of Rights: an addition made to the Constitution of the United States in 1791 that guarantees certain rights to the people, including freedom of speech and freedom of religion. It also prohibits the police and other government officials from searching people's homes or offices or seizing property without good reason and proper authority. Page 5.

Bill(s) of Attainder: a legislative enactment by which a person is pronounced guilty, without trial, of an alleged crime, originally a serious crime such as treason. Such an enactment is prohibited in the United States by the Constitution. *Attainder* means the loss of civil rights or the confiscation of the property of a person who has been sentenced to death for a serious crime. Page 64.

Bismarck: Otto von Bismarck (1815–1898), German political leader responsible for unifying the many small German states into an empire. He became the first chancellor (chief of government) of Germany, from 1871 to 1890. Bismarck declared that the great problems of his time must be settled by "blood and iron" instead of by speeches and resolutions. Page 205.

"black book," little: a book of names of people who are in disfavor with someone in authority and who are liable to be penalized. Page 5.

Black Caucus, Congressional: a group of African-American members of the United States Congress that focuses on issues of particular interest to black Americans. It was formed in the early 1970s. A *caucus* is a group within a legislative body seeking to represent a specific interest or influence a particular area of policy. Page 232.

Blain, Daniel: (1898–1981) American psychiatrist. In 1948, Blain became the first medical director of the American Psychiatric Association. Page 106.

blind eye, turned a: deliberately ignored or refused to take notice (of some state of affairs or situation); purposely overlooked (something). From an incident during a naval battle in 1801 when British Admiral Horatio Nelson (1758–1805), although second in command, took charge of the British operations. At the height of battle, the flagship of the fleet raised a signal to withdraw. Disagreeing with the signal, Nelson raised his telescope to his blind eye (one he had lost the sight of during an earlier battle) and told his men he saw no signal. He carried on with the attack, resulting in a major victory for the British. Page 19.

Bloc, Eastern: the group of countries (bloc) that consisted of the Soviet Union and its allies. *See also* **Soviet Union.** Page 194.

bloodlust: a strong or uncontrollable desire for bloodshed or killing. Page 3.

blot: a small or passing mention. Literally, a *blot* is a spot or stain, especially of ink on paper. Page 11.

blow: disappear or go, as if by an explosive action. Page 85.

bobbing: moving suddenly so as to appear or disappear. Page 75.

Bolshevik: of or having to do with the radical majority group within the Russian Socialist Party, which formed the Communist Party after seizing power in the 1917 revolution. Page 63.

bombast: figuratively, a term used to mean language that is loud or obvious. Page 139.

bona fides: the official papers, documents or other items that prove authenticity, legitimacy, etc., as of a person or organization. Page 24.

bonkers: an informal term for mad; crazy. Page 94.

books, in (one's) bad: out of favor; disliked (by someone). Page 147.

books, on the: entered in a list; on record. Page 232.

bounty hunter: somebody who pursues wanted persons in order to receive a financial reward (bounty). Page 231.

Bowart, Walter: Walter Howard Bowart (1939–2007), author of the book *Operation Mind Control,* an investigative report published in 1978 that detailed government mind control through the use of drugs such as LSD, behavior modification, hypnosis and the like. Page 194.

bow to: accept something and yield to it, often unwillingly. Page 168.

Brady, James: James Scott Brady (1940–), press secretary to the White House under US President Ronald Reagan. Brady was shot and permanently disabled in 1981 during an assassination attempt on Reagan. *See also* **Hinckley, Jr., John.** Page 204.

branded: labeled or marked as if with a *brand,* a mark formerly put upon criminals with a hot iron. Page 64.

Bray, Minister: a made-up name for a minister, characterized as uttering harsh, loud sounds like a donkey. Page 49.

brethren: an older word for *brothers,* used in referring to the members of a specific group. Page 26.

bright-eyes visionary: a dreamer or one whose ideas, plans, etc., are impractical or too fantastic and who is characterized as having *bright eyes,* eyes that show a strong desire for doing, obtaining or pursuing something. Page 94.

Britain's recent colonies, ritual murders such as those of: a reference to the human sacrifices and ritual murders practiced by some groups and religions native to West Africa and carried out in the former British colonies of the Gold Coast (now Ghana) and Nigeria. Both countries gained their independence from Great Britain in the mid-twentieth century. Page 114.

British Empire: the group of countries and territories throughout the world formerly connected with and controlled by Great Britain, which at its peak during World War I (1914–1918) covered 20 percent of the world's land area. After World War I various colonies began to demand and fight for independence. Since World War II (1939–1945), most areas of the former empire have achieved independence and are no longer under British rule. Page 143.

brush wars: warfare carried out by guerrillas (small defensive forces of irregular soldiers, usually volunteers, making surprise raids). Page 95.

bulwark: something serving as a defense or safeguard; literally, a wall or embankment raised as a defensive fortification. Page 236.

bunk: short for *bunkum,* talk that is empty, foolish or merely for effect; nonsense. Page 98.

Burgess: Guy Burgess (1911–1963), British diplomat who spied for the Soviet Union during and after World War II (1939–1945). As a British Broadcasting Corporation correspondent, member of British intelligence and member of the foreign office from 1944, he supplied large quantities of information to the Soviet Union. In 1951, Burgess was asked to resign because of his increasingly unstable behavior. He and fellow spy Donald Maclean were then warned that a counterintelligence investigation was closing in. Both mysteriously vanished and appeared five years later in Moscow, where they announced their defection from Great Britain. Page 124.

C

callous: without regard for the feelings or welfare of others; indifferent to the suffering of others. Page 10.

cap: provide a fitting climax or conclusion to. Page 134.

Capitalism: an economic system in which a country's businesses and industry are controlled and run for profit by private owners rather than by government and where money (capital) is invested or loaned in return for a profit. Page 86.

Capitol Building: the white-marble, domed building in Washington, DC, where the United States Congress meets. *See also* **Congressional.** Page 2.

carbon copy: somebody or something that is identical to or very much like somebody or something else; literally, a duplicate of written or drawn material that is made by using *carbon paper,* paper used for making copies, coated on one side with a waxy pigment that often contains carbon. Page 77.

card-carrying: having a membership card of a specified organization, especially of the Communist Party. Page 198.

carrier bags: a chiefly British term for large plastic or paper shopping bags with handles, especially ones supplied by a store. Page 230.

Carr, Sir William: (1912–1977) president of a British newspaper known as *News of the World*. Page 109.

case in point: a relevant example or illustration of something. Page 4.

case(s): a general term for a person being treated or helped. It is also used to mean the entire accumulation of upsets, pain, failures, etc., residing in a person's mind. Page 53.

caste: a social class separated from others by distinctions of hereditary rank, profession or wealth. Page 42.

Castro, Fidel: (1926–) ruler of Cuba from 1959 to 2008. Born on a large estate to a wealthy family, Castro came to power through armed revolution in 1959, overthrowing the military government. After seizing all property and businesses owned by Cubans and foreigners, he created a Communist state and established himself as dictator. Page 88.

catalyst: something that stimulates a reaction, development or change. Page 236.

catatonic: a person suffering from *catatonia,* a condition characterized by periods of inertia (an inability or unwillingness to move or act) or an apparent dazed state and solidity of the muscles. Page 185.

catchword: a popular or effective word or phrase, repeated so often that it comes to be identified with a particular idea, belief, school of thought or the like. Page 5.

cat was out of the bag: the secret has been disclosed; data priorly hidden has been made known, sometimes at the wrong time or accidentally. This phrase dates back to the eighth century when, in some areas, religious law forbade the selling and eating of pork. Pork lovers had to purchase their suckling pigs hidden in bags in the dark. In some instances, dishonest farmers would substitute a cat for a valuable pig. When the customer got home and the bag was opened, the trick would be disclosed and, literally, the cat would be out of the bag. Page 178.

caught wind of: found out (about something) indirectly. Page 109.

cellular colonies: groups of cells (the smallest structural units of an organism that are capable of independent functioning) formed together into connected structures and living or growing in close association with each other. Page 217.

Celtic: a reference to the Celts and their culture that thrived throughout much of Europe and as far west as the British Isles from several hundred years B.C. until being conquered by the Romans, especially during the first century B.C. and the first century A.D. The Celts are today represented chiefly by the Irish, Scottish, Welsh and Bretons (inhabitants of *Brittany,* a region of northwestern France). Page 113.

censorship: the system or practice of removing or prohibiting anything considered to be inappropriate for public knowledge. Page 49.

Center, Dr.: Dr. Abraham Center of a Savannah, Georgia, mental asylum where much early Dianetics research was conducted in the late 1940s. The whole of the Savannah "charity list," some twenty men and women in all, were eventually discharged from the asylum following LRH employment of Dianetics procedures. Page 118.

Central Intelligence Agency: a United States Government agency created in 1947. The stated purpose of the CIA is to gather information (intelligence) and conduct secret operations to protect the country's national security. Page 36.

chain banks: a series of banks that share the same name and whose activities are supervised or coordinated by a centralized management body. Chain banks usually consist of many bank branches. Page 53.

Chamber of Deputies: a *chamber* is a legislative body in some countries. In Mexico, the *Chamber of Deputies* is one of the two legislative bodies of the national government. Page 236.

Chambers, Whittaker: (1901–1961) confessed Soviet spy who was the United States' chief witness in the 1949 perjury trials of former US State Department official Alger Hiss (1904–1996). Chambers accused Hiss of membership in a Communist espionage ring that he himself had been a part of and he produced microfilms of confidential government documents that he stated Hiss had given him in the 1930s to send to the Soviet Union. Page 155.

championing: protecting, defending, supporting or fighting for. Page 18.

charlatan(s): one who pretends to have expert knowledge or skill; a fake. Page 141.

charter: a formal written statement describing the rights, special privileges, immunity and exemption granted to a particular person or group. Page 134.

chastised: criticized or condemned severely. Page 89.

check: stop or slow the progress of. Page 86.

chicanery: trickery or deception. Page 10.

chilling: causing a feeling of dread or horror. Page 107.

chin, take it on the: figuratively, receive a severe blow, likened to a boxer who is hit on the point of the chin. Page 178.

Chisholm, Brock: (1896–1971) a Canadian psychiatrist who held such positions as Canada's Deputy Minister of Health and Welfare in the mid-1940s and president of the World Federation for Mental Health in the 1950s. Page 33.

Church, Frank: Frank Forrester Church (1924–1984), United States senator from Idaho (1957–1981). In 1975, he served as chairman of the Select Committee to Study Governmental Operations with Respect to Intelligence Activities, a Congressional Committee that investigated abuses of power by the Central Intelligence Agency and the Federal Bureau of Investigation. The committee reported numerous instances of intelligence activities that "threatened and undermined the constitutional rights of Americans." Page 121.

Citizens Commission on Human Rights (CCHR): a public-benefit organization established in 1969 by the Church of Scientology that exposes psychiatric violations of human rights and actively works to eliminate harmful practices in the field of mental health. Page 126.

civil servant: a person working in the *civil service,* those government departments or agencies that are not legislative, judicial or military. Examples of this include postal workers and those who do city planning. Page 101.

clique: a small and exclusive party or group of people associated for unworthy or selfish ends, such as to impose themselves as supreme authority in a particular field. Page 10.

coercive: using force or threats to make somebody do something against his or her will. Page 49.

coffers: supplies or stores of money often belonging to a government or organization. From a box or chest, especially one for valuables or money. Page 205.

Cold War: hostilities short of armed conflict that existed after World War II (1939–1945) between the Soviet Union and countries supporting the Communist system, and the democratic countries of the Western world under the leadership of the United States. Page 6.

colonial Asia: regions of Asia that were *colonies,* countries or areas controlled by another country, such as parts of China, controlled by Japan; the Philippines, by the US; India, by the British; areas in Southeast Asia, by France. Following the Second World War, most of these colonies became independent countries. Page 3.

combine(s): a group of people or companies acting together for a commercial purpose. Page 90.

come to pass: happened; occurred. Page 5.

commensurate: corresponding in extent or degree; proportionate. Page 5.

Commissar: an official of the Communist Party in charge of political indoctrination and the enforcement of party loyalty. Page 89.

commitment (procedures, etc.): the steps taken to cause someone to be *committed,* confined in a mental institution. Page 63.

Commoner, Barry: American biologist and college professor (1917–) who helped initiate the modern environmental movement. Author of several books concerning damage to the environment caused by nuclear testing and by Capitalist technologies, he also founded a political party (Citizens Party) to forward his ecological message and ran for president of the United States in the 1980 election. Page 219.

Commonwealth: an association of countries including England, Wales, Scotland, Northern Ireland and various self-governing states (such as Canada, Australia, New Zealand, South Africa) that were formerly part of the British Empire. The Commonwealth was formally established in 1931 to encourage trade and friendly relations. Page 25.

Communism: the political theory or system in which all property and wealth is owned by all the members of a classless society and a single party with absolute power runs the economic and political systems of the state. Extensive restrictions are enforced on personal and religious liberties and freedom, and individual rights are overruled by the collective needs of the masses. Page 86.

Community Psychiatry: a branch of psychiatry concerned with the supposed detection, prevention and treatment of mental disorders within specific social, cultural or geographic areas. Page 151.

compass: literally, a device for finding directions, usually with a magnetized needle that automatically points to the north. Hence, figuratively, something that helps one find the correct course of action. Page 208.

Comte, Auguste: (1798–1857) French philosopher and a founder of sociology. He was secretary to socialist Claude Henri de Rouvroy, Comte de Saint-Simon (1760–1825), whose influence is reflected in much of Comte's work. Page 143.

Comte de Saint-Simon: Claude Henri de Rouvroy, Comte de Saint-Simon (1760–1825), French philosopher who advocated the creation of a social order directed by men of science and industry in which all people would work and receive rewards equal to their labor. No person could inherit wealth and all individuals would begin life on an equal basis. (*Comte,* or *count,* is a title of a nobleman.) Page 54.

concerted: jointly arranged or carried out; done with great effort. Page 230.

conditioning: a method thought to control or influence the way people or animals behave or think by using a gradual training process. Page 105.

Condon, Richard: (1915–1996) American novelist, playwright and crime writer best known for his novels *The Manchurian Candidate* (1959) and *Prizzi's Honor* (1982). *See also* **Manchurian Candidate, The.** Page 107.

confidence trickster(s): someone who is a professional swindler using *confidence tricks,* in which the victim is induced to hand over valuables or money as a "token" of trust in the swindler. Literally, playing tricks by gaining the confidence of the victim. Page 173.

confreres: fellow members of a profession; colleagues. Page 198.

confront: 1. present for acknowledgment, contradiction, etc.; set face to face. Page 63.
2. face without flinching or avoiding. Page 118.

con game(s): shortened form of *confidence game,* a method of professional swindling in which somebody obtains something of value by first gaining the trust of the victim, then betraying that person. Page 41.

Congressional: of or pertaining to *Congress,* the elected group of politicians that is responsible for making the law in the United States. It consists of two parts: the House of Representatives (the lower of the two lawmaking bodies) and the Senate (the higher of the two). Page 75.

Congressional Black Caucus: a group of African-American members of the United States Congress that focuses on issues of particular interest to black Americans. It was formed in the early 1970s. A *caucus* is a group within a legislative body seeking to represent a specific interest or influence a particular area of policy. Page 232.

Congressional Committee: a group composed of members of Congress that conducts investigations and considers, evaluates and recommends action on legislation. *See also* **Congressional.** Page 76.

Congress of Industrial Organizations: an association of labor unions formed in the late 1930s. It merged with the American Federation of Labor in 1955, forming the *AFL-CIO,* a labor organization made up of local unions throughout the United States. Page 76.

conscript: made up of persons who have been forced to join the army and fight. Page 21.

constitution: an instrument founding or modifying a government. *See also* **instrument.** Page 15.

Constitution: a document containing the fundamental laws of the United States that was put into effect on 4 March 1789. It establishes the form of the national government and defines the rights and liberties of the American people. Page 16.

contentious: causing or likely to cause argument, conflict or severe difference of opinion. Page 24.

convict labor: work imposed upon criminals in addition to imprisonment. Page 71.

coon: an offensive term for a black person. Page 69.

corn and games: food and entertainment; a reference to the practice in ancient Rome of feeding people and providing official public amusement (circuses in the arena) in an attempt to prevent unrest and to control the populace. Also called *bread and circuses. Corn* is a general term for all cereals, such as wheat, barley, oats, corn, rice, etc. Page 20.

corridor(s): literally, a main passage in a large building, often with a series of rooms opening onto it. Also used figuratively for a place of gossip or intrigue outside a meeting hall. Page 15.

Counterintelligence: the group of government and military bodies responsible for gathering information about enemy spies, blocking their activities and supplying them with false information. Page 75.

country, line of: an area of activity, involvement or the like. *Line* here is used to mean a course of conduct, action or procedure; an area of activity. *Country* means region, district or area and is used here figuratively in reference to a field of endeavor or pursuit. Page 34.

court-martialed: brought before a *court-martial,* a trial by a military or naval court of officers appointed by a commander to try persons for offenses under military law. Page 20.

court, upper: any court that can hear and decide on cases from other courts; a court of appeals. Page 71.

cow: frighten with threats or a show of force. Page 136.

cowered: crouched, especially for shelter, from danger or in timidity. Page 201.

crackpot: bizarre, eccentric and impractical; crazy. Page 211.

cram course: an intensive course of study designed to review or teach material needed for a specific purpose or, often, material previously taught but not mastered. Page 172.

credence: acceptance based on the degree to which something is believable or thought of as real or valid. Page 206.

credulous: too easily convinced that something is true. Page 38.

creed: a system or set of religious beliefs or opinions. Page 15.

crematorium: a furnace where bodies are incinerated (burned to ashes); a building with such a furnace in it. Page 174.

Cromwell: Oliver Cromwell (1599–1658), English military leader who defeated the forces of King Charles I and installed a government (1653–1658) run on strict religious principles. Viewed as a dictator who had done away with the traditional constitutional system, he had no widespread support and after his death England restored a king to the throne. Page 75.

crowned heads of Austria: a reference to ruling members of the Austrian monarchy during the early twentieth century. Specifically, Archduke Francis Ferdinand (1863–1914), heir to the Austrian crown, was assassinated on 28 June 1914. Then, following defeat in World War I (1914–1918) and the subsequent collapse of the Austrian empire, Emperor Charles I (1887–1922) was removed from power and banished from his homeland. Page 128.

cry is up: an urgent appeal, request or demand is happening at a particular time. Page 171.

crystallized: became fixed or definite. Page 220.

Cuban Revolution: a 1958 Cuban uprising that overthrew the military dictatorship of Fulgencio Batista (1901–1973) and brought the government of revolutionary leader Fidel Castro (1926–) to power. The revolution established the only Communist state in the Western Hemisphere and produced significant changes in the economic and social structure of Cuban society. Page 88.

curtain(s): used to indicate the end of something, as in *"the curtain fell"* or simply *"curtains,"* from a theatrical performance where the stage curtain is lowered to indicate that the performance is over. Page 20.

custodian: someone entrusted with the safekeeping, care and guardianship of something. Used ironically. Page 64.

cynicism: the attitudes or beliefs of a cynical person, someone who is doubtful or distrusting of the motives, goodness or sincerity of others. Page 20.

cytological: of, relating to or by the methods of cytology. *See also* **cytology.** Page 217.

cytology: the branch of biology dealing with the structure, function and life history of cells. Page 220.

czar: one having great power or authority in a particular field, from the former emperors of Russia, who ruled with complete authority. Page 97.

Czar: a reference to Nicholas II (1868–1918), who was the last czar (emperor) to rule Russia. He reigned from 1894 to 1917, when the Russian Revolution was at its height and he and his family were imprisoned. Eight months later they were assassinated, bringing an end to the Russian monarchy. Page 128.

Czarist Russia: Russia under the *czars,* Russian emperors who had absolute power. Czarist Russia existed from the mid-1500s until the 1917 Russian Revolution. The revolution overthrew the czar and established a Communist government. Page 42.

Czechoslovakia: a former republic in Central Europe, in existence from 1918 until 1993 and bounded by Poland, Germany, Austria, Hungary and Ukraine. In 1993 it divided into the Czech Republic and Slovakia. Page 42.

D

Dachau (concentration camp): a German concentration camp organized in 1933 and ended in 1945. It held more than 160,000 slave laborers and had facilities for mass murder and cremation of the camp's inmates. It was also a medical research center where experiments were carried out on more than 3,500 inmates. Dachau is a town 10 miles (16 kilometers) northwest of Munich, Germany. Page 168.

dark: characterized by evil or wickedness. Page 16.

Dark Ages: the period in European history from the A.D. 400s to the 1000s. The term refers to the intellectual darkness, such as lack of learning and schooling during this period, the loss of many artistic and technical skills, and the virtual disappearance of the knowledge of the previous Greek and Roman civilizations. This period was also marked by many wars, gruesome executions and general brute force. Page 174.

Das Kapital: a book written by German philosopher, economist and socialist Karl Marx (1818–1883), dealing with economic, social and political relations within the society. In the book Marx attacked Capitalism as evil and laid out the political theories of Communism. He demanded that all industries be controlled by the state and urged an end to private ownership of public utilities, transportation facilities and means of production. Containing the basic beliefs of Communism, the book became the bible of the Communist Party. Page 86.

D-day: the day chosen for the beginning of a military operation or other major venture, from the date (6 June 1944) when the Allied forces landed in northern France to begin the liberation of occupied Europe in World War II (1939–1945). Page 144.

death camp(s): a reference to a concentration camp for the incarceration of political prisoners or opponents, civilians, religious dissenters, etc., in which the inmates are unlikely to survive or to which they have been sent to be executed, such as those used for exterminating prisoners under the rule of Hitler in Nazi Germany during World War II (1939–1945). Page 109.

death-kiss: characteristic of a *death kiss,* an act or association that seems harmless but that ultimately causes ruin, from the betraying kiss with which Judas (one of Jesus's disciples) pointed out Jesus, leading to his arrest and crucifixion. Page 128.

death march: a song of mourning or grief, especially one about death or intended for a funeral. Also called a *funeral march.* Page 9.

decamp: leave a place abruptly or secretly; run away. Page 69.

decimated: killed off or destroyed in large numbers. Page 144.

decorated: given a medal or other honor or award to acknowledge bravery, dedication or achievement. Page 3.

decry: speak out against strongly and openly; denounce. Page 36.

definitive: having a fixed and final form; providing a solution or final answer; satisfying all requirements. Page 162.

defying belief: being extreme or very strange and therefore impossible to believe. Page 42.

degenerates: people who have declined, as in morals or character, from a standard considered proper and acceptable. Page 136.

Delaware: a state in the eastern United States, on the Atlantic coast. Page 167.

delegation: one or more persons appointed or chosen to represent others, as in a conference. Page 163.

delusional: relating to, based on or marked by delusions (false, persistent beliefs maintained in spite of evidence to the contrary). Page 155.

demilitarized: deprived of military organization or potential. Page 195.

Democratic National Convention: a large meeting held by the Democratic Party every four years, prior to the presidential election, to select candidates and adopt the principles and policies for the party. The Democratic Party is one of the two main political parties in the United States (the other being the more conservative Republican Party). The Democratic Party follows a liberal program favoring a strong central government and traditionally represents organized labor and minorities. Page 16.

demoniac: possessed, produced or influenced as if by a demon. Page 128.

depersonalize(d): deprive of personality or individuality; make somebody lose his or her sense of personal identity and external reality. Page 21.

depression: a period of drastic decline in the national economy, characterized by decreasing business activity, falling prices and unemployment. The best known of such periods is the Great Depression, which occurred in the 1930s. Page 90.

deprivation: the act of taking away or preventing from having. Page 33.

descend (on, upon): arrive at a place suddenly or in a way that brings something to notice. Page 16.

despotism: the exercise of absolute authority. Page 44.

detainee(s): a person who is held in custody. Page 34.

determinism: the action of causing, affecting or controlling. Page 122.

detonator, torpedo: a device used to explode a *torpedo,* a cylindrical self-propelled missile that is launched from an aircraft, ship or submarine and travels underwater to hit its target. Page 76.

Dewey: John Dewey (1859–1952), American philosopher, educator and author who was strongly influenced by modern psychology and the theory of evolution. The poor performance of today's educational system has been traced by many to changes introduced by Dewey. Page 86.

Dianetics: Dianetics is a forerunner and substudy of Scientology. Dianetics means "through the mind" or "through the soul" (from Greek *dia,* through, and *nous,* mind or soul). It is a system of coordinated axioms which resolve problems concerning human behavior and psychosomatic illnesses. It combines a workable technique and a thoroughly validated method for increasing sanity, by erasing unwanted sensations and unpleasant emotions. Page 59.

dictation: the giving of authoritative orders or commands. Page 53.

Diogenes: (412?–323? B.C.) Greek philosopher who rejected social conventions and was said to have lived in poverty, begged for food and used a barrel for shelter to show his disregard for possessions. According to tradition, he once lit a lamp in broad daylight and went through the streets looking for an honest man. Page 165.

dislocated: persons who have been put out of their usual place, position or relationship. Page 4.

dismemberment: the action of reducing, reorganizing or discontinuing the services or parts of (a company, government agency, etc.). Page 194.

Disraeli: Benjamin Disraeli (1804–1881), British writer and prime minister (1868 and 1874–1880) who for more than three decades exerted a profound influence on British politics. While maintaining a conservative stance, he supported policies ranging from extension of voting privileges to the working class, to diplomatic measures that raised England's influence internationally. Page 10.

dissent: disagreement with the methods or goals of a group, organization, official decision or the like. Page 177.

dissenter(s): people who disagree with the methods or goals of a group, organization, official decision or the like. Page 136.

dissident: one who is *dissident,* differing, often in a quarrelsome manner, with an established political system or belief of a country or people. Page 16.

dissolution: termination or destruction by breaking down, disrupting or dispersing. Page 89.

dizzy: so high as to make somebody giddy. Used figuratively. Page 167.

DNA: a substance found in all living organisms, responsible for passing along hereditary characteristics from one generation to the next. DNA is an abbreviation for *d*eoxyribo*n*ucleic *a*cid. Page 219.

docile: quiet; unlikely to cause trouble; easy to manage. Page 98.

dog boy: literally, the boy in charge of the dogs. Used figuratively for someone overseeing those people who, like "good dogs," are bland, mild and not at all aggressive. Page 147.

dog, good: characteristic of a person who is bland, mild and not at all aggressive. Page 7.

dog-in-the-manger: characteristic of one who will neither use something himself nor let another use it; an allusion to the fable of the dog that stationed himself in a manger and, though unable to eat the hay in the manger himself, would not let the ox or horse eat it either. Page 164.

dogma: a set of beliefs, opinions, principles, etc., that are laid down and held as true and not subject to question. From the Greek word *dogma,* opinion. Page 223.

doling out: distributing something. Page 116.

donning: putting on (an item of clothing). Page 60.

dope: of or relating to illegal drugs, especially marijuana, that induce a state of extreme excitement and happiness or satisfy an addiction. Page 33.

dossier: an accumulation of records, reports, pertinent data and documents bearing on a single subject of study or investigation. Page 53.

dramatizing: thinking or acting as would an actor playing his dictated part and going through a whole series of irrational actions. Page 209.

dropped in: paid a casual or unexpected visit. Page 76.

droves: very large numbers of people. Page 141.

drying out: of a drug addict or alcoholic, undergoing a course of treatment designed to break dependence on a drug or alcohol. Page 183.

due process of law: the courses of legal proceedings established by the legal system of a nation or state to protect individual rights and liberties. No citizen may be denied his or her legal rights and all laws must conform to fundamental, accepted legal principles, as the right of the accused to confront his or her accusers. Page 201.

Dunsany, Lord: Edward John Moreton Drax Plunkett Dunsany (1878–1957), Irish poet, dramatist and novelist. Many of his writings deal with "the mysterious kingdoms where geography ends and fairyland begins." Dunsany employed this background to satirize human behavior in a simple, charming style. Page 186.

dwells: has a place in, as if by living there; resides. Page 236.

E

Eastern Bloc: the group of countries (bloc) that consisted of the Soviet Union and its allies. *See also* **Soviet Union.** Page 194.

École Polytechnique: French engineering school founded in 1794 for training civil and military administrators. It is considered one of the most prestigious institutions of higher education in France. Page 143.

Ecstasy: an illegal amphetamine-based synthetic drug used to create an artificial feeling of well-being or joy. *Amphetamines* are any of a group of powerful, habit-forming drugs, called stimulants, that act on the central nervous system (the brain and the spinal cord), increasing heart rate and blood pressure while reducing fatigue. Serious mental problems can develop from repeated use. Page 204.

egregious: remarkable or extraordinary in a bad way; outstanding for undesirable qualities. Page 231.

Eire: the Irish name for Ireland. Page 45.

élan vital: according to the philosophy of Henri Bergson (1859–1941), a creative life force present in all living things. In French, the word *élan* means forward thrust or impulse; motion inspired by strong or intense feeling. *Vital* means of life. Page 219.

elbow of, at the: very close to a person, group or the like. Page 53.

electroconvulsive: of or having to do with the psychiatric "treatment" of *electric shock,* a barbaric procedure wherein an electric current is applied to the person through electrodes placed on the head. It causes a severe convulsion (uncontrollable shaking of the body) or seizure (unconsciousness and inability to control movements of the body) and results in memory loss and permanent physical damage, leaving the person an emotional vegetable. Page 34.

embody: give a tangible or visible form to (an idea or quality) through words, actions, etc. Page 6.

E-Meter: an Electropsychometer, a specially designed instrument that helps the Scientology auditor locate areas of spiritual distress or travail in a person. The Electropsychometer is a religious artifact and can only be used by Scientology auditors or auditors in training. It does not diagnose or cure anything. (An auditor is a Dianetics or Scientology practitioner. The word *auditor* means one who listens; a listener.) Page 24.

eminently: notably; extremely; very. Page 198.

encroaching: intruding gradually or stealthily, often taking away somebody's authority, rights or property. Page 37.

endocrine: of or having to do with the system of glands which secretes hormones (chemical substances) from certain organs and tissues in the body. These glands and their hormones regulate the growth, development and function of certain tissues and coordinate many processes within the body. For example, some of these glands increase blood pressure and heart rate during times of stress. Page 220.

engender: bring into existence; produce. Page 16.

enigma: something that is not easily understood; a puzzling or unexplainable situation, event or occurrence. Page 114.

enumerate: name or mention one by one; specify. Page 205.

Equestrian order: in ancient Rome, a specially privileged class of prominent citizens. Originally, members of the Equestrian order were those who had served in the cavalry of the Roman legions. They were called *equites,* a Latin word meaning horsemen or knights. Over the centuries, the financial and political power of this class expanded at the expense of the common people. Page 29.

equitable: fair and reasonable in a way that gives equal treatment to everyone. Page 23.

espionage: the use of spies by a government or organization to discover the military, political or technical secrets of other nations or organizations. Page 34.

espouse: make one's own; adopt or embrace. Page 50.

Establishment: the group of people who hold power in a society or social group and dominate its institutions. Page 9.

ethics: a system of moral principles governing the appropriate conduct for a particular group, profession, etc. Page 223.

evocatively: in a manner that brings strong images, memories or feelings to the mind. Page 4.

execrated: declared to be evil or detestable; denounced. Page 127.

executive branch: one of the three main sections of the United States Government. The executive branch, headed by the president, is in charge of executing plans, actions or laws and of administering public affairs. These functions are distinct from those of the other two main sections: the *legislative branch,* which makes the nation's laws, and the *judicial branch,* which interprets the laws if questions arise. Page 5.

executive order: an order having the force of law issued by the president of the United States to the army, navy or other part of the executive branch of the government. For example, Executive Order 9066, issued during World War II (1939–1945) by President Franklin D. Roosevelt, authorized the military to exclude whomever they felt necessary from military areas. This order served as the basis for the removal of approximately 120,000 ethnic Japanese—two-thirds of them American citizens—from the Pacific coast, resulting in their being relocated to ten camps set up in the interior of the US. Page 42.

exhorted: urged strongly; advised; warned. Page 208.

expatriate: situated outside a native country, as some governments during World War II (1939–1945) that were set up outside the boundaries of their native countries and from there worked to overthrow the occupation forces of Nazi Germany. Page 20.

exponents: people who are representatives or symbols of something or who speak out in favor or support of it. Page 127.

express elevator: an elevator that is direct or fast, especially one that makes few or no intermediate stops. Page 210.

extermination camp: a camp for the mass murder of human beings, applied especially to the camps set up by Nazi Germany during World War II (1939–1945). Page 20.

extortion: the obtaining of money from someone by using force, threats or other unfair or illegal methods. Page 117.

eye to, with an: with a view to; with the object or intention of. Page 106.

F

fabric, social: the framework or basic structure of society. Page 7.

fallacious: deceptive or liable to mislead people; erroneous. Page 64.

False Data Stripping: a procedure that helps a person sort out the true facts regarding a subject from the conflicting bits and pieces of information or opinion he has acquired. This eliminates the false data and lets him get on with it. Page 207.

fanfare: a noisy or showy display, from the use in music of a *fanfare,* a short, loud dramatic series of notes played on trumpets, as in marking the start of an event, the entrance of someone important or the like. Page 159.

Fascism: a governmental system, led by a dictator having complete power, that forcibly suppresses opposition and criticism and regiments all industry, commerce, etc. Page 77.

fascistic: of or relating to Fascism. *See also* **Fascism.** Page 60.

Federal Bureau of Investigation: a bureau of the United States Government that deals with matters of national security, interstate crime and crimes against the government. Page 5.

Federal Emergency Management Agency: abbreviation *FEMA,* an agency of the United States Government formed in 1979 to coordinate the activities of several other disaster agencies. FEMA has the purpose to coordinate federal disaster relief activities for events such as hurricanes, earthquakes, floods, wildfires and terrorist attacks. Page 53.

Federal Marshal: a US federal law enforcement officer who carries out court orders in a given federal judicial district and whose duties are similar to those of a local sheriff (the chief law enforcement officer of a county, charged in general with the keeping of the peace and the execution of court orders). *Federal* means having to do with the central government of the United States. Page 223.

fellow: a member of a learned society. Page 131.

festering: of a sore, becoming increasingly infected and thus worsening. Used figuratively to describe a dangerous, harmful or evil influence that is becoming increasingly severe. Page 173.

feudal baron(s): a lord or nobleman during the Middle Ages who held land in exchange for military and other services given, as laid out in the *feudal system,* a social and political system in which the land, worked by peasants who were bound to it, was held by low-ranking nobles in exchange for military and other services given to high-ranking nobles. Page 89.

fiber: an element that imparts strength, toughness or durability. Page 200.

fiddle the books: alter or falsify the financial or business records of a company, government, etc., for dishonest gain. Page 172.

fifth column: during the Spanish Civil War (a war between 1936 and 1939 involving rebel forces under Spanish General Francisco Franco and the Spanish Government), a group of sympathizers within Madrid worked secretly to help rebel forces overthrow the government. These sympathizers were called the *fifth column* in 1936, when one of Franco's men made a radio broadcast in an attempt to demoralize government forces, stating, "We have four columns on the battlefield against you and a fifth column inside your ranks." *Fifth column* has since come to mean any group of secret agents or traitors at work within a country. A *column* is a military formation of troops in which elements proceed one after the other. Page 105.

Filipino: a native or inhabitant of the Philippine Islands. Page 71.

First Book: *Dianetics: The Modern Science of Mental Health,* the basic text on Dianetics techniques, written by L. Ron Hubbard and first published in 1950. Page 221.

fiscal: of or relating to government expenditures, revenues and debt. Page 83.

Flaming Youth era: the time period of the 1920s, when young people in America adopted a lifestyle characterized by vigorous and unrestrained behavior or ways. Young women cut their hair short and wore short skirts. The favorite haunts were nightclubs where young people drank illegal liquor (Prohibition was in force from 1920 to 1933), listened to jazz (the latest musical craze) and danced. Page 184.

fledgling: young, new or inexperienced. Page 229.

flight surgeon: a medical officer in the US Air Force who is trained in aviation medicine. Page 25.

flimflam artist: someone who attempts to cheat or swindle someone through skillful persuasion or clever manipulation of the victim. Page 186.

flout: openly disregard; show contempt or scorn for. Page 44.

fly-by-night: temporary and unreliable, said of a person, corporation, etc. This phrase originated in the late eighteenth century to describe someone who, to escape creditors, sneaks or "flies" away at night. Page 167.

Food and Drug Administration: the United States federal agency that is responsible for trade in and safety of food and drugs. Page 24.

foodstuff(s): a substance that can be eaten, especially one of the basic elements of the human diet. Page 4.

fool some of the people: a reference to an old saying (or any of its variations) that has been used by many writers since ancient Greek times: "You can fool some of the people some of the time, but you can't fool all of the people all of the time." Page 136.

foray: invade something such as a group or organization in order to search out and take profits. Page 235.

foreclose: take possession of a mortgaged property as a result of someone's failure to keep up mortgage payments. A *mortgage* is an agreement by which someone borrows money from an organization or individual against security of some kind. To guarantee the loan will be paid back, the loaning organization or individual has the right to take possession of property (usually land, buildings, etc.) owned by the person receiving the loan if he fails to pay back the money. Page 86.

foreshadowing: coming earlier and being an indication of what is to come. Page 3.

"for it": about to suffer unpleasant consequences, especially of one's own actions or omissions. Page 141.

forum: an open discussion (or a place for such discussion) about matters of general interest. Originally, a *forum* was a public square or marketplace in ancient Roman cities where business was conducted and the law courts were situated. Page 37

foster: promote or encourage, as in terms of growth, development or the like. Page 46.

Founding Fathers: American statesmen of the Revolutionary period (late 1700s) who advocated and fought for fundamental principles, such as that all people are created equal and with certain rights, that governments exist to protect these rights and that they receive their power to rule only through agreement of the people. Many of these statesmen came together as delegates to the Constitutional Convention in Philadelphia in 1787 (four years after the American Revolution) and set down their ideas of government in the Constitution of the United States. Page 10.

franc(s): the basic monetary unit of France until 2002, when it was replaced by the *euro,* the main monetary unit of most European countries. Page 98.

fraying: becoming weakened or strained, likened to a piece of cloth that becomes worn at the edge. Page 7.

***Freedom* magazine:** a magazine published by the Church of Scientology since 1968 that is renowned for its exposure of human rights abuses and investigative journalism. *Freedom* has broken important stories on the forced drugging of schoolchildren, government chemical and biological warfare experimentation and psychiatric brutalities. Page 1.

Freedom of Information Act: a law enacted in 1966 requiring that government records (except those relating to national security, confidential financial data and law enforcement) be made available to the public on request. Page 18.

free enterprise: an economic system or practice of permitting individuals and private businesses to operate in competitive markets with a minimum of governmental control, primarily limited to protecting the rights of individuals rather than directly supervising the economy. Page 88.

free hand: complete freedom to take action or make decisions. Page 60.

"free" world: an ironic reference to the *free world,* the nations of the world that function chiefly under democratic systems rather than under Totalitarianism or Communism. Page 69.

French National Institute of Health and Medical Research: a scientific research organization dedicated to public health. It was created in 1964 with the objective to improve understanding of human diseases. Page 217.

French Revolution: a revolution in France (1789–1799) that overthrew the French monarchy and aristocratic class, and the system of privileges they enjoyed. Page 88.

Fromm-Reichmann, Frieda: (1889–1957) German psychoanalyst and psychiatrist. Trained in Freudian techniques, she immigrated to the United States in the early 1930s. Her book *Principles of Intensive Psychotherapy* (1950) described how a therapist should work with a patient and stressed the need for understanding between the therapist and the patient and the ability to share feelings and considerations. Page 124.

front: a stated area of activity or operations. Page 15.

front group(s): a group that serves as a cover or disguise for some other group or activity, especially one that is disreputable or illegal in nature. Page 26.

frontman: an apparently respectable person who lends his prestige to a group as its public representative or leader while acting as a cover for illegal or secret activities. Page 25.

fruitful: abundantly productive (of anything, whether beneficial or harmful). Page 1.

function: intellectual powers; mental action; thought, as contrasted with *structure,* how something is built or its physical design. Page 220.

futility: lack of usefulness or effectiveness; pointlessness. Page 42.

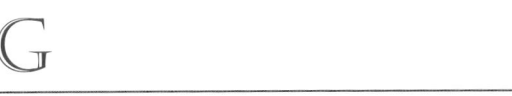

gainfully: in a manner that is profitable or by which something can be gained. Page 223.

General Assembly: the main deliberative body of the United Nations, composed of delegations from member nations. Page 235.

Genghis Khan: (ca. 1162–1227) Mongol emperor and general. Under his military leadership, the Mongols conquered vast portions of northern China and southwestern Asia. Page 170.

genus: origin. From the Latin *genus,* meaning origin, birth or race. Page 31.

geopolitical: of or pertaining to *geopolitics,* political relations among nations, especially as they involve claims and disputes pertaining to borders, territories, etc. Page 1.

germ: something that serves as a source or initial stage for subsequent development; basis. Page 95.

glib: thoughtlessly superficial and shallow. Page 198.

G-Man (G-Men): an agent for the Federal Bureau of Investigation. *G* is an abbreviation of *government.* Page 60.

gold dollar-based: based on a dollar that has a value defined by that of gold. Until 1971 the US dollar, which was used for most international commercial and financial transactions, had a fixed value in terms of ounces of gold and, by law, US dollar banknotes could be converted into gold upon demand. This, however, meant that the number of dollars in circulation was fixed and dependent upon the amount of gold physically owned by the US Government. This created tremendous difficulties in the face of economic growth and, starting in 1971, the United States phased out of this system. The US dollar subsequently was not based on any commodity. Page 83.

Golden Years: *golden* here means characterized by great prosperity, happiness and achievement. The term *Golden Years* has been used in reference to the period of high economic growth that followed World War II (1939–1945) and ended in the early 1970s. Page 83.

Goldwater, Barry: (1909–1998) American politician. After two six-year terms as senator from Arizona, Goldwater ran as the Republican candidate for president, losing the election to Democrat Lyndon B. Johnson. He then returned to the Senate from 1968 until his retirement in 1986. Page 155.

good dog: characteristic of a person who is bland, mild and not at all aggressive. Page 7.

good for: (of a person) that may be relied on to pay so much, as in *"he isn't good for any more."* Page 118.

good hats, guys in the: the people whose behavior conforms to certain standards of ideals, morality and virtue; those without corruption. Page 110.

good measure, for: as something extra to what is required, especially to make sure of something. Page 134.

graft: the acquisition of money, gain or advantage by dishonest, unfair or illegal means, especially through the abuse of one's position or influence in politics, business, etc. Page 168.

grain and cane: a reference to the wheat and sugar cane that are grown in Russia and Cuba, respectively. These agricultural products have traditionally formed a large part of the production of these countries. Page 88.

grandeur: the quality or state of being great or grand; very impressive or magnificent. Page 20.

grass-roots: of, concerning or originating with the common or ordinary people, especially as contrasted with the leaders. Page 232.

Griebl-Voss-Hofman-Rumrich ring: a reference to Dr. Ignatz Griebl, Otto Hermann Voss, Johanna Hofman and Guenther Gustave Rumrich, members of a Nazi spy ring operating in and around New York City from 1935 until the ring's eventual discovery and arrest in 1938. All four were found guilty of spying and given prison sentences. Page 76.

grievously: in a manner causing or characterized by severe physical pain or suffering; severely. Page 3.

grinding: causing extreme hardship; difficult to bear; severe. Page 3.

grit one's teeth: use all one's determination to continue in spite of difficulties. Page 94.

gross income: the total amount of money received over a period of time before any usual deductions, such as expenses, have been made. Page 90.

grounded: familiar with the essential details or data of a subject; having training in or knowledge of a subject. Page 223.

Guillotine, Dr.: French physician Joseph-Ignace Guillotin (1738–1814). He recommended that executions use a machine for beheading people, which eventually came to bear his name. It consisted of two posts grooved on the inside to guide a weighted blade down onto and through a person's neck. He considered this a quick and merciful way to die. The guillotine was used in France during the French Revolution (1789–1799) and until the late twentieth century. Page 98.

guise: a false outward appearance. Page 209.

Gulag: a prison or labor camp, especially one for political prisoners, as in Russia under Communist control. The word represents the first letters of Russian words meaning Chief Administration of Corrective Labor Camps. Also used figuratively to mean any place or situation similar to such a prison or labor camp. Page 105.

Gung-ho Group: a group composed of local Scientologists, interested friends and general public members. *Gung-ho* means pull together in Chinese. The group has the purpose of pulling together other groups in the community to work towards the betterment of society and of the area. The group's program works on the motto that a community that pulls together can make a better society for all. Page 37.

H

Haight-Ashbury: a neighborhood in San Francisco, California. During the 1960s Haight-Ashbury became a center for the hippie movement, also known for widespread use of drugs. Page 107.

half-wit: one who does not have all his mental abilities or intelligence; a stupid or senseless person. Page 10.

hallowed: regarded with great respect or reverence. Page 9.

Hamilton, Alexander: (1757–1804) American lawyer and statesman. As the first treasury secretary (1789–1795) of the United States, he established the first *Bank of the United States,* a private corporation operating under a federal charter and authorized to issue money. Page 10.

hampered: kept from moving or acting freely; hindered; impeded. Page 164.

hand, take (someone) in: deal with or undertake the discipline of (someone). Page 124.

hanged, drawn and quartered: the death penalty given to a criminal in England prior to the fifteenth century, usually for a major crime. It consisted of dragging the criminal behind a horse to the site of execution, hanging him briefly, disemboweling him (drawing), beheading him and then chopping the body into four pieces (quartering). Page 201.

hard labor: heavy manual work imposed upon criminals in addition to imprisonment. Page 71.

hardly: 1. barely or to almost no degree; almost not at all. Page 155.
2. in a hard manner, with energy, force or strenuous exertion; vigorously. Page 217.

hard science(s): any science in which data can be precisely determined, calculated or expressed and theories tested. For example, physics, chemistry and biology are hard sciences. Page 217.

harebrained: foolish or reckless. Page 10.

hatched: brought into existence or devised secretly, usually something illegal. Page 16.

have done with: stop having anything to do with. Page 129.

hazarding: tentative or uncertain explanation or guessing about something. Page 219.

H-bomb: short for *hydrogen bomb,* a bomb, more powerful than an atomic bomb, that derives its explosive energy from the fusion (combining) of hydrogen atoms. Page 171.

headshrinker: a humorous reference to a person who deals in the treatment of mental or emotional disorders. Page 53.

heads ready for the basket: a reference to the executions that occurred during the French Revolution (1789–1799), when thousands of people were beheaded under the guillotine, with a basket made ready to receive the severed heads. Page 72.

health minister: the official in charge of the *Ministry of Health,* the former British Government organization responsible for providing information, raising health awareness and education, ensuring the accessibility of health services and monitoring the quality of health services provided to the citizens. A *minister* is a senior member of the British Government who is in charge of a government department or a branch of one. Page 19.

health ministries: governmental agencies or departments responsible for providing information, raising health awareness and education, ensuring the accessibility of health services and monitoring the quality of health services provided to the citizens of their country. They are headed by a health minister or the equivalent for that country. Page 34.

Hearst: William Randolph Hearst (1863–1951), controversial American publisher who established and built the largest chain of newspapers in the United States. His papers were noted for journalism that gains or holds the interest of readers by printing or headlining news stories that are sensational or scandalous, or that involve ordinary news sensationally distorted. Page 50.

heavyweights: people or things with considerable power or influence. Page 106.

heed, pay little: to pay little attention to or notice of (someone or something). Page 11.

Hegel: Georg Wilhelm Friedrich Hegel (1770–1831), one of the most influential German philosophers. His aim was to set forth a philosophical system so comprehensive that it would encompass the ideas of his predecessors and create a conceptual framework in terms of which both the past and future could be philosophically understood. In his written works and published lectures he attempted to present a unified solution to all philosophical problems. Page 10.

heinous: shockingly evil or wicked. Page 23.

hellhole: a terrifying, unbearable or evil place. Page 235.

henchmen: loyal supporters or followers of criminals or corrupt political leaders. Page 136.

heroin: a compound derived from morphine (a drug used in medicine to relieve pain) that is illegally used as a powerful and addictive drug causing a lessened sensation of pain, slowed breathing and depression. Withdrawal symptoms include cramplike pains in the limbs, sweating, anxiety, chills, severe muscle and bone aches, fever and more. If overdosed, it can be fatal. Page 107.

hierarchy: a controlling group of any kind; a body of persons having top authority, sometimes in a system arranged in rank, grade, class, etc. Page 161.

Hilton: of the *Hilton Hotels Corporation,* an American hotel chain operating hundreds of hotels worldwide. Page 147.

Hinckley, Jr., John: John Warnock Hinckley, Jr. (1955–), attempted assassin of United States President Ronald Reagan. In 1981 as the president was leaving a hotel in Washington, DC, Hinckley, a psychiatric patient who was in the crowd, fired several shots, wounding the president and two others. He was tried and found not guilty of the crime by reason of insanity. His violent attack was later attributed to the psychiatric drug Valium, which he had been taking while receiving treatment prior to the assassination attempt. Page 204.

Hiss, Alger: (1904–1996) a former United States Government official who in 1950 was convicted of perjury for denying his association with confessed Soviet spy Whittaker Chambers (1901–1961). Chambers accused Hiss of membership in a Communist espionage ring that he himself had been a part of and produced microfilms of confidential government documents that he stated Hiss had given him in the 1930s to send to the Soviet Union. Hiss was convicted and sentenced to five years in prison, all the while continuing to profess his innocence. Page 177.

hitherto: up to this time; until now. Page 50.

Hitler: Adolf Hitler (1889–1945), German political leader of the twentieth century who dreamed of creating a master race that would rule for a thousand years as the third German Empire. Taking over rule of Germany by force in 1933 as a dictator, he began World War II (1939–1945), subjecting much of Europe to his domination and murdering millions of Jews and others considered "inferior." He committed suicide in 1945 when Germany's defeat was imminent. Page 33.

hocus-pocus: complicated nonsense; something that confuses or destructively misleads. *Hocus-pocus* is an expression without particular meaning, used traditionally in performing magic. Page 98.

holdings: property owned; financial assets. Page 50.

hollow: thorough or complete. Page 3.

holocaust: wholesale or mass destruction of any kind, specifically, in World War II (1939–1945), the systematic extermination by the Nazis of millions of Jews and others deemed "unacceptable." Page 236.

Home Office: the British Government department dealing with law, public order, public safety, immigration, fire, passports, prisons and the police. Page 24.

hoodlum: a gangster or violent criminal. Page 31.

hood(s): an abbreviation for *hoodlum,* which here means a tough-looking, violent young person. Page 31.

hoodwink(ing): deceive or trick. Page 139.

hook, off the: out of trouble, embarrassment or a state of burdensome responsibility; free of a situation that seems difficult or troublesome. Page 147.

Hoover, J. Edgar: (1895–1972) United States Government official and director of the Federal Bureau of Investigation (1924–1972). Page 5.

horde(s): a large number or group (of people, etc.). Page 127.

hovel(s): any small, miserable dwelling; hut. Page 201.

Hubbard Communications Office: the Office of L. Ron Hubbard, originally organized with the purpose of handling and expediting the communication lines of LRH. HCO was later made the division of a Church of Scientology that builds, holds, maintains and mans the organization. It obtains personnel, assigns posts and trains staff, routes incoming and outgoing communications, and maintains ethics and justice among Scientologists on staff and in the area. Page 37.

humanitarian: 1. showing concern for or seeking to improve the welfare and happiness of people. Page 2.
2. someone who has concern for and helps to improve the welfare and happiness of people. Page 2.

humanities: branches of learning concerned with human thought and relations, as distinguished from the sciences; especially literature, philosophy, history, etc. (Originally, the humanities referred to education that would enable a person to freely think and judge for himself, as opposed to a narrow study of technical skills.) Page 128.

human rights: the basic civil, economic, political and social rights of every person, as of freedom, justice and equality. Page 1.

hunger: feel a great need or desire for something; crave. Page 51.

hurumph: used to show a clearing of the throat, especially in a pompous way. Page 185.

hypocrisy: the false claim to or pretense of having admirable principles, beliefs or feelings. Page 34.

I

ice pick: a reference to a psychiatric operation in which an ice pick (a hand tool with a needlelike spike for chipping ice) is forced through the back of the eye sockets, piercing the thin bone that separates the eye sockets from the frontal lobes. The tip of the ice pick is then inserted into the frontal lobes and the nerve fibers connecting these to the rest of the brain are severed, resulting in the patient becoming an emotional vegetable. Page 117.

idealism: the cherishing or pursuit of high or noble principles, purposes, goals, etc. Page 50.

ideology: the doctrines, opinions or way of thinking of an individual, class, etc.; specifically, the body of ideas on which a particular political, economic or social system is based. Page 67.

idle: being without a basis or foundation in fact; groundless. Page 46.

ignoble: not noble in character or quality; dishonorable or mean. Page 88.

ilk: kind, sort or class. Page 209.

ill-fated: ending in, or doomed to, disaster. Page 24.

immunity: exemption or protection from something unpleasant, such as a duty or penalty, to which others are subject. Page 189.

imperiled: brought into danger of harm or loss, especially harm or loss that is likely to happen without delay. Page 152.

inalienable: that may not be taken away or transferred. Page 15.

incipient: beginning; coming into, or in, an early stage of existence; in an initial stage. Page 236.

incisive: sharp, keen, penetrating. Page 1.

incriminating: making (someone) appear guilty of a crime or wrongdoing. Page 60.

incumbent: a person currently holding an indicated position, post, role, office, etc. Page 10.

indict: charge with having committed an offense, a crime or the like. Page 63.

indiscriminate: done without thought about what the result may be, especially when it causes people to be harmed. Page 176.

inept: not in keeping with what is right or proper for the circumstances; likely to fail. Page 20.

inequity: lack of fairness or justice; favoritism or bias. Page 2.

infamy: the disgrace to someone's reputation caused by shameful, criminal or outrageous acts. Page 76.

infiltrate: (of something harmful) penetrate or enter an area, substance, group, etc., as if by spreading over or passing into. Page 50.

inquiry: an official investigation of a matter of public interest to determine the facts. Page 24.

instigator: a person who gets something started. Page 45.

instrument: 1. something that is used for the performance of an action and that serves or contributes to the accomplishment of a purpose, often a tool used for precision work. Page 24.
2. a formal legal document whereby a right is created or confirmed, or a fact recorded; a formal writing of any kind, as an agreement, record, etc. Page 45.

insurgent: rising up against established authority; rebellious; designating or of a revolt or rebellion. Page 21.

intelligence community: people involved in gathering intelligence (secret information about an enemy), such as members of government departments or of the military, whose object is to obtain information, especially by means of a system of spies. A *community* in this context is a group sharing common characteristics and perceived or perceiving itself as distinct in some respect from the larger society within which it exists. Page 6.

interloper: someone who enters a place without any right to do so; an intruder. Page 29.

Internal Revenue Service: the division of the US Department of the Treasury responsible for the collection of income and other taxes and the enforcement of tax laws. Page 16.

International Monetary Fund: an agency of the United Nations that began operating in 1947, responsible for promoting international monetary cooperation and facilitating the expansion of international trade. A key function of the fund is authorizing short-term loans to member countries. Page 95.

International Telephone & Telegraph (ITT): an American telecommunications company, established in 1920. The company expanded internationally and soon became a major telecommunications manufacturer. Throughout the mid-1900s, ITT, as it was most commonly known, acquired more than 250 other companies, including hotels, insurance companies and casinos. Page 59.

Interpol: a private, quasipolice organization (full name, *International Criminal Police Organization*) established to promote mutual cooperation between police authorities around the world. Originally set up in the 1920s in Vienna, Austria, Interpol was taken over by the Nazis during World War II (1939–1945). After the war, the organization relocated in France. As of the end of the twentieth century, Interpol claimed more than 170 member countries. Page 77.

intimating: indicating or making known indirectly; implying. Page 45.

intrinsic: belonging to something as one of the basic and essential elements that make it what it is. Page 18.

Iron Curtain: an impenetrable barrier to communication or information, especially the political, military and ideological barrier erected by the Soviet Union to seal off itself and its eastern European allies from open contact with the West and other noncommunist areas, existing from 1945 at the end of World War II until the fall of eastern European Communist governments between 1989 and 1991. Page 126.

-isms: a distinctive belief, theory, system or practice, from words with the ending *-ism*. Page 88.

J

Jefferson Memorial: a memorial site of prominence in Washington, DC, in the United States, featuring a statue of and honoring Thomas Jefferson (1743–1826). Jefferson was the author of the Declaration of Independence in 1776 and the third president of the United States (1801–1809). Page 60.

Johannesburg: a city located in northeastern South Africa. It is the most important industrial and commercial city in the country. Page 105.

joyride: a course of conduct or action marked by a seeking of pleasure with a reckless disregard of cost or consequences. Literally, a *joyride* is an automobile ride merely for pleasure, often at a reckless speed and in a stolen car. Page 178.

judiciary: the system of courts of law for the administration of justice. Page 67.

juju: a witch doctor who uses *jujus,* objects of any kind superstitiously revered by some African native peoples and used as charms or means of protection. The term *juju* also refers to the supernatural or magical power attributed to such objects or the system of observances connected with them. Page 173.

Jung: Carl Gustav Jung (1875–1961), Swiss psychiatrist and psychologist who first collaborated with Sigmund Freud but parted company and founded his own independent school of thought because he believed Freud placed too much importance on sexual instincts in human behavior. Jung theorized that all humans inherit a "collective unconscious" which contains universal symbols and memories from their ancestral past. This shared unconsciousness causes people to react to situations in ways similar to their ancestors. As an example, he interpreted contemporary phenomena in relation to some aspects of Druidism. Page 113.

jurisprudence: the science or philosophy of law; the systematic knowledge of the laws, customs and rights of men in a state or community necessary for the due administration of justice. Page 59.

Justice Department: an executive department of the United States Government. It enforces federal laws and provides legal advice for the president and the heads of the government's other executive departments. One of the largest agencies within the Department of Justice is the FBI (Federal Bureau of Investigation), which investigates violations of federal laws. Page 5.

K

Kaiser: Wilhelm II (1859–1941), the last emperor of Germany, who pursued an aggressive program of commercial and colonial expansion and who led Germany into World War I (1914–1918). *Kaiser,* the title used by rulers of Germany until 1918, is the German form of the Latin word *caesar,* meaning emperor. Page 132.

keep up appearances: maintain an outward show of acceptable behavior, well-being or the like. Page 98.

Keynes: John Maynard Keynes (1883–1946), English economist and writer. His economic theories, *Keynesian economics,* advocate using government policies and programs to increase employment through vast government spending in times of recession. Page 95.

KGB: abbreviation for *Komitet Gosudarstvennoj Bezopasnosti* (Russian for "Committee for State Security"), the former Soviet Union's secret police, espionage and security agency. Its responsibilities included covert intelligence operations, the protection of Soviet political leaders and border patrol (to keep intruders out and citizens in). Page 143.

kicks: thrills; pleasure; fun. Page 117.

King, Cecil: Cecil Harmsworth King (1901–1987), British newspaper publisher, director of the Bank of England and head of the UK National Association for Mental Health. Page 109.

knoll: a small rounded hill. Page 144.

Korea: a country in East Asia that was divided into two countries in 1948, North Korea (Communist) and South Korea (noncommunist). In June 1950 war broke out between the two countries when North Korea invaded South Korea. Communist China aided North Korea while the United States and numerous other countries aided South Korea. During the war the Chinese and North Koreans used brainwashing techniques on American prisoners in an attempt to convert them to Communism. Page 139.

Kraepelin: Emil Kraepelin (1856–1926), German psychiatrist who developed a classification system for "mental illness." He made distinctions between disorders that he felt were of external origin and thus treatable and those he thought had biological causes and thus incurable. Kraepelin continued to refine his classification, issuing numerous revisions of his several-volume psychiatric textbook, *A Textbook of Psychiatry.* Page 185.

Kutzbrain, Dr.: a humorous made-up name, alluding to the psychiatric practice of cutting (operating) on people's brains. Page 10.

L

labor union: an organization of wage earners that is set up to serve and advance its members' interests in terms of wages, benefits, working hours and conditions. Page 76.

Labour officials: in the United Kingdom, people holding public office who are members or supporters of the *Labour Party,* one of the main political parties, created to support the interests of working people and to promote government ownership of key industries, such as railroads, coal mines, etc. The Labour Party was in power during the late 1940s and again in the 1960s. Page 114.

Lafayette, Marquis de: (1757–1834) French aristocrat and statesman who fought for American independence and was a prominent leader in the early stages of the French Revolution (1789–1799), which overthrew the reigning king. Born into a wealthy family, he had already inherited a huge fortune by 1774. Page 88.

landing card: an identification card issued to a traveler for presentation to the immigration authorities. Page 25.

landmark: marking a significant change or turning point in something. From *landmark,* an event, idea or item that represents a significant or historic development. Page 134.

large, at: as a whole; in general. Page 205.

Lasswell, Harold D.: Harold Dwight Lasswell (1902–1978), American political scientist known for studies of the relationship between personality and politics and for promoting propaganda as a means of convincing the populace that those in power should be followed. Page 135.

Latin: the language of ancient Rome and its empire. Latin was also used in Europe (especially during the Middle Ages, from the 400s to the 1400s) as the language of government officials, doctors, lawyers, scholars and priests. Page 147.

lavishly: in a manner characterized by generous or excessive giving or spending. Page 143.

law of supply and demand: a principle in economics that the price for a product is determined by the level of demand and the quantity available. For example, if the demand exceeds the supply, the price rises, operating to reduce the demand and so enable the supply to meet it and vice versa. Page 173.

lay in: put in place; put in position for action or operation. Page 122.

lead boot: a medieval instrument of torture used for getting confessions from prisoners. One such device consisted of a long iron "boot" in which a prisoner's feet and legs were inserted. Wedges were then driven between the legs, serving to crush the legs and shatter the bones. The lead boot was once a common form of torture used in Scotland, Ireland and France. Page 201.

Lebensohn, Zigmond: (1910–2003) American psychiatrist, a chief advocate of electroshock and chairman of the Department of Psychiatry at Sibley Memorial Hospital, a private hospital in Washington, DC. Page 59.

leftist: favoring radical, reforming or socialist views. Page 194.

legion: constituting a large number; many. Page 231.

legislature(s): an official body of persons, usually chosen by election, with the power to make, change or undo laws. Page 53.

Leipzig: a city in east central Germany, the location of Leipzig University where Wilhelm Wundt (German psychologist) and others developed "modern psychology" in 1879. Page 131.

Lend-Lease: a system established by the US Government in 1941, by which the United States supplied weapons, food, equipment, etc., to some of its allies during World War II (1939–1945) on the agreement that such aid would be repaid after the war. However, after the war objections arose to demanding repayments by some who said, for example, that these US contributions had been offset by the sacrifices made by other countries. Page 97.

lettre(s) de cachet: a letter bearing an official (as a royal) seal and usually authorizing imprisonment without trial of a named person. Page 20.

leveled: aimed or directed at or toward. Page 42.

levied: of a tax, imposed or collected through government authority. Page 90.

Lewis, John L.: John Llewellyn Lewis (1880–1969), American labor leader. From 1920 to 1960 he was head of the United Mine Workers, a labor movement to improve conditions for mine workers. During the late 1930s he helped form the Congress of Industrial Organizations, an association of labor unions, and also served as its first president. Page 76.

libel: any false or damaging written statement about somebody. Page 69.

liberality: the quality or state of being liberal in attitude or principle. *Liberal* refers to a political philosophy that in its theory stresses individualism, rejects authoritarian government and defends freedom of speech, religion and the right to own property. It advocates governmental guarantees of individual rights and civil liberties with tolerance of the ideas and behavior of others. Page 41.

Liberty, Fraternity and Equality: a reference to the national motto of France: "Liberté, Égalité, Fraternité" (Liberty, Equality, Fraternity). This phrase was originally the motto of the French Revolution (1789–1799) and was used by the leaders of the revolution to inspire those who were fighting. Page 143.

light-years: a very great distance, especially in development or progress. Literally, a *light-year* is the distance light travels in one year, which is approximately 5.88 trillion miles (9.46 trillion kilometers), about 63,000 times the distance of the Earth from the Sun. Page 122.

listlessly: in a manner showing little or no interest in anything; uncaringly, apathetically. Page 5.

little people: people who are typical in having a small or average income and minimal power and influence; the common people, especially workers. Page 71.

lobbied: influenced or attempted to influence with regard to policy decisions. Page 59.

lobotomies: psychiatric operations carried out by boring holes into the skull, entering the brain and severing the nerve pathways in the two frontal lobes, resulting in the patient becoming an emotional vegetable. Page 232.

Lodge, Henry Cabot: (1850–1924) American statesman and Republican senator for more than thirty years (1893–1924). Page 97.

lofty: noble, important and admirable. Page 110.

longshoremen: people who work along the shore, on the docks, loading and unloading ships. Page 25.

looms large: appears in a large or significant way. From the literal meaning of *loom,* appear, take shape or come into view. Page 6.

loony bin: an insane asylum or the psychiatric ward of a hospital. Page 212.

lot: 1. a distinct group of anything, such as of people. Page 20.
2. one's condition or experiences in life as determined by luck, fate or chance. Page 211.

LSD: a drug that causes a person to have changes of thought processes, mood and perceptions. In addition to causing frightening experiences, LSD also causes *flashbacks,* visual disturbances that occur long after one has taken the drug. *LSD* is an abbreviation for the chemical compound *lysergic acid diethylamide.* Page 107.

Ludwig: Karl Friedrich Wilhelm Ludwig (1816–1895), professor of physiology at several universities, including Zurich, Vienna and Leipzig. Page 131.

Lycurgus: eighth century B.C. Greek lawmaker. When asked to develop a new form of government for Sparta, he redistributed the land and banned money, thus supposedly making all citizens equal. But control remained in the hands of only a few of its citizens. In the social system created by Lycurgus, strict supervision from birth enforced discipline and military training. Page 86.

lynched: put to death, especially by hanging, by mob action and without legal authority. Page 69.

Macedonian Party: a reference to supporters of foreign conqueror Philip of Macedon (382–336 B.C.) within the Greek senate. While Greece was a democracy, the king of neighboring Macedonia, Philip II, who had already conquered several Greek cities by force, used his money to bribe influential supporters in Athens and obtain a seat in the Greek senate. Now able to exercise his influence over other Greek cities, he set upon a course of military conquests that eventually put an end to Greek liberty. Greece did not regain its freedom from foreign occupation until the early 1800s. Page 51.

Maclean: Donald Maclean (1913–1983), British diplomat and member of the British Foreign Office who supplied information to the Soviet Union on atomic development and on the formation of the North Atlantic Treaty Organization (NATO). *See also* **Burgess.** Page 124.

Madison Avenue: a street in New York City that once was the address of many of the major advertising agencies and public relations firms of the United States. Over the years Madison Avenue has come to be synonymous with the advertising industry in general and the methods, practices, principles and attitudes of mass communications and advertising. Page 89.

Mafia: a secret Italian organization allegedly engaged in smuggling, trafficking in narcotics and other criminal activities in Italy and elsewhere. Page 117.

magnate: a person of great influence, importance or standing in a particular enterprise, field of business, etc. Page 50.

make of: understand, judge or interpret the meaning, truth, nature, etc., of, as in *"That's all I can make of this."* Page 26.

maladjusted: badly or unsatisfactorily adjusted, especially in relationship to one's social circumstances, environment, etc.; unable to cope with the stresses of everyday life. *Adjusted* in this sense means able to deal with and handle the mental and physical factors in one's life with regard to one's own needs and the needs of others. Page 159.

malaise: a condition of general bodily weakness or discomfort, often marking the onset of a disease. Page 191.

malcontent(s): someone who is not satisfied or content with currently prevailing conditions or circumstances. Page 9.

Manchu: a people who originally came from Manchuria (a mountainous region of northeastern China) and set up a powerful dynasty that lasted from the seventeenth century until the beginning of the twentieth century. Page 184.

Manchurian Candidate, The: a novel by American novelist, playwright and crime writer Richard Condon (1915–1996), also released as a motion picture. The story tells of a group of American soldiers in the Korean War who are captured by Chinese Communists and brainwashed. Returned to the US, they have no memory of their capture; however, one of the soldiers has been programed to kill and is part of a Communist assassination plot against various powerful political figures. Page 107.

Manson, Charles: (1934–) infamous and widely sensationalized criminal of the late 1960s; he had a following who lived communally on a ranch in California, practicing free love and taking drugs. He and his followers brutally murdered seven people. Manson was finally caught, found guilty and imprisoned for life. Page 107.

marginal: (of a group within society) having no power or influence because of being forced by those in power to occupy the *margin,* the edge of the group, away from the center of power. Page 232.

mark, taking a: cheating or swindling someone who is a *mark,* a person easily deceived or taken advantage of. Page 186.

Marx, Karl: (1818–1883) German political philosopher, whose theories were a form of *Socialism,* the type of economic system in which the production and distribution of goods are controlled by the government rather than by individuals. Marx stated that the working class would revolt and overthrow Capitalist governments, replacing them with a classless society. His ideas led to the formation of twentieth-century Communism. The summarizing statement of his philosophy is the famous line "From each according to his ability, to each according to his needs." Page 86.

Maryland: a state in the eastern United States on the Atlantic coast, surrounding Washington, DC, on all but one side. Page 168.

material science(s): any of the sciences, such as physics and chemistry, that study and analyze the nature and properties of energy and nonliving matter. *Material* means of or pertaining to matter; physical. Page 217.

matter: the substance, or the substances collectively, out of which a physical object is made or of which it consists. Page 219.

mayhem: unrestrained destruction; infliction of violent injury upon a person or thing. Page 5.

MD: abbreviation of Latin *Medicinae Doctor,* Doctor of Medicine; a physician. Page 223.

mean trick, no: a *trick* is a cunning action or plan that is intended to cheat or deceive. *No mean trick* refers to a trick that is "not shabby" or not a minor accomplishment. Page 178.

Medicare: in the United States, a health insurance program partially funded by the government and covering medical care and hospital treatment for the elderly. It was set up in the mid-1960s. Page 176.

megalomaniac: an individual supposedly affected by a mental disorder characterized by delusions of grandeur (false beliefs concerning one's personality or status, which is thought to be more important than it is) and delusions of wealth, power, etc. Page 155.

mental image picture(s): a picture which is a complete recording, down to the last accurate detail, of every perception present in a moment of pain and partial or full unconsciousness. These mental image pictures have their own force and are capable of commanding the body. Page 221.

mercury: a poisonous, heavy, silver-white metal that is liquid at room temperature. It is used in such things as thermometers, pharmaceuticals, dental fillings and lamps. Also called *quicksilver* or *liquid silver*. Page 151.

Mesmer: Anton Mesmer (1734–1815), Austrian physician who sought to cure people by use of a magnet and a magnetic influence that he felt resided within him, which he could spread to others by touch (often by stroking the arms of the person downward from the shoulder), putting them into a trance. Although his method (an early form of hypnotism) was discredited, others were able to induce this trance state, which eventually came to be called *mesmerism*. Page 122.

methamphetamine(s): a very addictive stimulant drug that is extremely harmful to the central nervous system. It brings about loss of appetite, rapid and irregular heartbeat, increased blood pressure, irritability, anxiety, confusion, convulsions and even death. Page 107.

MI5: (in the UK) the governmental agency (Military Intelligence section 5) responsible for internal security and counterintelligence on British territory. Page 76.

militant: using strong and violent action. Page 194.

militarism: the tendency to regard military efficiency as the supreme ideal of the state and to subordinate all other interests to those of the military. Page 205.

mind-set: a set of beliefs or a way of thinking that determines a person's behavior and outlook; attitude or inclination. Page 116.

ministerial investigation: a reference to the government inquiry into malpractices and violations of human rights in psychiatric hospitals ordered by the South African Minister of Health in 1995. *Ministerial* means relating to a government minister or the minister's department. Page 134.

mirror mazes: systems of paths lined with mirrors, built for amusement and designed to confuse persons trying to find their way out. Used figuratively. Page 220.

misdemeanors: minor criminal offenses. Page 64.

misunderstood: in Scientology, any error or omission in comprehension of a word, concept or symbol. Misunderstoods result in a subsequent inability to perform in those fields in which the misunderstood word, concept, symbol, etc., was encountered. Page 86.

Mitchell, John N.: John Newton Mitchell (1913–1988), attorney general of the United States (1969–1972). His conviction on conspiracy charges for his role in the Watergate scandal led to imprisonment (1977–1978). *See also* **Watergate.** Page 59.

mode: a particular type or form of something. Page 29.

mogul(s): a dominant person in a particular business or field. Page 173.

monetary: of or relating to money or to the organizations and the means by which money is supplied to the economy. Page 1.

moniker: a nickname for something. Page 105.

mores: the customs, social behavior and moral values of a particular group. Page 136.

morgue(s), newspaper: a room or file in a newspaper office containing miscellaneous pieces of information kept for future reference. Page 205.

mortgage: an agreement by which someone borrows money from an organization or individual against security of some kind. To guarantee the loan will be paid back, the loaning organization or individual has the right to take possession of property (usually land, buildings, etc.) owned by the person receiving the loan if he fails to pay back the money. Page 86.

motif: a dominant theme or central idea. Page 198.

mountebank: someone who deceives other people. Page 21.

muddle: a confused or disordered condition; mess. Page 190.

muddle along: cope more or less satisfactorily. Page 88.

munitions: materials used in war, especially weapons and ammunition. Page 168.

murder will out: something will be suddenly disclosed or a mystery will be solved; a misdeed will be made known, usually applied to one of a serious nature. From the literal concept that the crime of murder is so horrible that, no matter how hard someone attempts to hide it, in the end it will always become known. Page 26.

myriad: an indefinitely great number; innumerable. Page 238.

N

Napoleon: Napoleon Bonaparte (1769–1821), French military leader. He rose to power in France by military force, declared himself emperor and conducted campaigns of conquest across Europe until his final defeat by armies allied against him in 1815. Half a million men died in the Napoleonic Wars of 1799–1815. Page 135.

nary: not any. Page 232.

National Guard: in France, an armed force of citizens during the late 1700s, organized for general defense. Page 98.

National Guardsmen: in the United States, soldiers serving in the *National Guard,* the military forces of the individual states, who can be called into active service for emergencies, for national defense, as a police force or the like. Page 59.

National Institute of Mental Health: a United States Government center for research and funding of research on mental illness, established in the late 1940s. The institute is one of several agencies within the Public Health Service of the United States. Page 107.

nationalism: loyalty and devotion to a nation; especially, an attitude, feeling or belief characterized by a sense of national consciousness and an emphasis on loyalty to and the promotion of the culture, interests and political independence of a nation. Page 50.

Nationalist China: also called *Republic of China,* a republic consisting mainly of the island of Taiwan off the southeast coast of mainland China. *Nationalist* refers to supporters of the *Nationalist Party,* a political party that controlled much of China in the early twentieth century. In the late 1940s, with the Chinese communists gaining more territory throughout mainland China, the Nationalists moved to Taiwan and set up a government there that has continued to be separate from the People's Republic of China, the government on the mainland. Page 101.

"National" Mental Health groups: a reference to *National Mental Health Associations,* private, profit-making organizations established in various countries. They are under the World Federation for Mental Health. They work to get laws passed that will enable psychs to pick up people freely and put them into mental hospitals. By using the word *national* in their name, these groups pretend that they are part of a government, but they are not. Page 33.

Naval Intelligence, Office of: the military intelligence agency formed in 1882 to provide for the intelligence, counterintelligence, investigative and security requirements of the United States Navy. Page 75.

Nazi: of or about the National Socialist German Workers' party, which in 1933, under Adolf Hitler, seized political control of the country, suppressing all opposition and establishing a dictatorship over all activities of the people. It promoted and enforced the belief that the German people were superior and that the Jews were inferior (and thus were to be eliminated). The party was officially abolished in 1945 at the conclusion of World War II (1939–1945). *Nazi* is from the first part of the German word for the name of the party, *Nati(onalsozialistische),* which is pronounced *nazi* in German. Page 19.

nervously: in a way that relates to the nerves or the *nervous system,* the network of nerve cells that conveys nerve impulses between parts of the body. Page 131.

net income: the total amount of money left after all necessary expenses, such as taxes, etc., have been paid. Often contrasted with gross income. Page 90.

New Jersey: a state in the eastern United States, on the Atlantic coast, near New York. Page 176.

New Physics: a body of work in theoretical physics that points out the faults in earlier mechanical descriptions of the universe. Arguing instead that the universe has a meaningful design, the New Physics develops theories exploring the connection between physics and such fields as philosophy and religion. Page 217.

New Yorker: a weekly American magazine first published in 1925, known for its literary items and humor. Page 186.

New York Times: a daily newspaper published in New York City since 1851 and, today, distributed nationally. Page 186.

9/11, tragedy of: the destruction, death and suffering that occurred on September 11 (9/11), 2001, at the World Trade Center, a complex in New York City that included twin skyscrapers (the tallest in the US at 110 stories). These buildings were destroyed when two jetliners, hijacked by terrorists, were flown into them, causing the worst building disaster in recorded history and the deaths of some 2,800 people. Page 116.

1984: a famous satirical novel by English author George Orwell (1903–1950), published in 1949. The novel is set in the future in a supposed "perfect society," but where freedom of thought and action have disappeared and the world is dominated by a few totalitarian states. The government maintains continual surveillance on its people, denying any privacy, with placards proclaiming "Big Brother [the all-powerful dictator of the state] Is Watching You." Page 37.

1941 war: a reference to the United States' entrance into World War II (1939–1945) immediately following the 7 December 1941 Japanese attack on the US naval base at Pearl Harbor in Hawaii. Page 50.

1917 revolution: the Russian Revolution of 1917 that overthrew the czar (emperor of Russia). It consisted of two distinct revolutions, one in February of 1917, in which a temporary government came to power, and the other in October, in which this government was replaced by the Soviet Government led by the Communists under Vladimir Lenin (1870–1924). Page 131.

Nixon, Richard M.: Richard Milhous Nixon (1913–1994), US politician. He served as vice-president (1952–1960) and then ran for president, losing to John F. Kennedy (1917–1963), thirty-fifth president of the United States (1961–1963). Nixon ran again in 1968 and won this election, becoming the thirty-seventh president of the United States. He ran again in 1972 and was elected but resigned in 1974 under threat of being removed from office in disgrace for his role in authorizing burglary of the offices of the opposing candidate's party during the 1972 election. Page 16.

no-knock: of or relating to police entry into private premises without knocking and without identifying themselves. Page 77.

Nuremberg Code: a human-rights-based document on medical ethics, written in 1947 in Nuremberg, Germany, during the trial of Nazi war criminals who had committed numerous crimes and inhumane experiments on human beings in concentration camps. The code, which was ultimately signed by all nations, states that a human subject must be informed of the nature, duration and purpose of any medical experiment and that voluntary consent is absolutely essential. Page 21.

Oak Knoll Naval Hospital: a naval hospital located in Oakland, California, USA, where LRH spent time recovering from injuries sustained during World War II (1939–1945) and researching the effect of the mind on the physical recovery of patients. Page 220.

obscene: offensive to morality or decency; shocking. Page 107.

obstinate: firmly or stubbornly refusing to change one's opinion or chosen course of action; not yielding to argument or persuasion. Page 10.

occupational forces: the troops assigned to maintain control of a newly conquered region until the conclusion of hostilities or establishment of a settled government. Page 3.

odious: arousing dislike or intense displeasure; detestable. Page 67.

Office of Naval Intelligence: the military intelligence agency formed in 1882 to provide for the intelligence, counterintelligence, investigative and security requirements of the United States Navy. Page 75.

Office of Naval Research: an office within the United States Navy, established in 1946 with the purpose of planning and encouraging scientific research for the maintenance of naval power and the preservation of national security. The office directs research in such areas as engineering, biology, physics, electronics and cognitive science (the study of intelligence, perception, memory, judgment, etc.). Page 221.

offset: counterbalanced or compensated for. Page 95.

old saw: an old saying, often repeated. Page 136.

old school: people who adhere to old-fashioned, outmoded or obsolete values and practices that are unacceptable by present standards. Page 124.

oligarchy: a form of government in which the ruling power is confined to a few persons or families who act on their own interests to the exclusion of the welfare of the people they govern; government by the few. Page 10.

ologies: plural of *ology,* meaning study or knowledge, usually used in reference to a science or other branch of knowledge. Page 139.

omnigod: *omni* is a combining form meaning all. Thus *omnigod* is having the full power of a god. Used figuratively. Page 77.

onerous: burdensome, oppressive or troublesome; causing hardship. Page 97.

opium: an addictive drug prepared from the juice of a poppy (a plant with large red, orange or white flowers). Page 184.

opportunistic: characterized by taking advantage of opportunities or situations to gain money or power, without thinking about whether the actions are right or wrong. Page 9.

organized crime: powerful, ruthless, large-scale networks of professional criminals. Page 77.

Orwell, George: pen name of Eric Arthur Blair (1903–1950), well-known English author who gained a reputation for his political shrewdness and his sharp satires. Writing both novels and essays, Orwell first achieved prominence in the 1940s for his two most well-known books, *Animal Farm* and *1984*, both of which reflect his lifelong distrust and disagreement with dictatorial government. Page 37.

Oswald, Lee Harvey: (1939–1963) accused assassin of President John F. Kennedy. Oswald was arrested after the assassination on 22 November 1963 but, before standing trial, was fatally shot by Jack Ruby, a Dallas nightclub owner, who claimed to be distraught over the president's assassination. Page 77.

other-determinism: having one's actions determined by someone or something other than oneself; something else giving one orders or directions. Page 122.

outcrop: figuratively, something that emerges or comes out of (something else). Literally (of a layer of rock), emerge or come to the surface; come out and appear, as on the side of a slope or mountain. Page 19.

outdistanced: literally, left behind, as in some kind of competition such as running. Figuratively, surpassed by a wide margin, especially through superior skill, knowledge or method. Page 195.

outlandish: peculiar, unusual or bizarre; strange or odd. Page 230.

outstripped: achieved more and moved at a faster pace than something else. Page 171.

overarching: embracive and all-encompassing, likened to a curved structure (arch) that spans or extends across the entire width or space of something. Page 3.

Overholser, Winfred: (1892–1964) American psychiatrist and a superintendent of *St. Elizabeths Hospital*, a government-funded psychiatric hospital (state institution) for the mentally ill and criminally insane, founded in the mid-1800s in Washington, DC. Page 59.

P

Pacific Fleet: the naval fleet of the United States Navy stationed in the Pacific Ocean. During the raid on Pearl Harbor, Hawaii (7 December 1941), Japanese forces sank or seriously damaged eight battleships and thirteen other naval vessels. The attack severely crippled the Pacific Fleet and cost the lives of more than three thousand personnel, prompting the entrance of the US into World War II (1939–1945). Page 77.

pamphleteer: a writer of pamphlets attacking something or urging a cause. A *pamphlet* is a small leaflet or paper booklet, usually unbound and coverless, that gives information or supports a position. Page 201.

pandemic: general; universal. Page 106.

pantingly: in the manner of people who long for something with breathless or intense eagerness. Page 127.

paragon: a model or pattern of perfection or excellence. Page 110.

paranoia: a psychiatric term for a mental condition characterized by delusions or hallucinations, especially of grandeur, persecution, etc. Page 185.

parliamentary: of or relating to *parliaments,* official or formal conferences or councils, usually concerned with government or public affairs, such as proposing to correct or create new laws. Page 24.

party-regulated: characterized as being controlled by the rules set up by a *political party,* an established organization of people who share the same broad political views and aims, usually attempting to elect members to government positions. Page 10.

patent medicine(s): a trademarked medicine sold without a prescription, traditionally viewed as being advertised with false claims of effectiveness. Page 151.

Pavlov: Ivan Petrovich Pavlov (1849–1936), Russian physiologist, noted for his dog experiments. Pavlov presented food to a dog while he sounded a bell. After repeating this procedure several times, the dog (in anticipation) would salivate at the sound of the bell, whether or not food was presented. Pavlov concluded that all acquired habits, even the higher mental activity of Man, depended on conditioning. Page 10.

Pearl Harbor: a harbor in Hawaii, site of a major United States naval base. A devastating surprise attack on Pearl Harbor by Japanese aircraft on 7 December 1941 prompted the United States to enter World War II (1939–1945). Page 76.

pedigree: the line of ancestors of an individual person. Page 31.

penal code: a body of laws concerned with various crimes or offenses and their legal penalties. Page 45.

penitentiary: a prison maintained in the United States by a state or the federal government for serious offenders. Page 40.

peoples' revolt: an instance of forcible overthrow of a government or social order, in favor of a new system, by the people of a country. Page 29.

perennial(ly): regularly repeated or continuing. Page 3.

peripheral: of secondary or minor relevance or importance. Page 6.

Persian attacks on Greece: attacks during the late 400s B.C. by ancient Persia (an empire in western and southwestern Asia) against the Greeks. In several key battles the Greeks defeated the Persians, thus ending the Persian attempts to push its empire westward. Page 195.

persona non grata: literally, person not acceptable. This phrase is used to refer to someone who, for some reason, is unacceptable, objectionable or unwelcome. Page 15.

perused: read or examined attentively. Page 222.

Philip of Macedon: (382–336 B.C.) king of Macedonia (359–336 B.C.), an ancient kingdom in northern Greece now divided among modern Macedonia, Greece and Bulgaria. Philip expanded his kingdom, eventually coming to rule all of Greece. He was assassinated in 336 B.C., following which his son, Alexander the Great (356–323 B.C.), conquered the Middle East, Egypt, Persia and parts of India. Page 51.

philosopher-king: according to Plato, the ideal ruler, one who is philosophically trained and enlightened. *See also* **Plato.** Page 135.

physical sciences: any of the sciences, such as physics and chemistry, that study and analyze the nature and properties of energy and nonliving matter. Page 171.

pillars: people viewed as vital to the continued existence of a society, state, organization, etc., through their support (financially or otherwise) of that society, state, organization, etc. Page 9.

plaintively: in a manner expressing sorrow or sadness. Page 4.

Plato: (427–347 B.C.) Greek philosopher whose work on the just state, entitled *Republic,* described the *philosopher-king,* the ideal ruler, philosophically trained and enlightened. According to Plato, individuals should be educated to the level compatible with interest and ability. Those who complete the entire educational process become philosopher-kings, those capable of making the wisest decisions. Page 135.

ploy(s): a tactic or maneuver, especially one calculated to deceive or frustrate an opponent. Page 50.

poignancy: the condition or state of being particularly penetrating and appealing. Page 3.

pointed: directly relevant or significant. Page 4.

point of fact, in: with regard to matters of fact. Page 83.

Policy Letter: same as *Hubbard Communications Office Policy Letter,* a type of issue written by L. Ron Hubbard and dealing with the know-how in running an organization. *See also* **Hubbard Communications Office.** Page 37.

political: of or having to do with *politics,* the science or practice of government; the regulation and government of a nation or state for the preservation of its safety, peace and prosperity. *Government* is that controlling body of a nation, state or people which conducts its policy, actions and affairs. Page 1.

political meal, untidy: a situation regarded as not politically advantageous because it is *untidy,* not neatly organized or carried out. *Political* in this context means concerned with power, status, etc., within a government, rather than with matters of principle. Page 4.

Poll Tax: *poll* means, literally, head, and is used here to mean a person. A *poll tax* is a tax of a fixed, rather than a graduated, amount per head, which is required of all adults, and payment of which is often made a requirement for voting. In the United States in 1905 a change in laws replaced poll tax with income tax, thus fining people for making a living. Page 46.

Polo, Marco: (1254–1324) traveler and author from Venice, Italy, whose account of his travels and experiences in China offered Europeans a firsthand view of Asian lands and stimulated interest in Asian trade. Page 2.

pomp: showy or excessively proud display, especially of dignity or importance. Page 178.

pompous: characterized by an exaggerated display of self-importance or dignity. Page 9.

ponderous: awkward or unwieldy because of size or quantity, here in reference to official procedure regarded as extremely detailed or overcomplicated. Page 63.

Popov, Dusko: Dusan "Dusko" Popov (1912–1981), Serbian-born British spy who worked for the British as a double agent during World War II (1939–1945). Page 77.

Port Orchard: a resort and fishing community located in western Washington State on *Puget Sound,* a long, narrow bay of the Pacific Ocean on the northwestern coast of the United States. Page 71.

postage-stamp: of very small area or size. Page 198.

posthypnotic suggestion: a suggestion made during hypnosis so as to be effective after (post) awakening. A *suggestion* here means the process of influencing a person to accept an idea, command, impulse, etc., without his conscious knowledge. Page 122.

postulate(s): that self-determined thought which starts, stops or changes past, present or future efforts. Page 101.

power elite: a closely knit alliance of military, government and corporate officials perceived as the center of wealth and political power in the US. Page 9.

Preamble: the Preamble of the Constitution of the United States, which states that the Constitution has the purpose "to form a more perfect Union, establish Justice, insure domestic Tranquility, provide for the common defence, promote the general Welfare, and secure the Blessings of Liberty to ourselves and our Posterity." Page 46.

preclear: from *pre-Clear,* a person not yet Clear; generally a person being audited, who is thus on the road to *Clear,* the name of a state achieved through auditing or an individual who has achieved this state. The Clear is an unaberrated person. He is rational in that he forms the best possible solutions he can on the data he has and from his viewpoint. Page 117.

preposterous: so contrary to nature, reason or common sense as to be laughable; absurd; ridiculous. Page 168.

present time: now; the current time or moment. Page 202.

present time problem: a problem that is going on at the present time, making demands on a person's attention. Page 85.

pretensions: claims made, especially indirectly or by implication, to some quality, merit or the like. Page 164.

Princeton University: a major American university and the fourth-oldest institution of higher learning in the United States, located in Princeton, New Jersey. Page 3.

PRO: the practice of trying to promote goodwill, often by creating a false impression. Literally, the initials for *Public Relations Office* or *Public Relations Officer*. Page 178.

processes: applies Dianetics and Scientology techniques (processes) to (someone). A *process* is an exact series of directions or sequences of action applied by a Dianetics or Scientology practitioner to help a person find out more about himself and his life and to improve his condition. Page 53.

processing: the application of Dianetics or Scientology techniques (called *processes*). *See also* **processes**. Page 164.

process of law: the courses of legal proceedings established by the legal system of a nation or state to protect individual rights and liberties. No citizen may be denied his or her legal rights and all laws must conform to fundamental, accepted legal principles, as the right of the accused to confront his or her accusers. Page 19.

produce: 1. agricultural products, especially fresh fruits and vegetables, as in *"threat…to his own irrigation, produce and land interest."* Page 50.
2. something that is brought forth or yielded either naturally or as a result of effort and work, as in *"spending more money than there is produce to absorb it."* Page 90.

produce year of food: the amount of food, especially in terms of agricultural products, during the period of one year. (*Produce* in this context means the amount that is produced; yield.) Page 95.

Profumo scandal: a scandal (1963) involving John Profumo (1915–2006), then British Secretary of State for War, who had an affair with professional call girl Christine Keeler. Keeler's employer Stephen Ward was in the employ of MI5 (British intelligence) in an effort to entrap Eugene Ivanov, a Soviet embassy official and probable intelligence agent. The ensuing scandal raised questions of national security (a British cabinet secretary and a probable Soviet spy were having an affair with the same woman) and also revealed wild parties and promiscuity involving many high figures in British society. Profumo resigned from his position amid the controversy. Page 114.

Prohibition (Act): a law in effect for a period in the United States (1920–1933) in which the manufacture, transportation and sale of alcoholic liquors for beverage purposes were forbidden by federal law. Many people ignored the national ban. Page 46.

proof of the pudding: a contraction of the phrase *the proof of the pudding is in the eating,* which means that only through actual trial or experience can the value or quality of something be tested; performance is the only valid test. This comes from the idea that the only way to know for certain that a pudding (dessert) is good is to taste it. Page 51.

prophet(s): a leading spokesman for a cause, doctrine or group. Page 54.

provocation: reason for attacking somebody. Page 136.

psychedelic: of or relating to the time period or culture associated with *psychedelic drugs,* those drugs (such as LSD) capable of producing hallucinations and other abnormal psychic effects resembling mental illness. Page 107.

Psychiatry: a psychiatric journal founded in 1938 by American psychiatrist Harry Stack Sullivan (1892–1949). Sullivan, who edited the journal, also founded Washington, DC's School of

Psychiatry and was involved in the founding of the World Federation for Mental Health in 1948. Page 135.

psychopathic: of *psychopaths,* those whose behavior is largely antisocial and without morals, who are characterized by irresponsibility, lack of remorse or shame, criminal behavior and other serious personality defects. Page 155.

psychopolitical cog: an element characterized by the interaction of politics and psychiatry or the psychiatric means of bringing about political ends. Page 6.

psychosomatic: *psycho* refers to mind and *somatic* refers to body; the term *psychosomatic* means the mind making the body ill or illnesses which have been created physically within the body by the mind. A description of the cause and source of psychosomatic ills is contained in *Dianetics: The Modern Science of Mental Health.* Page 191.

psychosurgery: use of brain surgery as a supposed treatment of mental disorders. Page 59.

psychotropic: affecting mental activity, behavior or perception. Page 204.

Public Enemies by number: criminals at the top of the FBI's list of the ten most wanted criminals, for example, Public Enemy Number 1. Page 75.

public servant: an appointed or elected holder of a government position or office. Page 42.

public-spirited: motivated by or showing genuine concern for others in the community. Page 110.

pudding, proof of the: a contraction of the phrase *the proof of the pudding is in the eating,* which means that only through actual trial or experience can the value or quality of something be tested; performance is the only valid test. This comes from the idea that the only way to know for certain that a pudding (dessert) is good is to taste it. Page 51.

punitive: inflicting, concerned with or directed toward punishment. Page 230.

puppet: one whose acts are controlled by an outside force or influence. Literally, a *puppet* is a small figure, such as of a human, often made with jointed limbs and moved by strings or wires from above. Page 34.

push-button: characterized by or as if by the use of a *push button,* a device that, when depressed, closes or opens an electric circuit; operating in an automatic manner. Page 159.

Q

queer: strange or odd; not quite right; unusually different. Page 53.

quicksilver: a poisonous, heavy, silver-white metal that is liquid at room temperature. It is used in such things as thermometers, pharmaceuticals, dental fillings and lamps. Also called *mercury* or *liquid silver.* Page 151.

quid: an informal British term for a *pound,* the basic monetary unit of the United Kingdom. Page 141.

R

rabble-rousers: people who stir up anger, violence or other strong feelings in a group or a crowd through emotionalism, especially for political reasons. Page 9.

rack: a former instrument of torture consisting of a framework on which a victim was tied by the wrists and ankles to be slowly stretched by spreading the parts of the framework. Page 201.

raptly: with extreme interest or fascination; holding one's attention completely. Page 128.

ration(s): food or meals; a specified or measured amount of something provided, especially food or drink. Page 92.

raw: brutal, harsh. Page 49.

reach, beyond one's: greater than one's power to get or achieve. Page 89.

Reagan, Ronald: (1911–2004) American statesman and fortieth president of the United States (1981–1989). As an actor, Reagan appeared in some fifty films. Following service in the US Army during World War II (1939–1945), he became involved in politics and became governor of California, a position he held during the late 1960s and early 1970s. He won the presidential election in 1980 and held office for two terms. In 1981 as President Reagan was leaving a hotel in Washington, DC, John Hinckley, Jr., a psychiatric patient who was in the crowd, fired several shots, wounding the president and two others. *See also* **Hinckley, Jr., John.** Page 204.

reasonable: using or showing reason or sound judgment; sensible. Page 64.

recession: a period of an economic contraction, marked by a decline in employment, profits and sales. Page 83.

recidivism: repeated or habitual relapse into criminal habits. Page 182.

recourse: the means by which one can obtain help or a solution to a problem. Page 69.

red revolution: a forceful revolution, intending sweeping social or political reform. *Red* means inciting or endorsing sweeping social or political reform, especially by the use of force; from the flag used by revolutionaries. A *revolution* is an overthrow or rejection and thorough replacement of an established government or political system by the people governed. Page 71.

reek: have a foul smell, as by being strongly pervaded with something unpleasant or offensive. Page 190.

re-engineering: the act of newly *engineering*, planning, supervising or developing something. Here referring to using chemical substances (drugs) to affect or change perceptions, moods or thought patterns. Page 7.

Rees, John Rawlings: (1890–1969) British psychiatrist, medical director of the Tavistock Clinic (an experimental psychiatric clinic in London) from 1934 and first president and director of the World Federation for Mental Health. Rees was an advocate of psychosurgery and shock treatment. Page 105.

referendum: the submission of a law, proposed or already in effect, to a direct vote of the people. Page 46.

regenerate: a person restored or raised again from a low condition. Page 155.

regime: a form of government or rule; political system. Also, a system, especially one imposed by a government. Page 10.

Reich, Wilhelm: (1897–1957) Austrian psychiatrist and social critic. After being ousted by the Communist Party, in 1937 he moved to the US, where he practiced for many years. In the last years of his life, Reich showed little interest in psychiatry, devoting his efforts instead to discoveries in the field of physics. He developed the orgone accumulator, which he thought would capture certain energy in the atmosphere (which he called *orgone*) that could cure cancer. In 1956 he was sentenced to two years' imprisonment for disobeying a government injunction that the Food and Drug Administration had obtained against him, ordering destruction of all orgone boxes, his journals and books. He died while in prison a year later. Page 223.

remonstrance: a statement or plea in protest, objection or disapproval. Page 109.

remorselessly: in a way that continues without lessening in strength or intensity. Page 90.

repatriated: characterized as having returned to one's country of origin or citizenship. Page 3.

repeal: officially state that a law, decision or agreement is no longer effective; withdraw formally or officially. Page 63.

repress: keep under control, check or suppress. Page 89.

repression: the condition that occurs when forceful control is used against such things as freedom of expression, thought, creativity or the like. Page 2.

reproached: criticized for having done something wrong. Page 167.

republic: a state in which the supreme power rests in the people and their elected representatives or officers, as opposed to one governed by a king or similar ruler. Page 10.

requiem: a solemn chant, song, poem or the like, as for the dead. Page 10.

retention: the ability to remember. Page 220.

retribution: punishment caused or inflicted for evil done. Page 136.

reverberating: having continuing serious effects. Page 53.

reviled: subjected to insulting and humiliating treatment or language; abused. Page 9.

rhetoric: language calculated to have a persuasive or impressive effect. Page 18.

Rhodesia: a former region in Southern Africa, now the country of Zimbabwe. Page 15.

riot stick: a special club carried as a weapon by riot police. Page 59.

roadblock: a fact or condition that blocks progress along a course or prevents accomplishment of an objective. Literally, a *roadblock* is a temporary barrier used to prevent vehicles from continuing along a road so that they can be checked or their drivers questioned, usually by police or military personnel. Page 178.

robber-baron: of or relating to lords or noblemen (barons) during the Middle Ages who held land in exchange for military and other services given. They engaged in stealing from people traveling through their lands. Page 201.

Robinson, Kenneth: (1911–1996) minister of health in Great Britain in the late 1960s. Robinson was the vice-president of the National Mental Health Association, a private group in the UK specializing in the "treatment" of families of aristocrats. He was one of the key figures behind the 1968 British attack on Scientology and was subsequently removed as minister of health for this unpopular campaign. Page 25.

rock, a poor: inadequate to serve as a *rock,* a firm foundation or support. Page 219.

rocks, on the: in great difficulties and likely to fail. This term originates from the nautical sense: a vessel that is on the rocks is in danger of being wrecked unless it is pulled away. Page 88.

rolled up: built something up by gradually adding to it. Page 132.

Roman arena: the central part of an ancient Roman amphitheater (a round or oval building with an open space surrounded by rising rows of seats), in which combats took place. Arenas were the site of gruesome battles to the death attended by thousands of spectators. Slaves, captives, prisoners of war and the like were forced to become swordsmen (called *gladiators*) and fight each other or wild beasts. Page 190.

Rome: the city (and later, the empire) of ancient Rome, which at its peak included western and southern Europe, Britain, North Africa and the lands of the eastern Mediterranean Sea and which lasted from the 500s B.C. into the A.D. 400s. The last years of the empire (fourth century and part of the fifth century) were marked by steady decline: economic disintegration, weak emperors, invading tribes and a central government providing few services and little protection while demanding more taxes. Page 20.

Roosevelt: Franklin D. Roosevelt (1882–1945), thirty-second president of the United States (1933–1945). He was the only president elected four times. Roosevelt led the United States through the economic depression of the 1930s and through World War II (1939–1945). Page 76.

root out: remove altogether; get rid of something completely. Page 232.

roseate: optimistic or idealistic, especially to an absurd degree; rose-colored, rosy. Page 37.

rosy: (of times, circumstances, etc.) bringing happiness; bright, promising and hopeful. Page 83.

route, goes the: figuratively, goes the same way; continues along the same path. Page 63.

Royal Commission Inquiry: in the United Kingdom, Australia and other Commonwealth countries, a committee formed by the authority of the monarch on the government's advice to inquire into an issue. Page 134.

Royal Society: the *Royal Society of London,* the oldest and most prestigious scientific society in the United Kingdom, through which the British Government has supported scientific investigation since 1662. Page 131.

run down: trace something; find the source of something. Page 174.

Rust Belt: the declining industrial heartland of the northeastern and midwestern states of the United States, where decreasing production of items such as steel and automobiles resulted in many aging and rusting factories. *Belt* in this sense means a geographic region that is distinctive in a specified respect. Page 5.

S

Saboteur forces: those who engage in *sabotage,* the deliberate damaging or destroying of property or equipment to weaken an enemy or to make a protest. Page 33.

sadism: a type of behavior in which a person obtains pleasure from hurting others and making them suffer physically or mentally. Page 44.

safety net: something intended to help people in the event of hardship or misfortune, especially something providing financial security, such as insurance or welfare payments. From the literal idea of a *safety net,* a net installed below a high place, such as a circus tightrope or trapeze from which somebody might fall or jump. Page 83.

Saint Hill Manor: a manor (a large house and its land) located in East Grinstead, Sussex, in southern England. Saint Hill Manor was the residence of L. Ron Hubbard as well as the international communications and training center of Scientology from the late 1950s through the mid-1960s. Page 7.

Saint-Simon, Comte de: Claude Henri de Rouvroy, Comte de Saint-Simon (1760–1825), French philosopher who advocated the creation of a social order directed by men of science and industry in which all people would work and receive rewards equal to their labor. No person could inherit wealth and all individuals would begin life on an equal basis. (*Comte,* or *count,* is a title of a nobleman.) Page 54.

sanitarium: an institution for the mentally ill. Page 98.

satellite countries: countries under the domination or control of another, specifically in reference to the eastern European countries, such as Hungary, Poland, Czechoslovakia and others, that were dominated and controlled by the Soviet Union (Russia) during the twentieth century. Page 198.

Savannah: a seaport on the Atlantic coast in Georgia, a southeastern state of the United States. Page 118.

saw, old: an old saying, often repeated. Page 136.

schizophrenia: a condition in which a person has two (or more) apparent personalities. *Schizophrenia* means *scissors* or *two,* plus *head.* Literally, *splitting of the mind,* hence, *split personality.* Page 185.

School of Military Government: a school of military government established at Princeton University, Princeton, New Jersey, in October 1944. The purpose was to train military officers so as to provide needed personnel for projected military government activities as well as for specialized civilian duties. Page 3.

Schopenhauer: Arthur Schopenhauer (1788–1860), German philosopher who believed that the will to live is the fundamental reality and that this will, being a constant striving, cannot be satisfied and only causes suffering. Page 86.

"science of saliva": an ironic reference to the fields of psychiatry and psychology and the roots of their theories lying in the experiments of Ivan Petrovich Pavlov (1849–1936), Russian physiologist, noted for his dog experiments. Pavlov presented food to a dog while he sounded a bell. After repeating this procedure several times, the dog (in anticipation) would salivate at the sound of the bell, whether or not food was presented. Pavlov concluded that all acquired habits, even the higher mental activity of Man, depended on conditioning. Page 6.

Science of Survival: a book written by L. Ron Hubbard in 1951 that provides the first accurate prediction of human behavior. Page 107.

Scientology: Scientology is the study and handling of the spirit in relationship to itself, universes and other life. The term Scientology is taken from the Latin *scio,* which means "knowing in the fullest sense of the word" and the Greek word *logos,* meaning "study of." In itself the word means literally "knowing how to know." Page 1.

scribblers: writers whose work has very little value or importance. Page 202.

scrupulously: in a way that is *scrupulous,* extremely honest; doing everything correctly and exactly as it should be done. Page 69.

scuffle about: struggle or fight for (something). Page 49.

seat, lose (one's): no longer be permitted a *seat,* a place in an elected parliament or council, as by being voted out of office. Page 163.

Second World War: also *World War II* (1939–1945), conflict involving every major power in the world. On one side were the Allies (chiefly Great Britain, the US and the Soviet Union) and on the other side Axis powers (Germany, Japan and Italy). The conflict resulted from the rise of militaristic regimes in Germany, Japan and Italy after World War I (1914–1918). It ended with the surrender of Germany on May 8, 1945, and of Japan on August 14, 1945. Page 3.

Secretary of State: a senior member of the British Government who is in charge of a major department. The title was originally given to an official conducting the royal correspondence of a king or queen. Page 24.

secretory: connected with or promoting *secretion,* the process of producing a substance from the cells and fluids within a gland or organ and discharging it. Page 131.

secret police: a police force that functions as the enforcement arm of a government's political policies and whose activities, which include surveillance, intimidation and physical violence as a means of suppressing disagreement with political policies, are concealed from the public. Page 10.

seeing a Red under every bush: finding a *Red,* a political radical or revolutionary, especially a Communist, hiding everywhere one looks. Page 198.

see the light: begin to accept or understand a point of view one formerly opposed. Page 23.

seething: in a state of agitation or turmoil, as with discontent, excitement or anger that is not fully expressed but might become so. Likened to the activity of a boiling liquid that is bubbling and surging. Page 77.

seizure laws: regulations concerning *seizure,* the act of taking a person into custody through the authority of a warrant or other legal power. Page 178.

self-determinism: the condition of being *self-determined,* having power of choice and the ability to direct self or to determine the actions of self. Page 122.

sen: a coin of small value in several currencies of Asia, from a Chinese word meaning *money* or *coin.* Page 101.

Senate: an assembly or council of citizens having the highest power to make important decisions, especially the lawmaking body of a state or nation. Page 51.

sentient: conscious or capable of perceptions; consciously perceiving. Page 90.

served: (of a legal document) delivered to somebody. Page 21.

1789, another: another *French Revolution,* a revolt in France from 1789 to 1799 that overthrew the royal family and the aristocratic class and system of privileges they enjoyed. The revolution was in part a protest against France's absolute monarchy, its firmly established and unproductive nobility and the consequent lack of freedom for the middle classes. During the revolution, thousands of people were beheaded under the guillotine. Page 72.

Shays' Rebellion: a revolt in Massachusetts (1786–1787) by farmers who faced imprisonment or loss of their property because they could not pay their debts. Led by Daniel Shays (1747?–1825), a former army captain in the American Revolution, the uprising was one of a number of protests during the economic depression that followed the war. The rebellion was eventually put down, those involved pardoned and laws passed doing away with oppressive taxes. Page 46.

sheds (some) light on: clarifies; clears up; helps to explain by providing further information. Page 209.

shelled: attacked by being fired at with *shells,* metal containers filled with explosives. Shells are fired from large guns over long distances. Page 4.

shepherd's pipe: the name given to a shepherd's oboe (a woodwind instrument consisting of a slim tube with a slightly flared end). The shepherd's oboe has a wider flare at the end and a wider mouthpiece than the usual oboe. The term is also used to refer to a kind of bagpipe. Page 144.

shoulder to the wheel, put (one's): characteristic of working vigorously, especially in the way of assisting; strive energetically and vigorously toward achieving an objective or completing a task; making a determined effort. This expression originally referred to literally putting one's *shoulder to the wheel* of a vehicle (wagon, cart, etc.) to free or release it from the mud or a rut or to get it over a hill, etc. Page 23.

shrug off: reject or disregard something as unimportant. Page 128.

Siberia Bill: a reference to the Alaska Mental Health Bill, a bill proposed in the mid-1950s to the United States legislature to enact as a law. The Siberia Bill proposed that a Siberian-type camp be created for mental health patients in a remote part of Alaska, a region much like Siberia. The bill proposed a "simplified commitment procedure," allowing any peace officer, friend, medical doctor and, of course, psychiatrist to start commitment proceedings on a person. It was worded in such a way that any man, woman or child could be seized off the street and transferred without trial to this Siberian-type camp. Churches of Scientology, along with other civil rights groups, joined forces to fight this proposal from becoming law. A campaign was launched to inform the public of what was happening. This, along with a massive letter-writing campaign, which inspired political opposition, succeeded in stopping the commitment section of the bill, leaving merely an act to authorize mental health funding to the territory of Alaska. Page 105.

Sicily: an island off the southern tip of Italy, the scene of fighting during World War II (1939–1945), when Allied forces captured the island (August 1943). From Sicily, the Allies were able eventually to continue northward through Italy, key to the final defeat of the Italian and German armies. Page 170.

side with: support in a conflict or dispute. Page 101.

simon-pure: completely genuine or authentic, short for *the real Simon Pure*. From the name of a character in the play *A Bold Stroke for a Wife* (1717) by English playwright Susannah Centlivre (1669–1723). In the play, Simon Pure is a preacher who must prove his identity against an imposter's claims. Page 189.

singular: remarkable; very noticeable. Page 51.

sinister: wicked, evil or bad, especially in some dark, mysterious way. Page 6.

skeleton-filled closets: a variation and intensification of *skeleton in the closet,* a dark secret or withheld source of shame or disgrace, an allusion to a situation where a person has been murdered and the body has been hidden in a closet unbeknownst to others. Page 178.

sliding scale: a system in which the amount that is paid for something varies according to particular conditions. Page 90.

social engineer: someone involved in the application of social science to the solution of social problems. *Social science* is the study of a particular area of human society such as economics, psychology, history, etc. Page 147.

social fabric: the framework or basic structure of society. Page 7.

Socialism: an economic system in which the production and distribution of goods are controlled by the government rather than by individuals. Page 86.

sociologist: one who engages in *sociology*. *See also* **sociology.** Page 144.

sociology: the study of the individuals, groups and institutions that make up human society, including the way the members of a group respond to one another. Page 83.

sodium bomb: an explosive that uses *sodium,* a highly reactive, silvery-white, soft metallic element. The metal is extremely active chemically; it never occurs in the free state in nature but only in combination with other elements. It decomposes (breaks up) water, producing hydrogen gas and a sodium compound; the reaction is extremely violent, producing so much heat that in many cases the hydrogen ignites. Page 76.

sold out: gave up or betrayed a cause, one's country or one's associates, etc., in order to obtain wealth. Page 51.

Southern Africa: the southern portion of the African continent, generally including the countries of Botswana, Lesotho, Namibia, South Africa, Swaziland and Zimbabwe (priorly called Rhodesia). Page 24.

Soviet Union: the world's first and most powerful Communist country, in full the Union of Soviet Socialist Republics, which existed from 1922 to 1991, when the Communist Party lost power. The Soviet Union consisted of fifteen republics, many of which, as new countries, formed the Commonwealth of Independent States after the breakup of the larger country. Page 126.

Sparta: a city in ancient Greece famous for its military power. With a militaristic government, every male belonged to the state from the time of birth and slavery was imposed on conquered peoples. Spartans led a communal life, with all people eating at a public dining hall, males compelled to live in barracks till the age of thirty and the majority of citizens holding state-owned plots of land. Page 86.

spatter: scatter or send (something) flying all over the place. Page 144.

spawned: brought forth; produced. Page 53.

special interest: short for *special-interest group,* which could also be called a "hidden" interest group. It is characterized by having some fixed idea, but advertising something else. They are composed of zealots who work to the exclusion of all other interest as well as the exclusion of the well-being of others who are not "aligned" with the fixed idea of that group. Page 37.

spectacle: a striking example of something. Page 42.

spoils: valuables, money, goods, etc., obtained, usually forcibly through war or robbery. Page 10.

"sport": sexual intercourse or sexually loose and unrestrained activity. Page 19.

Stalin: Joseph Stalin (1879–1953), premier of the Soviet Union from 1941 to 1953, who ruled by terror, allowing no one to oppose his decisions and under whom millions were executed or sent to labor camps. Included in those millions were most of those who helped him rise to power, as well as Soviet peasants who opposed his program of collective agriculture (government control of farms). Page 49.

stamps: marks a thing with a distinctive or lasting characteristic as if hit with the sudden blow of a die (a metal tool pressed into an object to give its finished shape or design). Page 128.

standard: the basis for the measure of value in a given monetary system; the commodity or commodities on which the value of a currency or monetary system is based. For example, in a *gold standard,* the monetary standard would be solely in terms of gold, in which the basic unit of currency is made equal to and exchangeable with a specified quantity of gold. Page 98.

stand for: 1. believe in something strongly and fight for it. Page 49.

2. tolerate or put up with something. Page 69.

staple: principally used. Page 194.

Star Chamber: a body that conducts its proceedings by arbitrary or unfair methods, from the *Star Chamber,* a former royal English court (abolished in 1641), notorious for its secret sessions without jury, its harsh and arbitrary judgments and its use of torture to force confessions. Page 26.

stature: degree or level of achievement; reputation. Page 86.

statute: a collection of laws established by legislature and formally written down. A *legislature* is an official body of persons, usually chosen by election, with the power to make, change or undo laws. Page 64.

steering committee: a group of selected people who decide agendas and topics for discussion and prioritize urgent business. Page 106.

stem: stop, check or restrain. Page 77.

stench: an extremely disgusting smell, especially a strong lingering one. Used figuratively. Page 174.

steps, thirteen: an allusion to the hangman's gallows. Traditionally, a gallows is built with thirteen steps. At the top of the steps is a platform with a trapdoor, above which is suspended a noose. The condemned person walks up the thirteen steps to his hanging. Page 136.

stigmatized: characterized or marked as disgraceful or very bad. Page 147.

stimulus-response: a certain stimulus (something that rouses a person or thing to activity or energy or that produces a reaction in the body) automatically giving a certain response. Page 132.

stockade: a prison, especially a military one. Page 128.

Stonehenge: two concentric circles of large upright stones located about 80 miles (130 kilometers) west of London, England, and thought to have been constructed between 2500 and 2000 B.C. In ancient times, it was used for religious ceremonies and sacrifices. Page 113.

Stop the Clock: the action of putting a halt to time, as by stopping a clock. A play on the name *Beat the Clock,* a popular American television game show during the mid-1900s, in which contestants attempted to perform a specified task within a given time limit (usually sixty seconds or less). For example, a contestant might be asked to arrange jumbled-up words on a magnetic board into a well-known phrase. A large clock on the stage ticked off the time as the stunt progressed. Those who managed to "beat the clock" won cash or merchandise prizes. Page 31.

stranglehold: power over something or somebody that is complete and prevents any change. Page 26.

stratosphere: literally, a very high region of the Earth's atmosphere. Used figuratively to refer to a very high position. Page 190.

strawberries: a reference to a comic story delivered by Willie Howard (1886–1949), a German-born American comedian. In the story he portrays a revolutionary saying, "Fellow workers, the time has arrived. Our cup of bitterness, it is filled to the brim! We must throw off the yoke of oppression…revolt! Revolt! Comes the revolution, ve'll [we'll] eat strawberries and cream!" A heckler yells he doesn't like strawberries and cream. Willie says, "You'll eat strawberries and cream and like it!" Page 144.

strewn: 1. has (something) scattered through it. Page 51.
2. scattered over an area. Page 206.

stricken: affected by something overwhelming, such as disease, trouble or painful emotion. Page 70.

strife: strong disagreement or fighting; conflict. Page 194.

stronghold: a place occupied or dominated by a group holding or supporting a particular belief. Page 113.

structure: how something is built or its physical design, the way in which parts are arranged or put together to form a whole as contrasted with *function,* intellectual powers; mental action; thought. Page 220.

stupefied: made stupid, dull or insensible. Page 4.

suave: polite and charming, especially in a way that seems insincere. Page 198.

subatomic: of or pertaining to a tiny particle contained in an atom. This includes those found in the nucleus of the atom, including a proton (a positively charged particle) or a neutron (a particle that carries no electric charge); or to any found outside the nucleus, such as an electron (a negatively charged particle). Page 217.

subservience: the state or condition of being prepared to obey others unquestioningly. Page 220.

subterfuge: a secret, dishonest way of doing something; an action designed to hide, avoid or escape something. Page 237.

subversion: the action, plan or activity of undermining or corrupting the principles of. Page 6.

subversive: tending or seeking to undermine, corrupt, overthrow or destroy an established government, institution, belief, etc. Page 10.

suffices: meets present needs or requirements; is sufficient. Page 10.

suffrage, universal: the right to vote (suffrage) for all persons over a certain age, usually eighteen or twenty-one, who in other respects satisfy the requirements established by law. Page 15.

Sunday-school teachers: individuals who teach *Sunday school,* a school held on Sunday with the purpose of religious instruction and teaching children, youth and adults about the Bible, Christianity, Christian behavior in daily living and various other topics. Page 117.

superior court: a court in states such as California that can hear and decide any civil or criminal case. Originally called *superior* (higher) because these courts were at a level above lower courts that heard and decided only certain types of cases. Page 106.

Superlaw: an excessive display of the control or power of rules or policies, referring to this control or power as exercised by one group over other groups in society. Page 44.

Superman caste: the highest class (caste) of society, made up of "Supermen." In the writings of German philosopher and poet Friedrich Nietzsche (1844–1900), a Superman is an ideal, superior being, a man of extraordinary power or ability who through creativity and integrity is able to rise above or go beyond good and evil and is the goal of human evolution. In his book *Thus Spake* [spoke] *Zarathustra,* Nietzsche presents the Superman as one whose unlimited willingness to destroy forms a desirable code of conduct. Page 42.

superselect: chosen (selected) for strict adherence to the extreme views of the Nazis, which included racial superiority, with the aim of destroying groups not considered worthy. Page 29.

supply and demand, law of: a principle in economics that the price for a product is determined by the level of demand and the quantity available. For example, if the demand exceeds the supply, the price rises, operating to reduce the demand and so enable the supply to meet it and vice versa. Page 173.

suppression: the actions or activities of squashing, sitting on, making smaller, refusing to let reach, making uncertain about reaching, rendering or lessening in any way possible to the harm of the individual; a harmful intention or action against which one cannot fight back. Page 1.

suppressive: relating to or of the nature of suppression. *See also* **suppression.** Page 90.

Suppressives: people who suppress other people in their vicinity. A Suppressive Person will goof up or vilify (make malicious and abusive statements about) any effort to help anybody and particularly knife with violence anything calculated to make human beings more powerful or more intelligent. The whole rationale of the Suppressive Person is built on the belief that if anyone got better, the Suppressive Person would be for it as the others could overcome him then. He is fighting a battle he once fought and never stopped fighting. Page 85.

Supreme Court: the highest court in the United States. The Supreme Court consists of nine judges appointed by the president who make decisions solely on constitutional matters. Page 41.

Swastika: a design of ancient origin in the form of a cross with four equal arms, each bent in a right-angle extension. This figure was the official emblem of the Nazi party. Page 19.

sway: prevailing, overpowering or controlling influence. Page 174.

swayed: persuaded or influenced to believe or do something. Page 50.

sweeping: wide in range or effect; general. Page 20.

swell: become greater in intensity or amount; expand. Page 71.

symbiotic: characterized by or resulting in a state of *symbiosis,* any interdependent or mutually beneficial relationship between two persons, groups, etc. Page 59.

System, the: the prevailing structure or organization of society, business or politics or of society in general; establishment. Page 9.

T

takeover, 1932 bank: the result of bank collapses during the *Depression,* the worldwide economic slump that began in 1929. In the United States approximately one-half of the then-existing twenty-five thousand banks had failed by 1933. A *takeover* is an acquisition or gaining control of a corporation through the purchase or exchange of stock. Page 53.

Tavistock: a psychiatric clinic in London, England, established in 1920. Since its founding, the Tavistock Clinic has been prominent in mental health research and experimentation. Page 105.

Taxpayers' Bill of Rights: legislation passed between 1988 and 1998 for the protection of taxpayers against abuses of the income tax system by the *Internal Revenue Service,* the division of the US Department of the Treasury responsible for the collection of income and other taxes and the enforcement of tax laws. A *bill of rights* is a formal summary of certain fundamental rights and privileges guaranteed to a people against violation by the state. Page 18.

teeming: full of, abounding with. Page 36.

telltale: serving to reveal or disclose something that is not intended to be known. Page 116.

temporizes: adapts decisions and actions to whatever the existing circumstances are, without reference to standards of good conduct. Page 10.

tenacity: the quality of being stubbornly persistent; determination; firmness. Page 92.

Texas School Book Depository: a multifloor warehouse for the storage of school textbooks and related materials, located in Dallas, Texas. The building figured in the assassination of President John F. Kennedy (1917–1963) when authorities found a rifle near a window in the building after the shooting. Page 77.

textbook: so typical as to be suitable for inclusion in a textbook; providing a model; classic. Page 195.

theaters: areas of land, sea and air that are or may become involved directly in war operations. Also called *theater of war*. Page 3.

thermonuclear: involving or concerning thermonuclear bombs, also called *hydrogen bombs,* explosive devices more powerful than atomic bombs, that derive their energy from the fusion (combining) of hydrogen atoms at extraordinarily high temperatures (several million degrees). Page 15.

Third Reich: a term adopted by Adolf Hitler during the 1920s to describe the thousand-year regime he intended to create in Germany by conquering Europe. *Reich* is a German word meaning state or empire. Page 33.

thirteen steps: an allusion to the hangman's gallows. Traditionally, a gallows is built with thirteen steps. At the top of the steps is a platform with a trapdoor, above which is suspended a noose. The condemned person walks up the thirteen steps to his hanging. Page 136.

thistle pasture: a pasture filled with *thistles,* any of various very prickly plants. Hence a *thistle pasture* would be a miserable or uninhabitable place for a grazing animal such as a cow. Page 90.

.357 Magnum: a cartridge designed for a handgun with a revolving cylinder of chambers, allowing several shots to be fired without reloading. The designation *.357* refers to the size of the cartridge or the barrel of the gun built to fire such, measuring approximately .357 of an inch. *Magnum* refers to a cartridge that has a larger charge and casing than other gun cartridges of the same diameter. Page 75.

Tibetan lamaseries: monasteries of *lamas,* priests or monks in *Lamaism,* a branch of Buddhism that seeks to find release from the suffering of life and attain a state of complete happiness and peace. Lamaism is practiced in Tibet, a land in south central Asia, and in areas such as Mongolia, a country to the north of China. Page 2.

tide, turning the: reversing the course of events, especially from one extreme to another. Page 181.

***Time* magazine:** an American weekly newsmagazine, first published in 1923 in New York City, New York. Page 114.

tinkerer: one who works at things clumsily and experimentally, especially under the guise of attempted repair or improvement. Page 172.

tinkering: adjusting or working with something in an unskilled, clumsy or experimental manner, especially under the guise of repair or improvement. Page 7.

tipped: gave someone confidential information. Page 76.

toady: act in the manner of a *toady,* one who flatters or does distasteful or unprincipled things to gain favor. Page 202.

tomes: books, especially very heavy, large or learned books. Page 89.

torch: a valuable quality, principle or cause that needs to be protected and maintained; literally, a stick of wood dipped in wax or with one end wrapped in combustible material, set on fire and carried, especially in the past, as a source of light. Page 238.

torpedo detonator: a device used to explode a *torpedo,* a cylindrical self-propelled missile that is launched from an aircraft, ship or submarine and travels underwater to hit its target. Page 76.

totalitarian: of or relating to a political regime based on subordination of the individual to the state and strict control of all aspects of the life and productive capacity of the nation, especially by coercive measures (as censorship and terrorism). Page 16.

touch upon: write or talk about something briefly during the course of a discussion. Page 15.

tractable: easily managed or controlled. Page 230.

tragedy of 9/11: the destruction, death and suffering that occurred on September 11 (9/11), 2001, at the World Trade Center, a complex in New York City that included twin skyscrapers (the tallest in the US at 110 stories). These buildings were destroyed when two jetliners, hijacked by terrorists, were flown into them, causing the worst building disaster in recorded history and the deaths of some 2,800 people. Page 116.

Tricky Dick: an unflattering nickname applied to politician Richard M. Nixon, in reference to his reputation for being *tricky*. See also **Nixon, Richard M.** Page 16.

Tuinal: a brand name for a drug used as a quick and relatively long-acting sedative or hypnotic. Page 134.

tumbril(s): a crude cart used during the French Revolution to carry condemned prisoners to the place where they were to be beheaded. Page 20.

tumult: violent and noisy commotion, uprising, riot or disturbance, as of a crowd or mob; uproar. Page 83.

Turrou, Leon: Leon George Turrou (1895–1986), Polish-born American FBI agent instrumental in rounding up a Nazi spy ring during the late 1930s. The film *Confessions of a Nazi Spy* (1939) was drawn from his writings. Page 76.

two hundred American cities erupting in riot: a reference to the wave of riots and violent demonstrations that took place during 1968 and 1969 in cities across the United States. In the summer of 1968 alone, race riots broke out in more than 100 US cities following the April assassination of civil rights leader Martin Luther King, Jr. (1929–1968). Widespread racial discrimination and the United States' role in the Vietnam War (1954–1975) were chief among the causes of protest. Page 5.

tyranny: cruelty and injustice in the exercising of power or authority over others. Page 2.

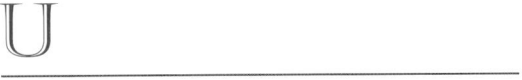

unblushingly: without feeling any shame or embarrassment. Page 46.

underscore: emphasize something, likened to marking with a score (line drawn or scratched) underneath the printed words on a page. Page 5.

unholy: 1. unnatural and potentially harmful. Page 42.
2. shockingly barbarous; malicious. Page 205.

unholy, the: persons having an evil, malicious character. Page 167.

unimpeachably: in a way that is not able to be *impeached,* challenged or discredited or called into question (as a person's honor or reputation, etc.). Page 198.

United Mine Workers: a labor union of coal-mine workers organized in 1890, one of the largest unions in the United States. Due to the importance of coal for the manufacturing industries, the UMW exercised a considerable influence in industrial matters. In the period from 1933 to 1950, the union's frequent strikes over wages, working conditions and other benefits resulted in work stoppages that threatened the nation's economy. Page 76.

United Nations: an international organization of countries created to promote world peace and cooperation. The United Nations was founded after World War II ended in 1945. Its mission is to maintain world peace, develop good relations between countries, promote cooperation in solving the world's problems and encourage respect for human rights. Page 18.

United Nations World Health Organization Technical Report Series No. 98: a document written in July 1955 entitled "Legislation Affecting Psychiatric Treatment." It was written by the World Health Organization and contained the collective views of an international group of supposed "authorities" on such things as psychiatric services, legislation, categories of patients, etc. Page 110.

Universal Declaration of Human Rights: an official declaration made in 1948 by the United Nations following the disregard of human rights resulting in the horrors of World War II (1939–1945). It sets forth the basic civil, economic, political and social rights and freedoms of every person, such as the right to a fair trial, the right to own property, the right to equal pay for equal work. It states all people are born free and equal in dignity and rights. Its introduction states the declaration is meant to serve as "a common standard of achievement for all peoples and all nations." Page 1.

universal suffrage: the right to vote (suffrage) for all persons over a certain age, usually eighteen or twenty-one, who in other respects satisfy the requirements established by law. Page 15.

unprincipled: acting contrary to moral principles; not doing right; immoral. Page 33.

unsavory: morally or socially objectionable or offensive; immoral. Page 174.

untenable: not fit to be occupied. Page 90.

usury: an excessively high rate of interest charged on borrowed money. Page 83.

Utopia: an impractical and usually impossibly ideal scheme, especially for social improvement. Originally a utopia was considered a place of ideal perfection in laws, government and social conditions. The name was the title of a book (1516) by English statesman and author Thomas More, who coined the word from the Greek *ou,* not, and *topos,* place, meaning nowhere. Page 34.

Utopian(s): those who speak of, promise or work toward a *utopia,* an impractical and usually impossibly ideal scheme, especially for social improvement. *See also* **Utopia.** Page 37.

V

vanguard: the leading position of a movement, field or cultural trend. Page 232.

vantage point: an actual or figurative position or location that provides a broad view or perspective of something. Page 83.

Verwoerd, Hendrik: Hendrik Frensch Verwoerd (1901–1966), political leader of South Africa, the main architect of the policy of racial separation known as apartheid. A professor of psychology during the 1930s, Verwoerd became a senator, rose to cabinet-level posts and eventually became prime minister in 1958. He was assassinated in 1966. Page 15.

vexatious: causing *vexation,* irritation, annoyance or something intended to harass. Page 64.

Vietnam: a tropical country in Southeast Asia, site of a major war from 1954 to 1975 between South Vietnam and Communist-controlled North Vietnam. The United States became involved in the mid-1960s, lending its support to South Vietnam. By the late 1960s, due to the length of the war, high US casualties and US participation in war crimes against the Vietnamese, American involvement became increasingly unpopular in the US and was strongly protested. In 1973, despite continuing hostilities between North and South Vietnam, the US removed all its troops. By 1975, the Communists had overrun South Vietnam and the war was officially ended, leading to the unification of the country (1976) as the Socialist Republic of Vietnam. Page 16.

vilified: subjected to false and malicious statements; spoken evil of. Page 198.

vindictive: characterized by a strong or unreasoning desire for revenge and intent to harm someone. Page 16.

Virginia: a state in the eastern United States, south of Washington, DC. Page 176.

virtue: 1. the worth, advantage or beneficial quality of something. Page 69.
2. behavior showing high moral standards. Page 110.

virulent: violent and rapid in its course; very deadly. Page 86.

visionary, bright-eyes: a dreamer or one whose ideas, plans, etc., are impractical or too fantastic and who is characterized as having *bright eyes,* eyes that show a strong desire for doing, obtaining or pursuing something. Page 94.

vital: 1. extremely important and necessary to the survival or continuing effectiveness of something. Page 20.
2. full of life and vigor; energetic. Page 23.

voilà: a French word used to call attention to or express satisfaction with a thing that has just been shown, proven or demonstrated. Page 98.

Volunteer Minister Program: established in the mid-1970s by L. Ron Hubbard, the Volunteer Minister Program is a worldwide grass-roots movement of people from all walks of life, dedicated to providing practical assistance to others in communities throughout the world. A *Volunteer Minister* is a person who helps his fellow man on a volunteer basis by restoring purpose, truth and spiritual values to the lives of others. Page 4.

vying: competing strongly in order to obtain or achieve something. Page 36.

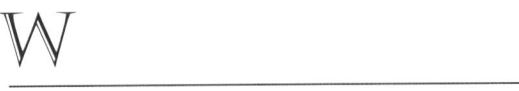

waning: decreasing in strength, power or influence; declining. Page 206.

want: the state or fact of lacking, or having too little of, something needed or desired. Page 5.

wardroom: on a warship, the dining room and lounge for the officers other than the commanding officer. Page 20.

Washington, George: (1732–1799) United States general and political leader. He was the commander of American forces during the American Revolutionary War (1775–1783) and first president of the United States (1789–1797). Page 10.

Washington Monument: the tall, white-marble, four-sided stone pillar tapering toward its pyramidal top located in Washington, DC, which honors George Washington (1732–1799), the first president of the United States (1789–1797). It is 555 feet (169 meters) in height and is one of the tallest stonework structures in the world. Page 6.

wash out: remove or get rid of as useless, unsatisfactory or the like. Page 118.

wastes: uninhabited, deserted or wild areas. Page 106.

water cure: a psychiatric treatment, purported to remove demons from a person, whereby the patient was stretched out on the ground and had water poured into his mouth from some height. Page 202.

Watergate: a building complex in Washington, DC, that included offices of Democratic Party headquarters. The name *Watergate* is used to designate the political scandal (1972–1974) that resulted in the resignation of then President Richard Nixon. The scandal came to light when burglars broke into the Democratic Party headquarters located at the Watergate complex. Investigation revealed the burglars had links to the Republican Party, which in turn led to officials high in the government and eventually to Nixon. It was found that key government officials, acting on orders from Nixon, had been spying on and plotting against people that Nixon considered to be his enemies. Attempts by these officials and the president to cover up the illegal actions were ineffective and Nixon finally resigned in 1974, when he was about to be removed from office because of the scandal. Page 5.

West, the: the countries of Western Europe and the Americas. Page 6.

Wheatstone Bridge: a reference to an early E-Meter that contained a *Wheatstone bridge,* a type of electric circuit used to determine an unknown resistance by comparing it with known resistances. This type of circuit was named after its inventor, Sir Charles Wheatstone (1802–1875), an English physicist. Page 223.

wheel: the imaginary wheel symbolizing fate or chance that is said to be turned by a mythical being known as Fortune. Page 10.

whim: a sudden thought, idea or desire, especially one based on impulse rather than reason or necessity. Page 20.

whiptail lizard: a lizard of North and South America characterized by great agility and alertness. Literally, a *whiptail* is a slender tail tapering from the base toward the tip. Page 107.

White, Harry Dexter: (1892–1948) American Government official in the US Department of the Treasury who was responsible for US foreign economic policy in the 1940s and who worked closely with English economist John Keynes. In 1948, he defended Alger Hiss in his espionage trial. White himself was accused of espionage by two admitted Communist spies, Elizabeth Bentley and Whittaker Chambers. When challenged with this data, White made a dramatic testimony denying the accusation. Three days later he died of a heart attack. Page 95.

white supremacist: having to do with the belief that government should restrict political, economic and social powers and opportunities to Caucasian people because they are supposedly superior to all other people and should therefore rule over them. *Supremacy* means the state of being highest in position or authority. Page 230.

Who's Who: the name of a famous reference work, first published in 1849, that contains biographical sketches of famous individuals and which is regularly updated. Page 77.

wild-eyed: extremely determined in a way that is slightly frightening; extremely irrational, senseless. Page 37.

Wilson, Woodrow: (1856–1924) twenty-eighth president of the United States (1913–1921). During the late 1800s, Wilson pursued a career as a historian and professor, writing several books on American history. Later, as US president, he worked to end World War I (1914–1918) and to form an international organization for keeping peace, the League of Nations. Page 155.

wind of, caught: found out (about something) indirectly. Page 109.

wiretapping: the practice of tapping (connecting a listening device to) a telephone line to monitor conversations secretly. Page 40.

witch doctor: a person in some societies who attempts to cure sickness and to drive out evil spirits from a person, place, etc., by the use of magic. Page 173.

withered: made to fall into a state of decay or decline; caused to lose force. Page 38.

wit, to: used to introduce a list or explanation of what one has just mentioned. Originally a phrase used in law, *that is to wit,* which meant that is to know, that is to say. Page 90.

World Federation for Mental Health (WFMH): an organization formed in 1948 by Canadian psychiatrist Brock Chisholm (1896–1971) and British psychiatrist John Rawlings Rees (1890–1969) to exert control on National Mental Health Associations throughout the world. Page 6.

World Health Organization: an agency of the United Nations established in 1948 with the stated purpose of improving the health of the world's people and preventing or controlling communicable diseases. Page 110.

worldview: a comprehensive conception or image of the universe and of humanity's relation to it; a conception of the course of events in and of the purpose of the world as a whole, forming a philosophical outlook on the universe. Page 2.

wormed (one's) way into: maneuvered (oneself) gradually into an area or position by devious or subtle means. Page 161.

wrapped up: put an end to. Page 76.

wraps, under heavy: in extreme secrecy; hidden. *Wraps* refers to secrecy or censorship. Page 76.

Wundt: Wilhelm Max Wundt (1832–1920), German psychologist and physiologist; the originator of modern psychology and the false doctrine that Man is no more than an animal. Page 127.

Y

yardman: a person who guards those who are confined, as to a mental institution. Page 129.

yardstick: any standard of measurement or judgment. Page 98.

"Yellow Peril": the alleged danger to Western civilization held to arise from expansion of the power and influence of Oriental peoples (as the Chinese and Japanese). Page 50.

yoke: something regarded as oppressive or burdensome. Literally, a *yoke* is a frame fitting over the neck and shoulders of a person, used for carrying pails or baskets. Page 20.

Z

zealots: people who show excessive enthusiasm for a cause; fanatics. Page 49.

zenith: highest point or state; culmination; climax. Page 206.

INDEX

A

aberration
    exposing lies and blowing, 85

accidents
    Scientology, one year with aircraft squadron and no, 25

accusations, false
    see **false accusations**

accusers
    confronting one with his, 69
    failing to confront one with his, 67
    pass legislation requiring accused to be confronted by accusers, 63

addiction, *see* **drug addiction**

Adler, 113

adultery
    psychiatrists and, 122, 189
    psychiatry and psychology advocate, 174
    psychoanalysts and, 210

agent provocateur
    tactics used by psychiatric front groups, 163

agriculturists
    Hearst and threat of immigration of Japanese, 50

Alaska Mental Health Act, 105–106, 109

America, 88
    people fond of Constitutional freedoms, 42
    reduction of, 198
    Russian Totalitarian State and, 143

American Gulag
    Siberia Bill and, 105

American Medical Association
    drugs and, 77

American Psychiatric Association, 6
    drugs and, 77

American Psychological Association, 6

American Revolution
    George Washington, 88

Americans
    Justice Department and, 75–78

Amtorg, 220

apartheid

    LRH working for one man, one vote versus, 24

appropriations

    psychiatric

        government and, 26

        shutting off, 34

argument

    how to win, 155

aristocracy

    France and Russia, 29

    pattern, 10

Aryanism, 31

Athens

    democracy undermined in, 51

atomic bomb

    made direct combat confrontation too dangerous, 196

attorney

    appointing each qualified attorney a judge, 63

auditors

    talking about cases, not publishers and politicians, 53

Austria

    absorbed into Russia, 132

    crowned heads of

        "very best people" and, 128

    death camps, 127

    psychiatry and psychology, 127

authority

    attracting criminals, 206

axioms

    Laws which are not generated by the mores and customs of a people..., 172

B

Bailey, Harry

    psychiatrist, exposed, 134

balance of payments

    cause of not balancing, 172

Balkans

    revolution and psychiatry and psychology, 174

bamboozlers, 186

bankers

    increased taxes and, 97

    psychiatric front groups and, 95

banking "Totalitarianism," 53

banks

    chain, 86

        obscuring the subject of economics, 86

    private banks smashed, 53

    US, 1932 takeover of, 53

barter, 89, 97, 98, 101

Beers, Clifford

    World Federation of Mental Health, takeover of, 178

behavioral control, 6

Belsen

    death camp, 174

Bergson, Henri

    "élan vital," 219

"best people," 31

    Adolf Hitler, 128

    crimes and injustices against the populations of Western nations and, 21

    crowned heads of Austria, 128

    Czar of Russia, 128

    denial of real justice, oppressive taxation and unreal, unworkable money standards, 98

    play a shepherd's pipe while the sheep quietly graze, 144

    population control and, 144

    psychiatric front groups and, 202, 203

    psychs, 34, 128, 178

    Republic and, 46

    revolution and, 34

    robber-baron castle ruled by, 201

    Russian Totalitarian State assisted by, 143

    slaughtered, 144

Bethesda, Maryland

    National Institute of Mental Health, 168

Bill of Rights

    American Government at odds with, 16

    corruption of, 5

    description, 41

    government departments and, 42

    Nixon and, 40

    "Preamble has no force in law," 46

    Taxpayers', 18

    ten amendments, 46

    tyranny versus, 44

    US Constitution, Penal Code and, 46

Bills of Attainder, 64

Bismarck

    psychiatry and psychology and, 205

blackmail, 136, 189

black people

    injustice and, 69, 71

Blain, Daniel, 144

    military mind-control experimentation, 106

bland personality, 147, 149

Bolshevik revolt

    1917, corruption and injustices, 63

boundaries

    psychiatry and psychology advocate the destruction of, 174

"bounty hunters"

    psychiatry enlisting bounty hunters to kidnap patients, 231

Bowart, Walter

    Operation Mind Control, 194

Brady, James

    shooting by psychiatrically treated John Hinckley, Jr., 204

"Bright and Stupid"

    "Good and Bad," 209

British Empire

    Russian Totalitarian State and, 143

bureaucracy, unconstitutional, 44

Burgess

    psychiatric treatment and, 124

C

Call, Joseph M.
　Superior Court Judge, 106

Canada, 18
　exposure of psychiatrist, 231

Capitalism, 88
　Communism and, 88
　Das Kapital to destroy, 86
　definition, 86
　Socialism and, 88
　twisting economics, 89
　world gets poorer, 88

Carr, Sir William, 109

Castro, Fidel
　Cuban Revolution, 88

"Cause and Prevention of Revolution, The," 2, 7, 9

CCHR, *see* **Citizens Commission on Human Rights (CCHR)**

censorship
　Totalitarianism and, 49

Center, Abraham
　arrogance of, 118
　Savannah, Georgia, 118

Central Intelligence Agency, 36, 121, 194
　LSD experimentation, 107

chain banks, *see* **banks**

Chambers, Whittaker
　labeled by psychiatrists, 155

Charter Behavioral Health Systems
　closure of, 232

Chelmsford facility
　exposure of "deep sleep," 134

chemistry
　Scientology and, 224

Chicago
　student protest of American involvement in Vietnam, 16

Child Medication Safety Amendments, 232

child molestation
　exposure of, 231

children
　attacking by making drug addicts out of bright children, 184
　psychiatric drugging of, 77
　psychiatrists and psychologists and, 212
　psychology and psychiatry taught in American schools, 127

China
　Communist, inflation and, 101
　overthrow of by importation of opium, 184

Chisholm, Brock
　Communist, 33
　psychiatric strategist, 208
　psychiatry and, 177
　right and wrong, psychiatric reinterpretation and eradication of the concept of, 105
　takeover of organization of Clifford Beers, 178

Christianity, 101
　psychiatrists and psychologists paralyzing and wiping out, 136, 181

Christ, Jesus
　labeled by psychiatrists, 155

churches
- destruction of, 198
- improvement of society, 190
- infiltration of churches in America, 76
- influence upon the state, 205
- psychiatric front groups and eradication of, 33
- psychiatric plans to knock out, 110
- traditional force of freedom and decency, 1

Church of Scientology
- aims, 53
- attacks
  - by psychiatry through press chains, 178
  - from psychiatric front groups, 128
- chemistry and, 224
- Creed of, 15
- drawn gun raid on Washington, DC, Church, 25
- economics, legitimate field for comment in, 86
- exposing psychiatric front groups, 34
- FBI surveillance of organization of, 60
- field of the mind and, 241
- flight surgeons and, 25
- force for human rights in government, 18
- game where everybody wins, 34
- handling of drug use, 184
- hidden secret of the attacks of nineteen years, 222
- highest respect for law, 23
- human rights demanded, 110
- intentions of, 163, 164
- movement, 241
- "Nixon Enemies List" and, 16
- physics and, 224
- pilots and, 25
- preservation of democracy and, 18
- psychiatric front groups' lies and attacks on Scientology, 34
- psychiatrists fighting with such terror, 124
- psychiatry discrediting and suppressing, 178
- reason psychiatric front groups attack, 109
- recognition of religious bona fides, 24
- scientific methodology and, 224
- secret and vicious war against, 174
- seeking to prevent collapse of Western civilization, 21
- source of attacks on Scientology identified, 178
- story of how it had to develop, 223
- totalitarian regime reaction to freedom and, 162
- way to rehabilitate the West, 63
- well, happy human beings and, 132
- worldwide human rights campaign, 18

CIA, *see* **Central Intelligence Agency**

CIO, *see* **Congress of Industrial Organizations**

Citizens Commission on Human Rights (CCHR), 176, 229
- award from United States Congress, 230
- documentary series, 236
- formation of, 134
- French health ministries and, 230

Index   321

Hungarian refugee, release of, 230

international headquarters, Los Angeles, California, 226–227

Italian government raids and closure of asylums, 231

Mexico, 232

"Principles, Guidelines and Guarantees for the Protection of Persons Detained on Grounds of Mental Ill-Health or Suffering from Mental Disorder," 235

public service awards and recognitions, 238

civil disorder

psychiatry, 190

see also **revolts; riots**

civilization

death of, description, 42

destroyed by psychiatry and psychology, 211

Hearsts of the world spoiling an era of, 51

Universal Declaration of Human Rights and, 20, 21

Western, destroyed by wild-eyed Utopians, 37

civil rights

destruction of, 34

LRH isolating the Why behind, 70

Siberia Bill and violation of, 109

clique

profit of, 10

Cold War, 6, 194

partnership between American military and psychiatrists, 15

"**combat conditioning,**" 105

COMINFIL

Communist Infiltration, J. Edgar Hoover and, 60

Commissar

twisting economics, 89

Commoner, Barry

Science and Survival, 219

Communism, 88

brainwashing and, 139

Fidel Castro in Cuban Revolution, 88

George Washington in the American Revolution, 88

Marquis de Lafayette in the French Revolution, 88

Super-Capitalist, 88

tool of the rich, 88

Communist China

inflation, 101

Communists

Hoover's office and "nothing can be done about," 76

infiltrators, FBI and, 60

"justice" and, 67

seven hundred and fifty million humans under the, 20

Communist Totalitarian State

psychiatry and psychology and, 143

see also **totalitarian state**

competent

redefined by psychiatric front groups, 34

Comte, Auguste

control of populations and, 143

Comte de Saint-Simon, 54

control of populations and, 143

Condon, Richard
> *The Manchurian Candidate*, 107

confidence tricksters, 186
> psychiatrists, 173
> psychologists, 173

con game
> constitutions being made into, 45

Congressional Committee
> listening to the enemy, 198

Congress of Industrial Organizations
> John L. Lewis and, 76

Constitution, 45
> American Government at odds with, 16
> Australian state Constitutions ignored, 46
> constitutional destruction, 33
> definition, 45
> Eire, binding on leaders and people, 45
> four parts composing, 45
> good versus bad, 46
> government employees not acting within framework of, 41
> Greece
>> some unwritten, 45
>> violation of, 46
>
> income tax is a violation of, 97
> justice written into, 71
> liberty, Bill of Rights and, 44
> no guarantee of constitutional government, 41
> omitting essential parts, 46
> psychiatric front groups and destruction of, 33, 53
> psychiatry and psychology advocate the overthrow of, 174
> South Africa, LRH calling for end of apartheid, 15
> US, Bill of Rights and Penal Code, 46
> World Federation of Mental Health
>> eradication of Constitution, 33, 168
>> unconstitutional actions in US, 168

control
> psychiatric front groups and control technology, 34
> terrorism and psychiatrists and psychologists, 136
> untried and insane concepts of total social, 37

control philosophies
> psychiatry, psychology, sociology, 144

control sciences
> psychiatry and psychology, 131
>> sociology and, 143

Coordinator of Law Enforcement Tactics
> Mitchell, 59

corruption
> Czarist Russia and, 63
> psychiatrists and psychologists, 136

counseling
> evaluative, lowers IQ, 210

country
> how a country can go down, 98

courage
> to speak out, 9

courts
> accepting no summonses for "public servants," 42
> liable to act on false reports, 67

psychiatric terms and, 185

psychiatry, psychology and, 173

"crazy"

disagreements with total social control and being labeled crazy, 155

"Create want!"

Keynes and, 173

Creed of the Church of Scientology, 15

crimes

auditors finding mental patients who have orders to commit crimes, 124

cause of, 211

Church of Scientology bringing to light, 21

criminals in charge and crime rate rising, 159

Justice Department and, 76, 77

lack of ready, speedy, inexpensive justice and, 64

lawless and irresponsible public attitude developed toward, 159

Prohibition Act and financed crime, 46

psychiatric front groups, *see* **psychiatric front groups**

psychiatry, 110, 117, 178

reaping social chaos and, 190

psychs and, 189, 205

"public servants" committing crimes with personal safety, 42

systems dying under senseless crimes, 10

why crime rate is rising, 161

criminal mind

law enforcement officer knowledge of, 161

psychiatrists and, 209

research on, 204

criminal offense

physical damage due to shock or brain surgery, 63

criminals

branded as, 64

crime rate and, 159

Hitler, 209

IQ, 209

Napoleon, 209

pain-drug-hypnosis and, 209

privileges and, 159

psychiatrists, 206

psychiatry and psychology advocate the release of criminals on the society, 174

psychologists, 206

reform of, 208

"treated" by psychologists and psychiatrists, 209

"crisis decades," 5

Cromwell

England's disastrous public official, 75

Cuba, 88

Cuban Revolution

Fidel Castro, 88

"Cultural Destruction," 195–200

Currency Exchange laws, 92

customs

Laws which are not generated by the mores and customs of a people..., 172

cynicism

displacing patriotism, 50

cytological experimentation, 217
    French National Institute of Health and Medical Research, 217

cytology, 220
    cellular memory, 220

Czarist Russia
    student revolts, 132

Czechoslovakia
    absorbed into Russia, 132
    psychiatrists and psychologists, 136

D

Dachau
    World Federation of Mental Health and, 168

Dark Ages
    mental science and, 174

Das Kapital
    Karl Marx and, 86

D-day, 144

death
    hypnotism under pain and drugs and bringing about one's, 122

death camps, 229
    Belsen, 174
    exposed, 181
    Kenneth Robinson advocating, 109
    Nazi, 122
    Poland, Germany, Austria, Russia, 127
    psychiatrists and, 110
    state-financed for dissenters, 136

"deep sleep"
    exposure of, 134

definitions
    Capitalism, 86
    Constitution, 45
    deflation, 89
    democracy, 46
    general-interest group, 49
    hypnotism, 121
    inflation, 89
    money, 86
    post-hypnotic-suggestion, 121
    quack, 151
    republic, 46
    special-interest group, 49
    totalitarianism, 49

deflation
    cause of, 172
    definition, 89

Delaware
    United States
        World Federation of Mental Health, 167

delusion
    psychiatrists screaming "It's just delusion," 124

democracy
    Athenian, 51
    breakdown of Western, 67
    candidate's campaign money, special-interest group and, 50
    Constitution and, 44
    definition, 46
    deteriorating into hands of special-interest groups, 50
    government directly by the people, 46

party-regulated "democracy," 10

people and government, 46

public servant in, 42

the more secrecy, the less, 18

Democratic National Convention

1968, 16

depersonalization

psychiatrists and, 122

depression

drug use and, 191

economics and, 98

US, 98

despotism

politicians reserving right of, 46

raw ruthlessness and, 49

detention centers

American intelligence community and, 53

Dewey, John, 86

tenets of, 132

US educator and follower of Wundt, 131

Diagnostic & Statistical Manual: Psychiatry's Deadliest Scam, 236

Dianetics, 221

attacks on Dianetics by psychiatry through press chains, 178

broadly applicable low-cost mental health, 192

FBI surveillance of, 60

handling of drug use, 184

psychiatry discrediting and suppressing, 178

source of attacks on Dianetics identified, 178

threat to healing income, 222

well, happy human beings and, 132

Dianetics: The Modern Science of Mental Health

attacks on L. Ron Hubbard after release of, 221

hypnotism not well understood before, 121

published, 221

remonstrance against psychiatric electric shock and surgery, 109

Diogenes, 165

diplomas

psychiatric facade to extort billions from government, 129

psychiatrists, 129

psychologists, 129

requirement for, 129

dissidents

labeling of those seeking to stem disaster, 77

DNA biological theories, 219

doctors

Hitler's intelligence service and, 168

Nazis and, 143

doom

genius to recognize approaching, 9

dope, *see* **drugs**

Double-Cross System in the War of 1939 to 1945, The

UK government publication, 77

drawn gun raid

description, 24

Washington Church of Scientology, 25

dream
    strange dream wherein everybody likes strawberries..., 144

drug addiction
    attacks by foreign intelligence agencies and, 184
    eradicating the cause of, 183
    failed psychotherapy and, 191
    intelligence subversion and, 196
    making drug addicts out of bright children, 184
    making drug addicts out of leaders, 184
    physical suffering or hopelessness and, 183
    pilot project in prison, 183
    psychiatry and psychology advocate, 174
    research, 182
    schools and, 33
    Scientology cooperating with governments to handle, 183
    unworkable psychotherapy and, 191

drug culture, 77
    "lost people," 4
    stupefied civilization, 4

drugs
    Charles Manson, mass murderer, 107
    deepening impact of commands, 122
    depression, pain, 191
    drying out, 183
    50,000-volt shocks and, 122
    getting unhooked, 184
    going blank at unexpected times after using, 184
    handling with Dianetics and Scientology, 184
    hypnotism and pain and death and, 122
    irresponsibility and, 184
    Justice Department, organized crime and, 77
    sickness and, 184
    terrorism and pain and, 122

Druidism
    psychiatry and, 113

dungeons
    psychiatry and, 201

Dunsany, Lord
    story about the day the temple fell, 186

duress
    hypnotism and, 122

DVDs
    An Industry of Death, 236
    Diagnostic & Statistical Manual: Psychiatry's Deadliest Scam, 236
    How Psychiatric Drugs Can Kill Your Child, 236
    The Marketing of Madness, 236
    The Untold Story of Psychotropic Drugging, 236

E

École Polytechnique
    destruction of, 143

economics, 83
    absence or misuse of, 173
    depression and, 98
    genus of, 90
    handling of, 92
    inflation, 98

mental science and, 174

misuse of the subject, 88

neglect of, 172

nine-tenths of life, 86

obscuring economics so as to take everything away from everyone, 88

one of the primary barriers to total freedom, 85

one of the standard equations of, 98

oppressive, 2

relationship of any man to, 94

science of, 89

subject obscured by chain banks, 86

subversion of, 196

theories of, 85

understanding of, 85

war and tax and, 95

weakening of, 195

economic slavery, 53

education

destruction of, 198

perverted by psychs, 136, 174

Rockefeller Foundation, 83

subversion of, 196

totalitarian state and, 144

trained in disloyalty and, 144

educators

John Dewey

follower of Wundt, 131

trained in Leipzig, Germany, 132

Wundt and, 131

Eire

Constitution, 45

electric shock, 19, 176

banning of, 134

exposing the myth of, 232

Hitler's development for dissident elements, 34

killing over 1,200 people in a year in US, 113

sanitariums and, 124

treatments with drugs, 122

electroconvulsive treatment, *see* **electric shock**

E-Meters

US Food and Drug Administration, seizure of, 24

endocrine experiments, 220

enemy

Congressional Committee listening to, 198

destruction of populations, 196

England, 88

crime rate and psychiatry, 127

Cromwell, disastrous public official, 75

photographs of L. Ron Hubbard at Saint Hill Manor, 7, 58, 82, 225

speed of contraction of, 198

universities going out of control, 132

epidemic

can start while one thinks about it, 3

Equestrian order of Rome, 29

espionage, 196

campaign, 196

Establishment, the, 9

arrogant, pompous and blind, 9

heedless in its blindness, 11

euphoric, 147

evil purposes

    research on, 204

exclusion

    revolt and, 31

F

false accusations

    basic breakdown of justice and, 67

    nations breaking down and, 63

    penalty for, 63

False Data Stripping

    psychiatrists and psychologists and, 207

false reports

    breaking down

        nation's structure, 67

        Western democracy, 67

Fascism, 78, 128

    J. Edgar Hoover and, 77

favors

    political holders of offices and, 10

FBI, *see* **Federal Bureau of Investigation**

FDA, *see* **Food and Drug Administration**

fear

    psychiatry and instilling, 15

    see also **terrorism**

Federal Bureau of Investigation

    corrupt, 5

    infiltration/surveillance and, 60

    intense federal harassment from, 16

    Lee Harvey Oswald and, 77

    surveillance of US civil and religious organizations, 60

Federal Emergency Management Agency

    detention centers, 53

Federal Marshals

    longshoremen posing as, 223

federal regulatory warnings, 232

FEMA, *see* **Federal Emergency Management Agency**

field of the mind

    Scientology and, 241

fifth column

    psychiatry, 105

Filipino

    injustice and, 71

finance

    destruction of a population, 196

    see also **economics**

fixed idea

    political life hardening into, 51

    special-interest group and, 49

Flaming Youth era of the Prohibition 20s, 184

flight surgeons

    Scientology and, 25

flimflam artists, 186

Food and Drug Administration

    US, seizure of E-Meters, 24

    Wilhelm Reich and, 223

Ford, Gerald, 40

Founding Church of Scientology

    Siberia Bill defeated by, 109

    US Food and Drug Administration seizure of E-Meters, 24

Founding Fathers (American), 45

    freedoms promised by, 42

France

    "lettres de cachet" and, 20

    upper classes of, 29

freedom

    economics and barrier to, 85

    fight for, 177

    Mankind and, 241

    mental science and, 174

    South Africa, LRH efforts and, 24

    threat to, fought by Scientologists, 34

    totalitarian regime reaction to, 162

Freedom Fighters, 7

Freedom **magazine,** 1

Freedom of Information Act, 230

    legislation, 18

freedom of speech

    government departments at war with, 42

free society

    violent opposition to, 143

French health ministries

    Citizens Commission on Human Rights (CCHR) and, 230

French Revolution

    control of populations versus, 143

    Marquis de Lafayette, 88

Freud, 113

    "mental diseases," 185

Fromm-Reichmann, Frieda

    book of warnings to psychiatrists, 124

function monitors structure, 220

G

general-interest groups

    definition, 53

    special-interest groups versus, 49, 51

genius

    recognizing approaching doom, courage and, 9

geopolitical study

    what plagues the world, 1

German intelligence, 195

German Intelligence Service

    John L. Lewis, 76

Germany

    death camps, 127

    Hitler, 49

        disastrous public official, 75

    Kaiser, destruction of, 132

    psychiatry and psychology, revolution and, 127, 136, 174

    see also **Leipzig, Germany**

"G-Man"

    school, 75

G-Men **magazine,** 75

God

    psychiatry and psychology

        there is no God, 132

gold

    can't eat it or have it, 98

    gold dollar-based world monetary system, 83

    money and, 86

reserves, 95

    International Monetary Fund and, 95

    Lend-Lease payments and, 97

Golden Years

  1960s and Western economics, 83

Goldwater, Barry

  labeled by psychiatrists, 155

"Good and Bad"

  "Bright and Stupid," 209

"good dog"

  mental state, 7

government(s), 15

  agencies failed to halt increase in drug taking, 184

  American, US Constitution at odds with, 16

  "best people" and, 31

  by special interest, 37

  by the few and oppression of the many, 29

  Church of Scientology and force for human rights, 18

  Constitution

    composition of, 45

    founding or modifying, 45

    versus actual conduct of, 45

  death of patriotism, 69

  democracy and the people, 46

  description of how a system is established, 10

  disbelief and disavowal of, 41

  economics and, 86

  enemy crushing people by using incompetent, 38

  financing psychiatry and psychology, 174

  forms of, 1

  handling of, 38

  influenced by psychiatrists, 110

  justice and, 71

  letters written to, 26

  loyalty dead due to no protection from, 69

  making it easy to seize people, 19

  men famous for stupid, obstinate devotion to, 10

  money handouts to buy support, 42

  Nixon brand of totalitarian, 16

  patriotism, loyalty and devotion of, 69

  policy

    "special interests" underlying, 50, 51

  prevention of domination by men who could never pass…, 181

  protesting groups and restoring wise policies in, 38

  psychiatric brethren and, 26

  psychiatry and psychology extorting huge sums from, 173

  psychiatry reaping social chaos and crime, 190

  revolt and, 29

  "right to override right of individuals' privacy," 59

  Scientology cooperating with governments to handle drug addiction in society, 183

  special-interest groups and, 50

  totalitarianism and detested form of, 49

  tyranny of, 2

unconstitutional, 41

unsafe, 67

vast majority of honest, decent people in, 44

violating Greek Constitution, 46

what almost all trouble in a country stems from, 41

why do governments support psychiatrists and psychologists, 210

why support psychiatry, 189

World Federation of Mental Health and why not acted upon by government agencies, 168

writing to, 25

Great Socialist

twisting economics, 89

Greece

Constitutions

some unwritten, 45

violation of, 46

exposure of psychiatric abuse in, 134, 231

Persian attacks on, 195

totalitarianism and, 51

Griebl-Voss-Hofman-Rumrich ring, 76

groups

minority

injustice and, 69

religious and racial, 69

political life of nation divided in two, 49

protecting from fallacious attacks, 64

psychiatric front groups, *see* **psychiatric front groups**

psychiatrists attacking decent social, 117

small, with fixed ideas, 51

H

Haight-Ashbury

drug experimentation among residents of, 107

Hamilton, Alexander, 10

happy

psychiatry and psychology, no approval of anyone being, 147

hate

special-privilege groups and, 29

healing societies

offered Dianetics and rebuffed it, 221

health

perverted by psychiatry and psychology, 174

Health Ministers, 26

attacks on Dianetics and Scientology, 178

World Federation of Mental Health, 167

Hearst

newspaper magnate and creation of 1941 war, 50

Hegel

psych research and, 222

Hinckley, Jr., John

psychiatrically treated, 204

Hiss, Alger

psychiatry and, 177

Hitler

criminal, 209

electric shocks to depersonalize dissident elements, 34

Germany, destruction of, 132

Germany's disastrous public official, 75

intelligence service of Third Reich and doctors, 168

Jewish people, whose industries and newspapers he needed, 51

primary weapon and the "incredible," 33

"very best people" and, 128

World Federation of Mental Health and, 168

holocaust

psychiatric roots of, 236

Home Office Immigration, 25

Hoover, J. Edgar, 75

compiling incriminating dossiers on presidents, 60

crimes, 77

donning of women's clothing and, 60

Interpol and, 77

Justice Department and, 76

little "black book," 5

planned attack on Pearl Harbor and, 77

political blackmail, 60

reaction to freedom and Scientology, 162

US disastrous public official, 75

How Psychiatric Drugs Can Kill Your Child, 236

human experiments, 229

humanities, 220

chaos in the field of, 223

obscured by authoritarianism, professionalism and dogma, 223

physical sciences and, 171, 174

political science and, 171

research into, 219

human rights

Church of Scientology and, 18

false report threatening, 69

Nazi violations of, 19

patriotism slain by deafness to, 21

preservation of, 1

psychiatric violations, 229

reforms in the field of, 20

Scientology demand for, 110

Universal Declaration of Human Rights, 1

violation of

seizure and, 114

Siberia Bill and, 109

hypnotism

death and, 122

definition, 121

drugs and pain and, 122

duress and, 122

fixating person's attention, 121

usual versus drug hypnosis, 122

hypocrisy

psychiatry, psychology and, 152

I

idealism

corrupted by special-interest group, 51

income tax, 88, 89

basis of, 90

no regard to Bill of Rights, 46

not vital, 92

oppressive, 97

violation of original US Constitution, 97

"incredible," the
Hitler's primary weapon and, 33

"incurable"
authoritative pose and, 185, 186

Industry of Death
DVD, 236

museum, 235

photographs, 228, 234–235

traveling exhibit, 236

inflation, 53
barter and, 97

cause of, 172

definition, 89

economics, 98

handling of, 92

not inevitable, 92

postage stamps, 101

primary factors behind, 173

suicide, 101

wipes out savings, 92

influence
those with authority and, 11

influence in high places
psychiatrists and, 189

injustice
bulk of American riots and, 71

Church of Scientology bringing to light, 21

insecurity and, 21

revolution and, 71

inmates
females sold as prostitutes, 174

Inquiry
UK Parliament stating no, 25

insanity
cleaning up the problem of, 181

physical disease, psychiatry and, 206

psychiatric "authority" using big words for forms of, 185

psychiatry, 190

increasing statistics of, 124

redefined as

anyone who is incompetent, 34

disagreeing with the social autonomy, 19

repealing all insanity commitment laws, 63

subversion of a population, 196

insecurity
injustices and, 21

personal, 69

revolution and, 42

institutions
men and women tortured in, 19

pain-drug-hypnosis, ordinary activity in, 122

psychiatric front groups and "treatment" in, 53

psychiatrists and

persons ruined by, 118

insurance fraud
exposure of, 231

psychiatric institutions and, 231

intelligence technology
against the West since 1948, 195

drug addiction widespread, 196

highly specialized, 195

miseducation and subversion of a population, 196

psychiatry and, 163

soaring crime rates, 196

International Monetary Fund

gold and, 95

Keynes and Harry Dexter White, founders, 95

International Telephone & Telegraph (ITT)

contribution to Nixon campaign, 59

Interpol

J. Edgar Hoover and, 77

IQ

criminals, 209

evaluative counseling lowers IQ, 210

Iron Curtain

psychiatric murder behind, 126

Western propaganda across, 194

World Federation of Mental Health "Congresses" and, 168

Italy

government raids and closure of asylums, 231

ITT, *see* **International Telephone & Telegraph (ITT)**

J

Japanese

Hearst and threat of, 50

Japanese intelligence, 195

conquering by making addicts out of leaders and bright children, 184

Jefferson Memorial

photograph by L. Ron Hubbard, 61

Jesus Christ

labeled by psychiatrists, 155

Jews

Hitler recruiting Jews whose industries and newspapers he needed, 51

Nazi death camps and, 122

why they killed other Jews under the Nazis, 122

judge

appointing every qualified attorney as, 63

Jung, 113, 114

jurisprudence

breakthrough in the field of, 67

ceasing to involve mental expertise with, 63

justice and, 59

swaying with long psychiatric terms, 185

just cause, a, 21, 23

justice, 67

basic breakdown of, 67

Church of Scientology and, 23

denial of real, 98

failing, links between psychiatry and, 59

fast, 63

for all, 21

inadequate, 2

judicial inequity, 5

jurisprudence and, 59

not affordable by all, riots and, 71

taken into one's own hands, 64

Western, as of 1969, 59

Western powers pulling up honor and, 69

Justice Department, 75

Americans versus, 75

attempting to expand to National Police Force, 75

breeding crime and lawlessness, 77

creating chaos, 77

crimes, 77

false dossiers on Americans, 77

Interpol and, 77

J. Edgar Hoover, star of, 76

Kennedy and, 77

labeling of "dissidents," 77

manufacturing dossiers for public leaders who had none, 77

protection of American president and, 77

K

Kaiser's Germany

destruction of, 132

Kennedy, John F.

assassination of, 77

Justice Department and, 77

Keynes

alteration of natural economic laws, 173

"Create want!," 98, 173

economic doctrine in West, 95

failure of Keynesian theories, 83

founding of International Monetary Fund, 95

planned inflation, 101

starvation and, 173

KGB

Russian Totalitarian State and, 143

King, Cecil, 109

King, Rodney

civil rights and, 70

Korea

brainwashing, 139

Kraepelin

scale of mental diseases, 185

Kutzbrain, Dr.

dealing with overactive mentalities, 10

L

Lafayette, Marquis de

French Revolution, 88

Lanterman-Petris-Short Act

Scientologists and the removal of, 34

Lasswell, Harold D.

plan to replace politicians and rulers with psychiatrists, 135

law

"above the law"

governments, 41

politicians, 45

psychiatrists and psychologists, 136

innocent until proven guilty beyond reasonable doubt, 64

J. Edgar Hoover instructing agents to violate, 60

Laws which are not generated by the mores and customs of a people..., 172 "men who know best" and, 45

psychiatrists and psychologists "above the law," 136

repealing all insanity commitment, 63

leaders

attacking by making drug addicts out of leaders, 184

Lebensohn, Zigmond

psychiatric presence in governing process, 59

legislators

bowing to psychiatry, 202

Leipzig, Germany

Ludwig, 131

origin of psychiatry, 177

psychologists, educators and psychiatrists trained in, 132

tenets of the school of psychologists and psychiatrists, 132

Wundt and men are animals theory, 131

see also **Leipzig University**

Leipzig University

Ludwig

nerve conditioning and, 143

psychology, psychiatry and educators from, 132

Wundt

nerve conditioning and, 143

see also **Leipzig, Germany**

"Let the Whistle Blow," 230

"lettres de cachet"

seizing and imprisoning people, 20

Lewis, John L.

head of labor union CIO, 76

liberty, 1

changes in Constitutions and limitations in, 46

LRH commitment to individual, 15

politicians pretending to guarantee, 46

revolution and destruction of, 34

unalert public and withered away, 38

Liberty, Fraternity and Equality

control of populations versus, 143

destruction of, 144

lies

aberrations blowing when exposing, 85

life

economics, nine-tenths and social-political, one-tenth, 86

research into, 219

loans

bank and state, 88

lobotomies

exposing the myth of, 232

Lodge, Henry Cabot

"With modernly armed armies no citizen revolt could ever succeed," 97

longshoremen

posing as marshals, Washington, DC, raid, 25

"lost people," 4

loyalty

disruption of, 67

LSD

mind control and, 107

psychedelic era, 107

psychiatry, 184

Ludwig, Karl Friedrich Wilhelm
   Leipzig, Germany
      nerves and physical reactions, 131
   nerve conditioning and, 143
   tenets of, 132

M

Macedonian Party
   covertly undermining Athenian democracy, 51

Maclean
   psychiatric treatment and, 124

Madison Avenue
   advertising, 89

"mad Russian doctor"
   portrayed in movies, 177

Mafia, 129
   psychiatrists compared to, 117

Man
   can be totally controlled
      psychiatry and psychology, 132
   cannot be changed
      psychiatry and psychology, 132
   has no will, is stimulus-response and irresponsible
      psychiatry and psychology, 132
   push-button stimulus-response robot, 159
   spiritual being, 224
   training of, 132
   see also **Man is an animal theory**

Manchu Dynasty
   overthrow of with opium, 184

Manchurian Candidate, The
   Richard Condon, 107

Manhattan
   study of American society (circa 1973), 4

Man is an animal theory, 29, 31, 127, 131, 132, 159, 174, 205, 206

Manson, Charles
   mass murderer, drug experimentation and, 107

Marketing of Madness, The, 236

Marx, Karl
   economics and politics, 94
   income tax, 90
   philosophy, 86

Massachusetts
   exposure of psychiatrist, 231

mass communication media
   destruction of a population using, 196

mathematics
   study of, 220

medical profession
   economic threat of, 163
   refused Dianetics and Scientology, 163

Medicare claims, 176

mental energy
   discoveries about, 220

mental healing
   psychiatry and crimes, 189

mental health
   castrating, torturing, seizing in the name of, 118
   psychiatric front groups facade, 53

see also **National Institute of Mental Health; World Federation of Mental Health**

mental "hospitals"

    shock, surgery, water "cures," drugs, 202, 203

    torture and crime, 202, 203

mental illnesses

    invention of, 236

mental image pictures, 221

mental "laws"

    seizure without law, 202

mental science

    Dark Ages and, 174

    most basic human science, 174

mental technology

    breakthrough in, 164

    Hitler and Germany, 127

    murder was being sold for mercy, 173

    never developed or approached prior, 173

    Stalin and Russia, 127

Mesmer, 122

Mexico

    Citizens Commission on Human Rights and curtailing child drugging, 232

MI5

    Nazi spy ring in America and, 76

military dictatorship

    pattern, 10

mind

    psychiatric groups preventing developments in field of, 34

    Scientology and the field of the mind, 241

    technology of

        never developed or approached prior, 173

        psychiatry and psychology sought to crush, 173

mind control, 6

    LSD and drugs, 107

    military mind-control experimentation, 106

Minister Bray, 49

minority groups

    injustice and, 69

miseducation

    intelligence subversion, 196

Mitchell, John N.

    Watergate accomplice, 59

monarchies

    Constitution and, 44

    pattern, 10

monetary systems

    structure of, 1

money

    definition, 86

    government handouts to buy support, 42

    increasing with property and goods increasing, 86

    produce and, 97

    psychiatry and, 83, 118

standards
> unreal, unworkable, 98
>
> worse off it gets, 173

moral code
> hypnosis and pain and drugs and, 122

mores
> Laws which are not generated by the mores and customs of a people..., 172

murder, 229
> charges, psychiatry and, 110
>
> politicians condoning, 33
>
> psychiatric kidnap, torture and, 117
>
> psychiatrists, 189

"My Philosophy," 3

N

Napoleon
> criminal, 209

Narconon, 182

national decay
> silencing of voices raised in protest, 198

National Institute of Mental Health
> Bethesda, Maryland, 168
>
> wasted funds and extravagance, 107

Nationalist China
> inflation, 101

nations
> assets grabbed, 53
>
> degenerating and dying, 42
>
> false accusations and breakdown of, 63
>
> false reports and
>> breaking down social structure of, 67
>
> tearing apart, 67
>
> special-interest groups and disaster, 51
>
> Western
>> dominated by one group, 53
>>
>> "Health" ministries and appointees in, 34

Nazis
> Aryanism and, 31
>
> death camps, 122
>> World Federation of Mental Health and, 168
>
> doctors and, 143
>
> false reports and, 67
>
> fighting for a world safe from Nazi extermination camps, 20
>
> Justice Department and, 77
>
> Man is an animal theory, 29
>
> spy ring in America, 76
>
> superselect, 29
>
> terror symbol, 122
>
> violations of human rights, 19

Nazi Totalitarian Germany
> German doctors and, 143

nerves
> severing the nerves, 132

newspapers
> psychiatrists and psychologists
>> pressure on owners of, 136

New York
> "experts" in the work of Wundt and Pavlov, 127
>
> photograph of New York City (1973) by L. Ron Hubbard, 5

New Yorker **magazine**
> psychiatric terms, 186

New York Times
    psychiatric terms, 186

New Zealand
    exposure of psychiatric abuse in, 134
    exposure of psychiatrist, 231

1984
    evil and, 118
    George Orwell's, 37
    headshrinkers taking over world and, 54

"Nixon Enemies List"
    LRH and Church of Scientology, 16

Nixon, Richard M.
    Bill of Rights and, 40
    exceedingly dark term as president, 16
    reaction to freedom and Scientology, 162
    secret discussions with ITT and, 59

Nuremberg Code, 21

O

Oak Knoll Naval Hospital
    research (1945), 220

Office of Naval Intelligence, 75

Office of Naval Research, 221

oligarchy
    pattern, 10

Operation Mind Control
    Walter Bowart, 194

opinions
    right of writing freely one's own, 15

opium
    overthrow of China by importing opium, 184
    overthrow of Manchu Dynasty, 184

oppression
    government and, 29
    groups in the West fighting, 37
    revolt and, 42

organized crime
    Justice Department and, 77

Orwell, George
    1984, 37
    headshrinkers and, 54

Oswald, Lee Harvey
    FBI and, 77

outlaws
    psychiatrists and psychologists, 136

Overholser, Winfred
    military mind-control experimentation, 106
    psychiatric presence in governing process, 59

P

Pacific Fleet
    J. Edgar Hoover and destruction of, 77

pain-drug-hypnosis, 121
    criminals and, 209
    effective on 100 percent of population, 121
    political threats of, 124
    psychiatrists and, 122
    Science of Survival, described in, 107

paragons of virtue, 189

paranoia, 185

Parliament
> UK, stating no Scientology Inquiry (1968), 25

patriotism, 19
> corrupted by special-interest group, 51
> dead, description, 69
> displaced by cynicism, 50
> governments worth, 20, 21
> government undermining, 42
> slain by false accusations, 21

Pavlov, Ivan Petrovich, 131, 132
> animal and death-camp practices, 127
> brainwashing techniques and, 139
> destruction of American schools and, 141
> destruction of the West and, 128
> false theories, 139
> Russia, 143
> UK Royal Society and, 131
> violent university revolution and murder of the Czar, 131

paycheck
> shrinking
>> primary factors behind, 173
> tax-shredded, 21

Pearl Harbor
> J. Edgar Hoover and, 77

penal code
> Constitution and, 45
> US Constitution, Bill of Rights and, 46

Persia
> attacks on Greece, 195

personality
> bland, 147

persona non grata
> South Africa and being made, 25

pharmaceutical industry
> psychiatry and, 106

philosophers
> contemporary, 9

physical sciences
> humanities and, 171, 174

physics
> Scientology and, 224
> study of, 220

"pillars of society," 9

pilots
> offer to halve pilot reaction time, 223
> Scientology and, 25

Plato
> philosopher-kings of, 181

Poland
> absorbed into Russia, 132
> psychiatry and psychologists, 127, 136
> revolution and psychiatry and psychology, 174

police
> brutality
>> eradicating, 64
> detesting psychiatrists and psychologists, 136
> psychiatric kidnapping, murder, torture and no action by, 117

police state, 136

political assassinations
> psychiatrists and, 124

political chaos, 5

political control

    psychiatry, psychology and, 222

political murders

    psychiatry, psychology and, 174

political prisoners

    psychiatry, psychology and, 174

political puppets

    wake up, 136

political science

    humanities and, 171

    ignorance of, 172

    mental science and, 174

    not used, 171

    politicians unaware of the subject of, 171

    teaching of, 171

politicians

    "above the law," 45

    blackmail by psychiatric front groups and, 163

    bowing to psychiatry, 202

    corruptible

        Russian Totalitarian State and, 144

    "National" Mental "Health" organizations replacing, 135

    political science, unaware of the subject of, 171

    "Preamble has no force in law," 46

    psychiatric front groups corrupting, 34

    psychiatrists and psychologists and, 159

        appropriations from, 139

    psychiatry, England, Germany, Russia and US promise to control men, 132

    special-interest groups and, 50

    swayed by special-interest group, 50

    wake up, 136

politics

    attacks on a country and increasing drug addiction, 184

    hollow stupidity of, 3

    political system for and by the people, 15

    political victory and enjoying the spoils, 10

Poll Tax

    decay of country and, 46

    1905 change in US Constitution and, 46

population

    accepting a Constitution, 46

    attacks on, 195

    Constitution

        as a bad thing and oppressing, 46

        as a good thing, 46

        persuading a population to accept, 45

    fast, inexpensive justice for, 63

    oppressed by special-interest men, 51

    psychiatry trying to remove active people from, 42

    revolt and force needed to control, 42

    special-interest groups are the minority of, 50

population control, 171

    psychiatry and, 163

        psychology and, 173

population explosion

    sterilization and, 101

positions of power

    attracting criminals, 206

postage stamps
   inflation, 101

post-hypnotic-suggestion
   definition, 121

power
   abuses of, 42
      officials sued or disciplined for, 64
   attracting criminals, 206
   going mad with, 44

power elite, 10

press
   politicians and, 110
   psychiatry and attacks on Dianetics and Scientology through press chains, 178

priests
   Druidism, Celtic inner circle of lawgivers and, 113

primitive cultures
   study of, 220

Princeton University, 170
   papers, 3

prisons
   death rate, 151
   pilot project on drug addicts, 183

Profumo scandal
   orgies by high officials and, 114

Prohibition Act
   beginning trend of financed crime, 46
   J. Edgar Hoover and, 75

propaganda
   special-interest group and, 49

prostitutes
   women inmates sold as, 174

psychedelic era
   Central Intelligence Agency LSD experimentation, 107

psychiatric drugging, 232

psychiatric front groups
   agent provocateur tactics, 163
   attacking Scientology, 128
      directing, 117
      reason for, 109
   bankers and, 95
   "best people," 202, 203
   blackmail of politicians, 163
   control technology used, 34
   corrupting politicians, 34
   crimes, 114
   destruction of
      Constitution, 33, 53
      morality on sex and, 33
   discovery of their crimes and, 114
   eradication of churches, 33
   exposing, 34
   lies and attacks on Scientology, 34
   mental health facade, 53
   reason for attacks on Scientology, 109
   redefinition of competent, 34
   seizure of people and, 33
   special-interest groups and, 53, 54
   stuck in 1450, 202
   terrorist textbooks and, 117
   totalitarianism and, 54
   "treatments" in institutions, 53
   turmoil created in schools, 34
   two-pronged campaign by 1950, 177
   United States, 15

universities, turmoil and, 34

Western destruction, 33

World Federation of Mental Health, 167

see also **special-interest groups; World Federation of Mental Health**

psychiatrists and psychologists

abuse of the soul, 211

adultery, 189

AMA and APA, drug pushers of America, 77

"authority" and tangled terms, 185

blackmail, 189

blood-soaked terror symbol, 21

bragging about sex orgies, 19

cause of crime, 211

children and, 212

Cold War partnership between American military and, 15

confidence tricksters, 173

corrupt pressure groups, 67

couldn't cure a pimple, 139

crimes, 159, 189

criminal mind and, 209

criminals, 206

cure nothing, 155

demand for rights violations, 229

depersonalization and, 21, 34, 122

diplomas, 129

exposing the crimes of, 229

exposure of child molestation, 231

False Data Stripping, 207

1450 and robber-baron castles, 201

freely admitting their murderous treatments, 114

guards for governments in a sort of cage, 26

Harold D. Lasswell and plan to replace politicians and rulers, 135

influence in high places and, 189

killing for sexual kicks, 117

knowing electric shock kills, 113

know nothing of the scientific method, 222

main reason fighting Scientology, 124

Man is an animal, *see* **Man is an animal theory**

murder and bury in the grounds, 189

not believing others change, 29

old-fashioned holdovers, 201

outlaws, 136

political assassinations and, 124

politicians and rulers of state and supplanting of, 135

preventing seizure of property by, 64

psychotics, 209

rape, 110, 117, 124, 178, 231

research fund activity (1948), 222

saying long words impressively, 186

Scientologists light-years above morally, 122

screaming "It's just delusion," 124

sexual perversion, 189

shocks, drugs, etc., 209

Siberia Bill half through US Congress, 109

sterilization of people and, 122

suicide, 189

terror in patients and, 122

terrorist textbooks and, 117

trained in Leipzig, Germany, 132

two serious mistakes, 136

Western governments and, 127

what is considered abnormal, 147

why are they supported, 210

psychiatry and psychology

    advocates

        adultery, 174

        destruction of boundaries, 174

        drug addiction, 174

        overthrow of constitutions, 174

        release of criminals, 174

    agent provocateur and intelligence tactics, 163

    Alger Hiss, 177

    attacks

        Church, 105

        law, 105

        medicine, 105

        teaching profession, 105

    basic tenet of, 206

    big words and, 185

    blackmail of politicians, 163

    "bounty hunters" to kidnap patients, 231

    Brock Chisholm, 177

    brutality and blackmail, 173

    chaos produced, 152

    civil disorder, 190

    Communist Totalitarian State and, 143

    control philosophy, 144

    courts and, 173

    crimes, 178, 205

    cutting nerves and, 132

    death camps and, 163

    describe rather than cure, 185

    discrediting and suppressing Dianetics and Scientology, 178

    "diseases" changing and no cures, 185

    drug addiction and, 184

    drugging, 232

    Druidism and, 113

    economic threat of, 163

    explanation of criminality and "irresistible impulse," 59

    failed, drug addiction and, 191

    failed technology, 127

    failing justice and, 59

    false subject, 206

    fifth column, 105

    first institute of, 131

    fraud, 107

    front groups by 1950, 177

    front groups stuck in 1450, 202

    government-financed control science, 131

    Harry Dexter White, 177

    heavily monied interests and, 83

    "incurable" diseases and authority, 185

    infiltration of society, 181

    insanity, 190

        physical disease, 206

    Kenneth Robinson, psychiatric frontman, 25

    KGB and Russian Totalitarian State and, 143

    LSD, 184

    Ludwig, 132

    Man is an animal, *see* **Man is an animal theory**

1960, zenith of, 206

no cures, 186

not intended to cure, 143

opposition to, 155

origin in Leipzig, Germany, 177

pervasive terror of, 2

pharmaceutical industry and, 106

policing frightened populations and, 15

political control and, 222

political murders, 174

political prisoners, 174

population control, 173

population oppression, 163

psychiatric patient assassinating Dr. Verwoerd, 25

public detesting, 110

public relations and, 174

reaping crime and social chaos, 190

redefining key words relating to the mind, 185

refused Dianetics and Scientology, 163

research funds used to pay out to friends, 222

Rockefeller Foundation support and, 83

Roman arena, 190

schools and, 144

seizing and killing tens of thousands of people, 110

selling women inmates as prostitutes, 174

Siberia Bill, 105

spawned by an insanely militaristic government, 206

subversion and, 105

tangled terms, 185

terrorism, 116

"treatments"

    mayhem, murder, 210

trying to remove active people from population, 42

two-pronged campaign, 177

using people as though they were animals, 29

"very best people," *see* **"best people"**

watchdog over the activities of, 229

what it advocates, 174

why supported by governments, 189

worked for eighty years establishing above-law dominance, 177

Wundt, 131, 132

    father of, 131

see also **psychiatric front groups**

psychoanalysts

crime and, 210

urge wives to commit adultery, 210

Psychological Strategy Board, 144

nuclear counter-strike policies, 15

psychosurgery

exposing the myth of, 232

Soviet treatment and worst forms of, 59

psychotherapy

failed

    drug abuse and, 191

unworkable

    drug addiction and, 191

psychotics

numb, 147

psychiatrists, psychologists, 209

psychotropic drugs, 232, 236

    profits from, 236

Public Enemies

    J. Edgar Hoover and, 75

        searching for "Public Enemy No. 1," 78

"public opinion"

    special-interest groups and, 50

public relations

    psychiatry and psychology and, 178

public revolt

    primary factors behind, 173

Q

"quack"

    definition, 151

quackery and fakery, 151

R

racial warfare

    subversion of a population, 196

raid

    US Government on Washington office, 223

Reagan, Ronald

    shooting of, 204

recession

    cause of, 172

    inflationary, 83

Red Cross, 230

Reds, 198

Rees, John Rawlings

    psychiatrist, speech, 105

refunds

    psychiatrists and psychologists and, 151

Reich, Wilhelm

    FDA and, 223

religion

    government departments at war with, 42

Religious Freedom Week

    annual, 18

reporters

    press attacks on L. Ron Hubbard, 221

"Representative of the People"

    republic and, 46

republic

    "best people" and, 46

    Constitution and, 44

    definition, 46

    "good of the people," 46

    pattern, 10

research

    solving the economics of, 220

research funds

    hidden secret of the attacks of nineteen years, 222

revolts

    exclusion and, 31

    force needed to control population and, 42

    government and, 29

    insecurity, oppression and, 42

not the answer, 38

primary cause of, 45

primary factors behind, 173

spirit of, generated by Justice Department, 78

universities

    psychiatry, psychology and, 174

see also **civil disorder; revolution; riots**

revolution

"Cause and Prevention of Revolution, The," 2, 7, 9

destruction of liberty and ingredients of, 34

injustice, suppressed wrath and, 71

mechanics of, 69

political evolution rather than, 10

psychiatry and psychology creating, 174

psychiatry's planned, 135

see also **civil disorder; revolts; riots**

Rhodesia

LRH calling for the end of apartheid, 15

right and wrong

psychiatric reinterpretation and eradication of the concept of, 105

rights

all men created with equal, 15

Constitution and guarantee of, 41

    individual, 44

    violations of, 42

        psychiatry and, 42

riots, 71

American cities (1968 to 1969), 5

distribution of "Riots" to Los Angeles residents, 70

injustices and, 71

justice not affordable by all, 71

LRH isolating cause of all, 70

see also **civil disorder; revolts; revolution**

robber-barons

psychiatrists and, 201

Robinson, Kenneth

psychiatric frontman, 25

trouble for Scientology Churches in UK and, 109

vice-president of private psychiatric group, 19

Rockefeller Foundation

psychiatric funding, 83

Roman arena

psychiatry, 190

Roman Empire

what destroyed, 20

Rome

Druidism and suppression by, 113

Roosevelt, Franklin D.

John L. Lewis almost defeating, for presidency, 76

rulers

"National" Mental "Health" organizations replacing, 135

Russia, 88

Amtorg, 220

Austria, Czechoslovakia and Poland absorbed into, 132

Czarist

    corruption, injustices and, 63

    student revolts, 132

Czar, "very best people" and, 128

death camps, 127

enslaving the people, 132

psychiatry and psychology, revolution and, 127, 136, 174

Stalin, 49

disastrous public official, 75

upper classes of, 29

Russian Totalitarian State

America and, 143

British Empire and, 143

KGB and psychiatric agents and, 143

"Rust Belts," 5

S

"safe men," 9

Saint-Simon, Comte de, 54

"Saliva, Sciences of," 131, 139

San Francisco's Haight-Ashbury

drug experimentation among residents of, 107

sanitariums

electric shock and, 124

psychiatric terms and, 185

sanity

perverted by psychiatry and psychology, 174

route to, 122

schizophrenia, 185

schools

psychiatric front groups and turmoil in, 34

shootings in, 204

trained in disloyalty and, 144

see also **children; education; students; universities**

Schopenhauer, 86

science

humanities and, 171, 174

mental

most basic human science, 174

Science and Survival

Barry Commoner, 219

Science of Survival

pain-drug-hypnosis described, 107

"Sciences of Saliva," 131, 139

scientists

summary on Scientology for, 219

Scientologists

are everywhere, 241

feared by psychiatrists and why, 122

fighting powers of evil, 110

Freedom of Information legislation and, 18

intentions, 164

primary threat to freedom fought by, 34

secret and vicious war against, 174

Scientology Volunteer Minister Program

Something Can Be Done About It!, 4

Scotland

World Federation of Mental Health, 167

secrecy

democracy versus, 18

Secretary of State for the Home Office

lifting ban on Scientology, 24

secret police

psychiatrists' and psychologists' use of state-financed secret police, 136

security

false reports tearing down, 69

forces, psychiatric murders with no action by, 117

personal, undermining, 67

security branches

detesting psychiatrists and psychologists, 136

seizure

easy, psychiatry and, 19, 20, 33, 53, 69, 109, 110, 168, 178, 181, 202

illegal, of persons and property, 42

laws authored by psychiatry and psychology, 178

politicians condoning illegal, 33

preventing psychiatric seizing of property, 64

violations of human rights and, 114

without process of law, 118

self-determinism

hypnotism and, 122

Senator Belch, 49

sexual perversion, 117, 124, 178, 231

psychiatric front groups and destruction of morality, 33

psychiatrists, 189

orgies, 19

subversion of a population, 196

Shays' Rebellion, 46

Siberia Bill, 105–106, 109

smile

looked "for the smile and the warmth that was there once," 4

social control

disagreements with, labeled "crazy," 155

social decay, 5

social engineer

"acceptable personality" and, 147

Socialism, 88

Capitalism and, 86, 88

social-political

life and economics and, 86

social scientists, 191, 198

society

destruction of, 161

dying unless reformed, 23

understanding of economics and step forward for, 85

sociologists

psychiatrists and psychologists and, 144, 152

sociology

control philosophy, 144

schools and, 144

study of American society circa 1973, 4

Something Can Be Done About It!

Scientology Volunteer Minister Program, 4

soul

abuse of by psychiatrists and psychologists, 211

South Africa

exposure of slave-labor camps, 134

LRH

calling for the end of apartheid, 15

efforts toward freedom in, 24

photograph of L. Ron Hubbard in Johannesburg, 104

psychiatric abuse in slave-labor camps, 229

special-interest groups, 42, 50

    advertised purpose, 51

    buying a voice to press its special interest, 50

    campaign money and, 50

    citizen suspecting, 50

    corruption of patriotism, 51

    definition, 49

    democracy deteriorating into the hands of, 50

    description, 51

    fixed ideas, 49

    general-interest groups versus, 49, 53

    government and, 50

    government by, 37

    idealism corrupted by, 51

    minority of the population, 50

    nations and disaster, 51

    oppression of population, 51

    politicians and, 50

    propaganda and, 49

    psychiatric front groups and, 53, 54

    "public opinion" and, 50

    "Representative of the People" and, 46

    small minority of population, 50

    test of, 51

    see also **psychiatric front groups**

special interests, 50, 51

sphere of influence

    contraction of by covert means, 195

spies, 196

spirit

    Man is a spiritual being, 224

Spy/Counter Spy, 77

Stalin

    Pavlov and control of human beings, 131

    Russia, 49, 127

        disastrous public official in, 75

    Totalitarianism of, 53

    World Federation of Mental Health and, 168

state

    beware of state which neglects criminals and attacks decent citizens, 189

    Constitution and purpose of, 45

    psychiatry accelerating downfall of, 42

    why a government supports psychiatrists and psychologists, 210

sterilization

    population explosion and, 101

    psychiatrists and, 122

Stonehenge

    Druidism and, 113

strawberries

    strange dream, 144

strikes, 88

"Strong Voices in the Land," 9

students

    revolting, 128

    violence on American campuses (May 1970), 5

subversion

    psychiatric, 6, 105, 109

suffrage

    universal, LRH calling for, 15

suicide

    injustice and, 72

madmen and, 44

psychiatrists causing, 189

supply and demand, 89, 173

suppression

source of, field for comment, 1, 86

Suppressives

web of economic entanglement and, 85

Supreme Court

US, existing to reverse government unconstitutionality, 41

Swastika, 19

Switzerland

World Federation of Mental Health, 167

System, The, 10

self-seeking righteousness, 9

T

"Tangled Terms"

psychiatry, 185

tax audits

continual, 16

taxes

economics and war and, 95

for the socialist safety net, 83

income, 86

increasing, 173

oppressive, 4, 98

Taxpayers' Bill of Rights, 18

technology

of the mind

psychiatry and psychology sought to crush savagely, 173

psychiatric front groups and *control* technology, 34

terrorism

crushing all opposition, 51

drugs and pain and, 122

employed by psychs to control populations, 136

psychiatric, extending to the top, 117

psychiatric front groups and, 54

psychiatrists cause of, 122

psychiatry, 116

today's, 117

totalitarianism and, 49

Third Reich

Saboteur forces of, 33

thought

inalienable rights to think freely, 15

seeking to discredit any new, 9

torture, 229

politicians condoning, 33

totalitarianism, 51

banking, 53

being born, 51

definition, 49

evolution of, 49

psychiatric front groups and, 54

totalitarian regime

reaction to Scientology and, 162

totalitarian state

disagreement with and pronounced "insane," 155

"mental health" organizations and, 151

trade

weakening of, 195

trial

    detention without, 42

"Tricky Dick," *see* **Nixon, Richard M.**

truth

    though fought, always prevailing in the end, 24

Turrou, Leon G.

    FBI agent, 76

tyranny

    acting according to Constitutions versus, 44

    Constitution omitting any of four essential parts, 46

    description, 67

    setting up a new channel for, 46

    West being unmade by, 37

U

UK Royal Society

    Pavlov and, 131

"underprivileged" people

    criminals and, 159

understanding

    universal solvent, 1

unemployment

    across much of Western Europe, 83

"Unholy Stick Together, The," 167

United for Human Rights

    raising awareness on human rights, 18

United Kingdom

    universities going out of control, 132

    see also **England**, 132

United Mine Workers

    John L. Lewis and, 76

United Nations, 230

    Church of Scientology, human rights and, 18

    mental health "Bill of Rights," 134

    our intentions and, 163

    World Health Organization Technical Report Series No. 98

        planning to knock out churches in field of mental healing, 110

United Nations General Assembly, 235

United States

    Founding Fathers, 45

    gold reserves of, 95

    J. Edgar Hoover, disastrous public official in, 75

    offer to increase IQ and halve pilot reaction time, 223

    psychiatric front within, 15

    reduction of, 198

    religious and racial minority groups, 69

    universities in uncontrolled riot, 132

United States Capitol Building

    photograph by L. Ron Hubbard, 2

United States Congressional Black Caucus

    defeat of funding of experimental psychosurgery, 232

United States Department of Justice, 176

United States Naval Lieutenant, 3, 4

United States School of Military Government, 3, 170

Universal Declaration of Human Rights

    Church of Scientology and, 18

Freedom magazine and, 1

governments' survival and, 20, 21

universal solvent

understanding, 1

universities

psychiatric front groups and turmoil in, 34

psychiatry and psychology and revolts in, 174

taken out from under churches, 132

Untold Story of Psychotropic Drugging, The, 236

US civil defense manual, 53

US Freedom of Information Act, 18, 230

US Navy's Office of Naval Research, 221

US Prohibition, 172

Utopia, 34, 139

insanity and, 94

no planned airy-fairy, 64

psychiatrists and psychologists, 141

social and economic, 38

totalitarian, 147

V

Verwoerd, Dr. Hendrik

assassination by mental patient, 124

South African Prime Minister, 15

warning to, 25, 26

Vietnam

students protesting American involvement in, 16

Voice of America radio network

Central Intelligence Agency, 194

voices

strong voices in the land, 9

Volunteer Minister Program, 4

W

wars

degradation of a population instead of war, 195

economics and tax and, 95

fast transport, 196

incompetent foreign relations and, 20

internationalization of finance and, 196

mass communication media, 196

Washington, DC

photograph of Jefferson Memorial by L. Ron Hubbard, 61

photograph of United States Capitol Building by L. Ron Hubbard, 2

photograph of Washington Monument by L. Ron Hubbard, 6

raid of church, 24

Washington, George, 10

American Revolution, 88

Watergate, 5, 59

Way to Happiness, The

common sense moral code, 208

West

affairs in the hands of experimenters in social control, 38

attacks on every new development in the field of the mind, 128

Capitalism and Marx, 86

carefully planned things going wrong in, 38

crime and psychiatry and psychology, 128

destruction of, 196

"Golden Years" economically (1960s), 83

institutions infiltrated, 198

intelligence technology against the West since 1948, 195

leaders listening to psychiatry and psychology, 128

liberty and, 38

made by free men, 37

nations dominated by one group, 53

psychiatry, psychology and, 127

Scientology and rehabilitating, 63

security forces and Cultural Destruction, 198

WFMH, *see* **World Federation of Mental Health**

White, Harry Dexter

founding of International Monetary Fund, 95

psychiatry and, 177

WHO, *see* **World Health Organization**

Wilson, Woodrow

labeled by psychiatrists, 155

wiretaps

illegal, on suspected political dissidents, 59

wisdom

voices with, 11

world

deeply troubled

answers for, 2

"world which lost its bearings," 5

World Federation of Mental Health, 6

Constitution, eradication of, 33

death camps, 168

Delaware

United States, 167

delegates from Russia and Iron Curtain countries, 168

dope, death and easy seizure, 168

eradication of all boundaries and constitutions, 168

experimental surgery, 168

government graft funds and, 168

Health Ministers, 167

illegal

operations of, 167

legislation and, 168

munitions combine and, 168

"National" groups and, 167

psychiatric front group, 167

Russian origin of the technology they advocate, 168

salary of, 167

Scientology, attacks by WFMH, 168

Scotland, 167

seizures in the night, 168

Stalin and Hitler plans and, 168

status of, 167

suppression of beneficial treatment of the insane, 168

Switzerland, 167

takeover of organization of Clifford Beers, 178

target to eradicate the only new Western development in the field of the mind, 168

unconstitutional actions in US, 168

why not acted upon by government agencies, 168

World Health Organization

investigation in South Africa, 230

World War II

apathy, 20

interruption of research, 220

Justice Department taking over Counterintelligence, 75

most fighting under protest, 20

Wundt, Wilhelm Max

animal and death-camp practices, 127

destruction of the West and, 128

father of psychology, 131

Leipzig, Germany

men are animals, 131

nerve conditioning and, 143

tenets of, 132

"Yellow Peril"

Hearst and development of, 50

THE
L. RON HUBBARD
SERIES

"To really know life," L. Ron Hubbard wrote, "you've got to be part of life. You must get down and look, you must get into the nooks and crannies of existence. You have to rub elbows with all kinds and types of men before you can finally establish what he is."

Through his long and extraordinary journey to the founding of Dianetics and Scientology, Ron did just that. From his adventurous youth in a rough and tumble American West to his far-flung trek across a still mysterious Asia; from his two-decade search for the very essence of life to the triumph of Dianetics and Scientology—such are the stories recounted in the L. Ron Hubbard Biographical Publications.

Drawn from his own archival collection, this is Ron's life as he himself saw it. With each volume of the series focusing upon a separate field of endeavor, here are the compelling facts, figures, anecdotes and photographs from a life like no other.

Indeed, here is the life of a man who lived at least twenty lives in the space of one.

FOR FURTHER INFORMATION VISIT
www.lronhubbard.org

To order copies of *The L. Ron Hubbard Series*
or L. Ron Hubbard's Dianetics and
Scientology books and lectures, contact:

US AND INTERNATIONAL

BRIDGE PUBLICATIONS, INC.
5600 E. Olympic Blvd.
Commerce, California 90022 USA
www.bridgepub.com
Tel: (323) 888-6200
Toll-free: 1-800-722-1733

UNITED KINGDOM AND EUROPE

NEW ERA PUBLICATIONS
INTERNATIONAL ApS
Smedeland 20
2600 Glostrup, Denmark
www.newerapublications.com
Tel: (45) 33 73 66 66
Toll-free: 00-800-808-8-8008